ACTS
OF THE
EMISSARIES

A MESSIANIC COMMENTARY

ACTS
OF THE
EMISSARIES

THE EARLY HISTORY
OF THE
YESHUA MOVEMENT

RABBI BARNEY KASDAN

Lederer Books
An imprint of
Messianic Jewish Publishers
Clarksville, MD 21029

Printed in the United States of America
Graphic Design by Yvonne Vermillion,
MagicGraphix.com
Copy Editing by George Koch, copyedit.pro

ISBN: 978-1-951833-23-7

2022 1

Published by
Lederer Books
A division of
Messianic Jewish Publishers
6120 Day Long Lane
Clarksville, Maryland 21029

Distributed by
Messianic Jewish Resources Int'l.
www.MessianicJewish.net
Individual and Trade Order Line: 800-410-7647

Email: lederer@messianicjewish.net

To the Kasdan family, near and far.

From Minsk to New York to Louisville to San Diego and beyond.

To the many who have decided to continue the Jewish spiritual journey by including the first century understanding of Yeshua in our faith.

Since the name Kasdan is from Cohen (High Priest), may our family be a light through our service to our community and Mashiach.

CONTENTS

MAPS

GENERAL EDITOR'S PREFACE

Nearly all Bible commentators emphasize the importance of understanding the historical, cultural and grammatical aspects of any text of Scripture. As has been said, "A text without a context is a pretext." In other words, to assume one can understand what God has revealed through those who present his Word—prophets, poets, visionaries, apostles—without knowing the context is presumption. To really understand God's Word, it's essential to know something about who wrote it and to whom, what was actually said and what it originally meant, and when, where, and why it was written.

By now, everyone knows the New Testament is a thoroughly Jewish book, written almost entirely by Jews, taking place in and around Israel. The people written about—Paul, Peter, James, John, etc—were all Jews who never abandoned their identities or people. The topics covered—sin, salvation, resurrection, Torah, Sabbath, how to "walk with God," the Millennium, etc—were all Jewish topics that came from the Hebrew Scripture. The expressions were Jewish idioms of that day. So to fully understand the New Testament, it must be viewed through "Jewish eyes," meaning the Jewish historical, cultural, grammatical must be examined.

There are commentaries for women, men, teens, even children. There are commentaries that focus on financial issues in the Bible. Others provide archaeological material. Some commentaries are topical. Others are the works of eminent men and women of God. But until now, no commentary series has closely looked at the Jewish context of each of the New Testament books.

Some of the world's top Messianic Jewish theologians contributed their knowledge and understanding. Each has written on a book(s) of the New Testament they've specialized in, making sure to present the Jewish aspects—the original context—of each book. These works are not meant to be a verse-by-verse exegetical commentary. There are already many excellent ones available. But these commentaries supplement what others lack by focusing on the Jewish aspects along with explaining the book itself.

Several different authors wrote these commentaries, each in his own style. Just as the Gospels were written by four different men, each with his own perspective and style, these volumes too have variations. We didn't want the writers to have to conform too much to any particular style guide, other than our basic one.

You may see some Hebrew expressions or transliterations of Hebrew names in the New Testament. Thus, one writer might refer to the Apostle to the Gentiles as Paul. Another might write *Sha'ul*, Paul's Hebrew name. Still another might write *Saul*, an Anglicized version of *Sha'ul*. And some might write *Saul/Paul* to reflect, not reject, the different ways this servant of Messiah was known.

Another variation is the amount of reference material. Some have ample footnotes or endnotes, while others incorporate references within the text. Some don't have an enormous number of notes.

We have plans for a Messianic Jewish commentary series on the entire Bible. Though much has been written on the books of the Hebrew Scriptures, some by Messianic Jews, there hasn't been a full commentary series on the Tanakh, the "Older" Testament. But we hope to publish such a series in the future.

So, I invite you to put on your Jewish glasses (if you're not Jewish) and take a look at the New Testament in a way that will open up new understanding for you, as you get to know the God of Israel and his Messiah better.

RABBI BARRY RUBIN
General Editor and Publisher

INTRODUCTION

Maybe it's time to take a new look at something very old.

I t reminds me of the truth illustrated in a prism. The cut-glass filter has various angles to do its work of separating a light beam. From just one beam comes a plethora of colors from the spectrum. For centuries, Christians have looked at their faith through a particular prism of their culture and convictions. Meanwhile, many of us Jews have looked at the New Testament through our prism, often reaching very different conclusions than Christians. What I am attempting in this Acts commentary is to take the same beam of light but refilter from a different angle. Please note, it is the same light beam of old (biblical truth) that reflects a different color.

I am happy to say that in recent years that there has been a resurgence of interest in the Jewish background of the New Testament. This renewed interest in the Jewish Jesus is reflected by many who are using his original name, "Yeshua," and by the Jewish markers in his life—the lifecycle events he observed and all the Jewish holy days he celebrated. While the Jewish Yeshua continues to regain much of his rightful place in the religious world, the same cannot be said about his early followers. In the mind of many, Jesus is certainly a Jew, but the apostles branched off into a new religion called "Christianity." Yet even these presuppositions are being challenged in our day. In recent decades, *A New Perspective on Paul*

1

(see Krister Stendahl, E.P. Sanders, N.T. Wright) advocated for exploring the Jewish foundations of the Apostle and questioning some the conclusions put forth by the Christian reformers. This is evident in both Jewish and Christian scholarly explorations as illustrated in such recent works as Paula Fredriksen's *When Christians Were Jews: The First Generation.* Did the early Jewish disciples diverge from the Jewish focus of Yeshua? If not, then how did a Jewish sect eventually morph into a "Gentilized" church? A fresh analysis of first-century history is vital; and the Book of Acts is the key to this history. What is often overlooked is the contribution of contemporary Messianic Jews who are familiar with both the Jewish and Christian perspectives as Jewish followers of Yeshua (Jesus). As one of those Messianic Jews, I write this Acts commentary to add important elements to the current discussion.

Such a study of first-century history in Judea requires a renewed focus on the entire context. This religious movement of Yeshua did not start in the pagan corners of the Roman Empire but in the heart of the Jewish community. Jesus was born a Jew in the Jewish land of Israel. His early ministry was totally among the Jewish people as he preached and taught well-known Jewish themes. His first followers were fellow Jews who responded to his call, "Repent, for the Kingdom of God is near!" It was in the spirit of this prophetic message that large numbers of Jewish disciples responded by accepting Yeshua—not as the founder of a new religion, but as the promised Mashiach/Messiah of Israel. Because of this, they continued to live as Jews, albeit "Messianic" Jews, who added to their Judaism the conviction that Yeshua indeed fulfills the predictions of the coming Redeemer. The Book of Acts confirms this strong Jewish perspective that would ultimately have a great impact beyond the borders of Israel.

The 28 chapters of Acts teach three vital lessons our generation must reconsider:

#1. The early Jewish followers of Yeshua were convinced that he is the Messiah promised in the *Tanakh*/Hebrew Scriptures. Based on this conviction, they continued to live within their Jewish heritage, clearly documented in Acts. They continued with the

2

Jewish holy days like Shavuot (Pentecost) and Yom Kippur (Day of Atonement), as seen in Acts 2:1 and 27:9. These new Messianic Jews continued with practices like *kashrut* (kosher) and *brit-milah* (circumcision). See Acts 10:14, 16:3. They quite naturally attended local synagogues and even participated in the Temple offerings (cf. Acts 17:1–2, 21:20–24). Simply put, they were Jews who now added to their Judaism the faith in Yeshua as the Mashiach.

#2. The message of Yeshua as Messiah will also have an international appeal. Though the Book of Acts assumes this Yeshua-faith will naturally attract a significant number of traditional Jews, surprisingly, this faith would likewise attract many non-Jews throughout the Roman Empire. That this was unexpected can be seen through the dialogue and decisions recorded in Acts. The first nine chapters of the book (actually a letter written by Luke) mostly deal with the Jewish experience with this messianic message. But when it becomes clear that it is to expand beyond the Jewish community, the early *Sh'likhim*/apostles must be convinced through some dramatic events. Peter is given the shocking vision of the four-cornered sheet (possibly a *tallit*) with all sorts of unkosher food on it (cf. Acts 10). While Kefa/Peter is considering this picture, God makes it clear that he does not need to stop keeping kosher but that he should accept in fellowship the "unkosher" Gentiles. It had been predicted that faith in the God of Israel (and the Messiah) would be a life-giving message for the Nations/goyim/non-Jews (cf. Gen. 12:3, Isa. 49:6). These days of messianic redemption started in the Book of Acts. The Gentile branch of this nascent Yeshua movement is welcomed by the Jewish branch, and are reminded to always appreciate their inclusion in (not replacement of!) the promises to Israel.

#3. In recent decades, we have witnessed a renewed awareness in the Jewishness of the New Testament message. I believe this is a "God thing." How else can one explain the birth of hundreds of Messianic synagogues worldwide comprised of Jews from various backgrounds who include Yeshua in their faith? This phenomenon seems to parallel the physical rebirth of the modern nation of Israel and the reestablishment of the Jewish Jerusalem. In retrospect, it should not be surprising that this physical restoration has been accompanied by a spiritual resurgence among our people, just as the Prophets predicted (cf. Ezek. 36:24–27). Along with this Jewish curiosity about the historical Yeshua, many Christians are now realizing that their savior was a Jew all along. To best understand the message of the New Testament, many Christians are digging deeper into the original context of this faith. The result is a new appreciation for their Bible and their personal faith. I believe God is moving both the Jewish and non-Jewish sides closer together as we both take a fresh look at Yeshua of Nazareth and the early Yeshua movement. The Book of Acts is a treasure trove for anyone who desires to rediscover the original person and message of this One who changed the world.

Finally, a few notes on the format of this Messianic Jewish commentary.

As with my previous work on the Gospels (*Matthew Presents Yeshua, King Messiah*), I take a narrative approach to this volume on Acts. Of course, that fits quite naturally as the historian Luke records his account in a narrative fashion. Along with this, I include a fair amount of exegesis to try to understand many of the theological issues addressed in Acts. I use plenty of rabbinic texts and cultural background. These have often been the missing pieces. There have not been many Jewish commentaries that make these links.

Two things to keep in mind. First, I am not claiming the rabbinic sources are equivalent to Holy Scripture. The Talmud would not make such a statement about itself, but instead it is a number of rabbis and scholars debating with each other to better understand the meaning of Scripture. Second, though the rabbinic commentaries are not equal to the Written Torah, they are very helpful (I dare say essential) to understanding the cultural context of Scripture.

With these things in mind, I invite you to put on your yarmulke (*kippah* or skullcap) and Jewish glasses for an open-minded look at the message of Acts. I am writing with the hopes that this commentary will be a blessing to my own faith community of Messianic Judaism. Likewise, it is my hope that all readers from various backgrounds will have a fresh outlook on the message of the New Testament. I believe an awareness of the Jewish context of Acts will build new bridges of appreciation and love between the long-separated Jewish and Christian communities.

Whether you are a longtime believer in Yeshua, a newer believer, or just plain curious, may you find a blessing in understanding the history of the Yeshua movement among both Jews and Gentiles. Who knows? Maybe you will sense a new calling to become part of that history!

Dedicated to my rabbinic colleagues in the Union of Messianic Jewish Congregation (UMJC) and the Messianic Jewish Alliance of America (MJAA) and the many Messianic Jewish organizations worldwide. It is a blessing to walk together in the renewed Yeshua movement!

Chapter One

INTRODUCTION

Three things come unexpectedly: a find,
a scorpion, and the Messiah.

(Tractate Sanhedrin 97a)

I. The Miraculous Pesach – 1:1–3

The Book of Acts serves as a vital bridge of understanding during a tumultuous time of Jewish history. Y'hudah (Judea) was solidly entrenched in the Roman Empire, which presented multiple challenges. Caught between the political chaos of the house of Herod and the sectarian battles within Judaism, the first-century writer seeks to document the rise of an intriguing movement of Jews who embraced Yeshua (Jesus) as the promised Messiah. Several details confirm that this writer is Luke, Sha'ul's (Paul's) travel companion.

That this scroll is addressed to *Theophilos* shows a direct connection to Luke's Gospel recounting Yeshua's life and work in Israel (Lk. 1:1). This could be one person's proper name, meaning "friend of God." Or perhaps Luke uses this as a term of endearment for a respected Roman official. A third option is that Luke is using the term to address his broader reading audience—as in "to all 'friend[s] of God.'" That would include those of us reading his scroll even today. Any or all these options could apply to Luke's audience,

7

who were evidently familiar with the story of Yeshua *through the first book.* Bible scholars have also noted the stylistic similarities between the Gospel of Luke and the Book of Acts. Likewise, there are many internal references in Acts where the writer uses the first-person "I" or "we," which in turn is directly connected to Luke himself (16:10–17; 20:5–21:18; 27:1–28:16).

Many assume Luke is not Jewish based on one passage where he is not listed among "the circumcised" believers (Col. 4:11). Others conclude this because Luke is clearly a Greek as his name reflects. But these don't prove the case, and there's much evidence of his Jewish heritage. First, his writings in his Gospel and in Acts contain a wealth of Jewish background. Luke is the only Gospel writer who goes into detail about Yeshua's Jewish lifecycle celebrations, including his *b'rit-milah* (circumcision; 2:21), dedication at *Pidyon HaBen* (redemption of the firstborn; 2:27ff) and even bar mitzvah (2:41–42). Add to this Luke's minute details of the Temple service of first-century Judaism; this would be difficult for a non-Jew to explain (see Lk. 1:5–23).

Based on this internal evidence, Luke was either a Hellenistic Jew or at least a Greek convert to Judaism. I prefer the former, especially in light of his close friend Sha'ul, who confirms the Jews were the ones entrusted with transmitting the Word of God (Rom. 3:2). As for the when this scroll was written, most scholars embrace a time before 70 C.E. If it was after 70 C.E., the destruction of Yerushalayim and the Temple and would be documented. Likewise, Acts ends before Sha'ul's death during Nero's bloody reign in 64 C.E. Because of these indicators, most place the writing of Acts between 60–64 C.E.

Luke clearly states his intended purpose for writing Acts. Having already recounted Yeshua's earthly life, Luke wishes to document the *instructions to the emissaries* as they are to share this exciting arrival of Messiah. In describing Yeshua's ministry, Luke employs a common Jewish idea that the Messiah would have two distinct missions. The first is that the Messiah would reign as King over the restored Paradise, a kingdom of peace, blessing and fruitfulness on the renewed earth (Isa. 9, 11). Since Messiah is to be our greatest King, he is given the title "Mashiach ben David" (Messiah son of David). Like Israel's greatest ruler, King David, the Messiah will rule over all.

However, the rabbis also saw a contrasting picture of the coming Messiah. This Messiah would somehow suffer and even die for some rather mysterious reasons. The classical rabbis of the Talmud came to this conclusion after considering such biblical passages that describe Messiah's rejection, physical affliction and unjust death (Isa. 53 and Zech. 12:10 as quoted in Tractates Sanhedrin 98a and Sukkah 52a, respectively). They even debated the possibility that there may be two different messiahs to fulfill these two vastly different missions. This second Messiah, the suffering one, is aptly named "Mashiach ben Yosef" (Messiah son of Joseph) as he apparently has a parallel experience to Yosef in Genesis.

The opening paragraph of acts quickly addresses this idea of two Messiahs performing two distinct missions. Luke affirms that Yeshua of Nazareth indeed suffered as Mashiach ben Yosef as documented by *his death*. But instead of looking for another person to fulfill the function of ben David, Luke shows how the same Yeshua will be able to fulfill that role as well. He was resurrected from the dead and *showed himself to them and gave many convincing proofs that he was alive*. Instead of the Talmudic idea of two different Messiahs, the *B'rit Chadashah* (New Testament) gives another viable explanation: One Messiah can fulfill both missions since he is risen from the dead. It is no doubt a radical claim, but the rabbinic ideas aren't far from the Jewish explanation Acts proposes.

A closer look at the Torah and Jewish tradition reveals an amazing prophetic picture of the work of Messiah in this regard. God gave Israel holy days not just as times of enjoyment but also because each one contains a prophetic snapshot of what the Messiah will accomplish (Lev. 23). It is well-documented that Yeshua suffered in accordance with the detailed description of ben Yosef (Isa. 53; Tractate Sanhedrin 98a). Also, his suffering on the Roman cross took place, not coincidentally, on the very afternoon of *Pesach* (Passover). It was at the very hour of the *Minchah* ("gift") lamb offering for the entire nation that Yeshua died on that tree (Mt. 27:45–46). He thus fulfilled the work of ben Yosef not only suffering for the sins of the world but at the very hour of the Pesach redemption!

And that's not all. On the third day of Pesach is another Jewish holy day, *Bikkurim* (First Fruits). In another amazing "coincidence," it is on this third day of Pesach that Yeshua was resurrected as the first fruits from the dead (I Cor. 15:20). As the living Redeemer, Yeshua could now also fulfill the future mission of Mashiach ben David. We begin to appreciate Luke's description of the *many convincing proofs* that Yeshua of Nazareth is the perfect fulfillment of the messianic hope for both Jews and non-Jews. It was during the *forty days* before his ascension to the Father that Yeshua assured his Jewish disciples that he is both ben Yosef and ben David as he taught them more *about the Kingdom of God*.

II. The Anticipation of Shavuot – 1:4–8

Yeshua's Jewish followers had spent the last three-and-a-half years soaking in their rabbi's teachings. They learned how to be true disciples through study but also working together sharing the blessing of Yeshua with their fellow Jews. But before they could take it to the next level, the disciples would need some extra help. After all, their risen Messiah was soon to depart to the Father, the God of Israel. How could they accomplish their exciting work?

For this reason Yeshua *instructed them not to leave Yerushalayim* (Jerusalem) *but to wait for what the Father promised. Yochanan* (John) *used to immerse people in water* as preparation to get ready for Messiah. Yeshua lovingly reminds the Jewish group that they were always promised an immersion *in the Ruach HaKodesh* (Holy Spirit), who would enable them to be effective for their Kingdom work. The Ruach is quite prevalent in the history of Israel. From the earliest work of creation (Gen. 1:2) to the future work of redemption (Isa. 48:16), the Ruach has played a vital role.

The Jews understand the Holy Spirit not as an external power source, but a living reality, even a personal manifestation, of God himself. This promise of the Father has two angles. Yeshua shared this promise at the last Seder when he assured his disciples that the Father would send a Comforter to strengthen his people for their spiritual journey (Jn. 15:26). Once again the Father's promise can be seen in the picture of the Jewish holy days. As Yeshua died on the day of Pesach and rose precisely on the day of Bikkurim, so too the Father promised the blessing of the Ruach HaKodesh on the holy day of *Shavuot* (Pentecost; Lev. 23; Joel 2). This important festival takes place on the 50th day after Pesach. Yeshua reminds his followers in this 40-day period that even after the redemption of Pesach and the resurrection of Bikkurim, there is still another spring holiday to fulfill.

This exhortation raised some questions in the disciples' minds especially regarding the status of Israel. They ask, *"Lord, are you at this time going to restore self-rule to Isra'el?"* The Jews' position must have seemed perplexing even to his closest companions. Many people put great emphasis on the concept of ben David and anticipated the Messiah would cast out all oppressors like the first-century Romans. If Yeshua is in fact the Messiah, surely he would establish political independence for the Jews as the major thrust of his program. Yet with Yeshua also emphasizing his work as ben Yosef, the disciples wondered how all these things would be reconciled.

Some people berated the disciples for asking a "political" question instead of focusing on Yeshua's "spiritual" redemptive work. But Yeshua did not correct them or even imply the question was out of order. In fact, his answer actually affirms the big picture of their question. Certainly, the Kingdom of God is still coming to Israel as promised through Moshe (Moses) and the Prophets.

The Messiah focuses the answer on a different issue, saying they *don't need to know the dates or the times*. There is no change in God's plan for Israel and the Jewish people. How could there be when Yeshua said he came to fulfill, not annul, God's promises (Mt. 5:17–18)? With the limited information Yeshua's disciples had, they thought all phases of the messianic redemption would occur immediately. Yeshua tells them there will be a delay between the Messiah's two missions. The suffering aspects of ben Yosef were fulfilled before their eyes in first-century Yerushalayim, but there would be a necessary delay of the completed work of ben David. Yeshua's followers still had some holy work to accomplish in the interim: *"You will receive power when the Ruach HaKodesh comes upon you; you will be my witnesses…"*

It is amazing that this early Yeshua movement thus far was rather limited among Jews in first-century Israel. There were thousands of traditional Jews who embraced Yeshua as the promised Messiah and continued in their heritage (Acts 21:20). Even some Roman and Samaritan non-Jews had an unusual encounter with this Messiah. But all the way back to Abraham and through Moshe and the Prophets, we were told the messianic redemption would be a blessing to all peoples internationally (Gen. 12:1–3; Num. 23:7–12; Isa. 49:6). This is what Yeshua emphasizes as he reveals to his followers that now was the time to take this message worldwide to all peoples, to the Jew first and also to the non-Jew (Rom. 1:16). Israel was always called to be a witness to the reality of the one true God (Isa. 43:10). At this critical time in the first century, this early remnant of Jewish believers would fulfill that calling by testifying that they were eyewitnesses to the reality of the risen Messiah.

This was a daunting commission. No way it could be achieved by their own limited strength and resources. Hence the Ruach's power (*dunamis*, dynamite) is promised. Stop to reflect on this wonderful promise. Acts will document the powerful history of the early Yeshua movement, which was clearly directed by the Spirit's power. Some 2000 years later, messianic believers need to realize anew that we too need the Ruach's help. Too many things in this life are beyond our control or knowledge. One of the great promises included in Messianic Judaism and faith in Yeshua is that we also receive the power to walk his path today. Too many believers try to walk in their own power, to great frustration. No wonder Yeshua exhorts his followers to wait for the promise of Shavuot. Not surprisingly, many of the New Testament exhortations call us to be controlled by the Ruach for a successful, joyful journey with our Messiah (Eph. 5:18).

In this current dialogue, Yeshua also guides his disciples on how to spread this message of redemption and blessing. They are to start *in* Yerushalayim, their home and center for the Jewish community. This messianic redemption has long been a promise to the Jewish people, so it is logical that Messiah says to start there. The people of the promises should be the first to hear the fulfillment has come. From the Jewish capital, the New Covenant message should be shared with the larger Jewish area of *Y'hudah and Shomron* (Judea and Samaria). This is the biblical description of the land of Israel God gave the Jews, with Y'hudah in the south and Shomron to the north (Gen. 15:18–19; Deut. 30:1–6; Rom. 11:26–29).

This is Yeshua's way of saying this Good News must go forth to all the Jews even beyond Yerushalayim. He reminds his disciples that ultimately this message of the messianic kingdom is also to go *to the ends of the earth*. This mandate includes the larger non-Jewish world beyond the land of Israel, as was always predicted in the Tanakh. Again we are instructed that this New Covenant would not just stay within the Jewish community but would also be an open invitation to all non-Jews who would want to be directly connected to the God of Israel through the work of Messiah Yeshua.

This commission is to be taken quite literally. People often reference these verses to exhort modern-day disciples to go to their "personal Jerusalem." The common assumption is that we are to take this message to our own locality and expand from there. It is good to share our faith in our hometown, but the original context of Acts 1:8 is not of a "spiritual city" but a literal city in the Middle East.

Too often this spiritualizing has misled believers into a form of replacement theology, which espouses the idea that the Church (i.e., Gentile Christians) has replaced Israel (the Jewish people). As we'll see, the development of Acts debunks any replacement idea. It is informative that Sha'ul, even as the apostle to the Gentiles, invariably goes first to the local synagogue to share this messianic news with his Jewish brothers (Acts 13:13–16; 14:1; 17:1–4). He later explains his philosophy of outreach as "to the Jew first and also to the Greek" (Rom. 1:16). It is not a matter of favoritism but of God's justice. It only makes sense that the people who have the promises of the coming Messiah should be the first to hear of his arrival. As Sha'ul states in Romans, this good news should be shared with the Jewish community first *and also* (at the same time) with the non-Jewish community.

This methodology is key to understanding the explosive success in Acts. It could also partially explain why later church-history looks so different from first-century ones. It seems God put his blessing on these early believers as they followed his manner of outreach, to the Jew first. Perhaps the full blessing of God can return in our day as the Church realizes its ongoing debt to the Jewish people. Many churches today have significant mission budgets to take the Gospel to every tribe and tongue. That is good and vital. Hopefully every church would also have a designated effort to return the blessing of the Good News to their Jewish friends and the nation of Israel. Many Christians in fact appreciate being grafted into the rich olive tree of the biblical faith that came through Israel and so look for good opportunities to share the Jewish Yeshua with his Jewish cousins.

Embedded in Acts 1:8's amazing truth is Luke's working outline of his history of the early Yeshua movement. As we go through Acts, we see it begins in Yerushalayim (1–8), proceeds to Y'hudah and Shomron (8–12) and reaches to the ends of the earth (13–28). The Jewish remnant is to be empowered for this pivotal time in world history as the Father's promise is poured out on Shavuot.

It was now the end of the 40-day period from Yeshua's death to his subsequent resurrection appearances. This radical claim of the risen Messiah was not just a rumor of a few questionable people. It was to several hundred Jewish citizens of Yerushalayim on several occasions. This interaction with Yeshua in Acts is strong testimony, but there were other public encounters with his close disciples and even at one large public gathering of some 500 eyewitnesses (Jn. 20:24–31;

14

I Cor. 15:1–8). This 40-day period is contained within the traditional 50-day counting period between Pesach and Shavuot known as *S'firat HaOmer* (Counting the Omer). Since the days of Moshe, Jews have observed this time of thanking God for the early harvest of First Fruits and anticipating the blessing of Shavuot (Lev. 23:15–16). The early first fruits are represented by the barley harvest in Israel, while the later first fruits, 50 days later, acknowledges the wheat harvest of late spring. We already saw how Yeshua fulfilled all the spring holy days with his death on Pesach and resurrection on Bikkurim. It is now approaching the time for the next holy day of Shavuot to be fulfilled with the pouring out of the Holy Spirit on the Jewish believers.

After exhorting them to be his witnesses, Yeshua was *taken up before their eyes.* He was already in his resurrection body as the first fruits and the victor over death. Now it was time to ascend to the Father in heaven. This is actually a return to Messiah's eternal home at the right hand of the Father. The Talmudic rabbis debate this possibility as reflected in the below discussion about one of the angels, Metatron. This name means "precursor" or "next to the throne" and is given to one particular angel who makes some highly unusual appearances. He is held in especially high regard as the one who went before the Israelites in the wilderness (Ex. 23:20). So respected is this angel above the other angels that people are warned not to pray to him:

> *A Sadducee said to Rabbi Idit, "It is written, 'And unto Moses He said, Come up unto the Lord' (Ex. 24:1). It ought to have stated, "Come up unto Me"! He replied, "The speaker was Metatron, whose name is the same as his Master's, for it is written, 'My name is in him' (Ex. 23:21). "In that case," said the Sadducee, "we ought to pray to him!" "No," was the Rabbi's answer, "for the context declares, 'Do not exchange Me for him."* (Tractate Sanhedrin 38b)

This discussion shows the Angel of the Lord was seen by many as a unique being. Many considered Metatron as being at the Throne of God and yet revealed in Israel's history at various occasions. This fits with the New Testament description of Yeshua as the Messiah sent from God's presence to fulfill his mission as Messiah ben Joseph (Phil. 2:5–11). In the Book of Acts, we find Yeshua taken up again to the Throne of the Father after accomplishing his redemptive work.

Luke says *a cloud hid him from their sight*, so much so that *they were staring in the sky*. In context, this would not just be an ordinary cloud in the sky but likely a manifestation of the *sh'khinah* (Glory of God) at that encounter. This is confirmed by the fact that *suddenly they saw two men dressed in white standing next to them*. These men, appearing as radiant angels, make a startling pronouncement: *"This Yeshua, who has been taken away from you into heaven, will come back to you in just the same way as you saw him go into heaven."*

The story of Yeshua perfectly parallels the doctrine of ben Yosef as well as ben David. He came from heaven to fulfill the work of the Suffering Messiah, yet he was risen, so he could also fulfill the future work of King Messiah. The angels confirm that Israel and the world will see him return *in the same way*. This is important for several reasons. First, his return will be in the same physical, resurrected body as at his ascension. Through the ages, various sects and even cults have claimed Jesus has already returned but only they can see him! When Yeshua returns, every eye will see and there will be no question.

Second, Yeshua's physical return will take place at the same location as his ascension: *Har Ha-Zeytim* (the Mount of Olives) on the east side of Yerushalayim (Zech. 14:4; Acts 1:12). Too often Jesus is turned into an Indian guru, a Greek philosopher, and other cultural expressions from all over the world. The Scriptures testify that the historical Yeshua, the Jewish descendant of David, will return to the land of his birth in Israel. It has been a long 2000-year interlude, but his promise still stands. The disciples were greatly encouraged by this message, and we too can take great joy in knowing the true Messiah will return to his homeland in his own way. Some believers today are simply stuck staring into heaven! His promise is sure, but in the meantime, we, like those early believers, have some holy work to do.

Chapter Two

THE EARLY YESHUA MOVEMENT IN JERUSALEM

Every prophet only prophesied for the days of the Messiah and the penitent.

(Tractate Berakhot 34b)

III. The Upper Room – 1:12–26

That Yeshua's ascension took place on Har Ha-Zeytim is confirmed by what transpires next. The Jewish disciples returned *the Shabbat-walk distance* from that place to the city of Yerushalayim. This is one of Luke's Jewish details that reveal his intimate knowledge of Judaism, likely as a Hellenistic Jew. The term is a technical description of a rabbinic concept. The original problem derives from the fact that the Torah clearly says a Jew must not leave his "dwelling place" on Shabbat (Ex. 16:29). But we are told the Levites may walk 3000 feet outside to perform their religious duties (Num. 35:5). After considerable debate, the rabbis concluded this is three-quarters of a mile, an acceptable journey (Tractate Sotah 27a). This can even be expanded by having an *eruv* (boundary wire) around a city or neighborhood. The disciples returned *to the upstairs room where they were staying.* It is quite common to have such a

17

room even today in Israel as a place of study or prayer. The inclusion of the definite article "the" seems to indicate it was the same upper room used for the last Pesach Seder some 40 days previous.

A list of the Jewish disciples is given. These Hebrew names give a snapshot of who this inner circle included. *Kefa* (Aramaic, "rock") was also called *Shimon* (Hebrew, "hearing") and Peter (Greek, "rock"). All these individuals have multiple names, and this is still common practice among Jews. Every traditional Jew has at least two names: one Hebrew, the other from the local language where he/she lives. *Ya'akov* (James; Hebrew, "heel-grabber") and *Yochanan* (John; Hebrew, "God is gracious"), both sons of Zebedee. *Andrew* (Greek, "manly") is Kefa's brother and Philip (Greek, "lover of horses"). Next are *T'oma* (Hebrew, "twin"), *Bar-Talmai* (Aramaic, "son of Talmai"). *Mattityahu* (Matthew) means "gift of God," though many might dispute this since he worked for the Roman IRS! *Ya'akov Ben-Halfai* ("son of Alpheus") is recorded as well as *Shimon Ha-Kanai* ("Simon the Zealot"). Similarly listed is *Y'hudah Ben-Ya'akov* ("Judah son of James").

Included in this *minyan* ("number") are *some women, including Miryam (Yeshua's mother) and his brothers*. One need not study this list long to see the remarkable diversity of this inner circle of early followers. It would have led to some interesting small-group meetings with Matthew (the Roman employee) and Shim'on (the Zealot dedicated to assassinating Romans)! But this reminds us that Yeshua's call is to a higher Kingdom of God, not any earthly political agenda. In fact, they *devoted themselves single-mindedly to prayer*. This diverse minyan not only tolerated the differences in their midst but were actually unified through Yeshua's calling.

Too often today, there are divisions among believers because of differences between us: Jew/Gentile, Charismatic/non-Charismatic, conservative/liberal, even Republican/Democrat! We do well to learn the spiritual lessons from our early Messianic Jewish ancestors and focus on our unity in Yeshua even amid our diversity. In fact, Yeshua seemed to greatly appreciate these mixed dynamics, as he said others would know we belong to the Messiah by our unity (Jn. 17:23).

At this time this core group held an important meeting. *Kefa stood up and addressed* a group of about 120 Jewish disciples. Not coincidentally, Kefa is the main speaker; Yeshua himself gave him a special place of leadership in this first-century movement. Kefa is given the "keys of the Kingdom," which implies he will be used to open doors of new opportunities (Mt. 16:18–19). Indeed, as the history of Acts unfolds, Kefa is the mandatory representative as the Good News goes from the Jews in Yerushalayim (Acts 2) to Y'hudah and Shomron (8) and then to the non-Jewish world (10–11). At the meeting, Kefa talks to the group about the loss of Y'hudah. Shocking as his betrayal must have been to the group, Kefa shows how even that was part of God's great plan. The *Ruach HaKodesh spoke through King David about Y'hudah* because *the Tanakh had to be fulfilled. With the money he received for his evil deed, Y'hudah bought a field* (Hebrew *Hakal D'ma); and there he fell to his death.*

The enigma of Judas remains. He is often depicted as an evil man who rebelled against his God (as even the anti-Semitic "Passion Plays" of the Middle Ages depict). No doubt Satan moved him to do evil. But it is also possible Judas was a traditional Jew who looked for the messianic Kingdom. If so, maybe he grew disenchanted with his group as Yeshua increasingly spoke of his approaching death and the delay of the Kingdom. It doesn't justify Judah's actions, but the first-century Jewish experience makes it more understandable.

The graphic description of his death has led to much speculation about the details. Did Y'hudah commit suicide by hanging himself? Did the rope break and he fell? Was his body cast outside Yerushalayim's walls, as it would have rendered others unclean during the start of Pesach? We cannot be sure, but either way, it is an obvious fulfillment of the prophecies (Ps. 69:25, 109:8).

As Y'hudah was one of the original 12 *Sh'likhim* (apostles), *someone else [had to] take his place.* There were some obvious prerequisites for the replacement. First, he must be from *one of the men who have been with the emissaries continually* during Yeshua's earthly ministry. This must go back to *the time that Yochanan was*

immersing people until the day Yeshua was taken up from them.
Most importantly, the person had to be *a witness to the resurrection.*
He would be sent out as any eyewitness to Yeshua's life and
message as the risen Messiah. While the Greek *apostolos* means
"one sent out," the Hebrew *shaliach* has a stronger connotation. The
Talmud defines the person thus:

> *"A shaliach is equal to the sender himself"* (Tractate Berakhot
> 34a). *It was clear to the other Sh'likhim that these important
> qualifications were essential in order for the new emissary to
> minister as an eyewitness representative of Yeshua.*

With all this in mind, *they nominated two men—Yosef Bar-Sabba,
surnamed Justus* (Joseph Barsabbas), *and Mattiyahu* (Matthias). Not
surprisingly, they sought God's wisdom in prayer as they asked the
Father to show them *which of these two* to choose. To do this, the
emissaries turn to a traditional Jewish method found in the Tanakh as
they drew lots (Prov. 16:33). This practice involved writing names on
dice-sized pebbles, which were shaken in a jar until one fell out. To
the modern believer, this might seem a "dicey" way to determine
God's will. But remember, they were trying to hear from God at a
time before the giving of the Holy Spirit on Shavuot. Combined with
sincere prayer, the drawing of lots was implemented to reveal that
Mattiyahu was chosen to be *added to the eleven emissaries.*

Interestingly, some scholars have debated if the apostles made
the right decision. Some speculate that they should have waited to
include Sha'ul, who would come to faith in Yeshua in the months to
come. He himself noted he was appointed directly by Yeshua as a
shaliach as he too was a witness of the resurrected Messiah. He
laments that he was not part of the original 12 only because he was
"born at the wrong time" (I Cor. 15:8–9). Though Mattiyahu is
appointed, we never hear from him again in the Book of Acts.

IV. The Shavuot Encounter – 2:1–41

It was indeed an eventful 50 days between Pesach and Shavuot in that year 32 C.E. It has been customary since the days of Moshe to celebrate three major holy days each spring. Pesach, the feast of redemption, starts on the Jewish calendar on 15 Nisan, which usually falls in March/April. Technically, it is the first night (or first two nights outside of Israel) where the Pesach Seder meal is observed to recall our physical redemption from Egypt. This is followed by the seven days of the *Chag HaMatzot* ("Feast of Matzah"). It is so interconnected with Pesach that we usually refer to the entire eight-day period as Pesach. On the second night of Pesach, the Jewish world begins to count of the *omer* offering called *S'firat Ha-Omer*. There is a traditional blessing recounted every evening as we count the 50 days until Shavuot. On the third day of Pesach is another holy day that acknowledges the first fruits of the barley harvest. This is Bikkurim.

With great anticipation, the days are counted off until we reach the third holy day known as Shavuot, the Feast of Weeks. It is called this in the Torah as it designates its timeframe that is seven weeks + one day after Pesach, or 50 days (hence the name *Pentecost*). The focus of this holy day is the celebration of receiving the Torah at Mount Sinai and the hope for a fruitful summer harvest. All these spring holy days are described in great detail in the Torah and continue to be a central part of our Jewish faith (see Lev. 23).

Looking at the bigger spiritual picture, we see all these festivals point to the prophetic work of the coming Messiah (Kasdan, *God's Appointed Times*). As Pesach is the feast of our redemption, it is no coincidence that Yeshua died on the Roman execution stake on the afternoon of Pesach. As the barley offering was raised up on Bikkurim, so too was Yeshua raised from the earth exactly on the third day. As we saw in Acts 1, Yeshua exhorted his disciples to wait for the blessing of the Ruach to come upon them. And the Ruach is poured out on the Jewish remnant exactly on the day of Shavuot as they themselves became the early harvest within Israel.

So important are the Jewish biblical festivals that three are called the *Shalosh Regalim* ("Three Foot Festivals"), where Jewish men are required to make a pilgrimage to Yerushalayim if possible. The three prioritized feasts are Pesach, Shavuot and *Sukkot* ("Tabernacles"). The Holy City was always packed to overflowing at these times. The Jewish Roman historian Josephus testifies that over 250,000 Pesach lambs were prepared one year, which would represent over a million Jewish worshipers (*The Jewish War* 6.9.3). This detail is significant regarding the celebrations of 32 C.E.; Yerushalayim was certainly packed as Yeshua was executed by the Romans, and rumors of his resurrection permeated the larger Jewish community. The fulfillment of Pesach and Bikkurim was not done in secret but in a most-public way during the height of the holy day season. The third holy day now awaited its spiritual fulfillment in first-century Israel.

Consistent with the Jewish holy day season, *the festival of Shavuot arrived and the believers all gathered together* in Yerushalayim. The celebration would include prayers blessing God for the giving of the Torah at Mt. Sinai and thanksgiving for the first fruits, represented by the wheat harvest in Israel. It was a huge spiritual party with religious services in the *Beit Ha-Mikdash* (Temple) as well as feasting and sweet fellowship among all who gathered in the Holy City.

Amidst all the festivities in the diverse Jewish crowds were representatives from the newer Yeshua movement who convened *in one place.* This is one of the many reminders in Acts that the early Jewish believers naturally continued in their God-given heritage. They did not see themselves as converts to a new religion but as Jews who embraced Yeshua as the promised Messiah. They are later identified as followers of "The Way" and "Nazarenes," meaning they were followers of the branch (Hebrew *netzer*) from King David's lineage (Isa. 11:1; Acts 9:2, 24:5). They were Messianic Jews, to use the contemporary term, who continued to participate in Judaism's holy days and heritage. As the morning services were in full swing, *there came a sound from the sky like the roar of a violent wind.* Luke uses a simile that would certainly get the attention of any

Jew or Hebrew speaker. There probably was a literal wind that suddenly picked up on the Temple Mount. But the implied experience is deeper than that, as *ruach* can mean both "wind" and/or "spirit." That phenomenon was like a roar from the sky.

This Ruach manifestation is said to have *filled the whole house where they were sitting*. It is important to understand some of the implied Hebrew language. Many interpreters assume "the whole house" means the Upper Room of the Last Seder and post-resurrection gatherings. But we read that *many thousands* of Jewish worshipers engage with the Messianic disciples (2:41). No room in Yerushalayim, or anywhere else, could fit such a crowd. A better option is clarified when we see the Hebrew name of the Jerusalem Temple was *Beit Ha-Mikdash* ("The Holy House") or simply *Ha-Bayit* ("The House"). This better fits the context of the massive celebration of Shavuot on the Temple Mount in the first century.

Other spiritual manifestations were encountered at that Jewish celebration as the disciples *saw what looked like tongues of fire that came to rest on each one of them*. The manifestation is clearly not literal fire; it is "like" fire. It is a simile reminiscent of the spiritual world. Often the concept of fire is used to describe the sh'khinah. To anyone who knows Judaism, the connection between Shavuot, fire and the sh'khinah sounds familiar.

For over 2000 years there have been special, chanted readings for the synagogue and Temple service. It is logical that the long-established Torah reading for this holy day retells the giving of the Torah from Mt. Sinai along with the signs of fire and wind (Ex. 19–20). The *Haftorah* (reading from the Prophets) for Shavuot has long been from the amazing revelation of the *Merkava* (chariot) with its flashes of fire and dramatic wind (Ezek. 1:1–28, 3:12). This is still read today for its parallel connection to the sh'khinah experience at Mount Sinai. Ezekiel records some additional vital details. After the vision of God's glorious throne, the Prophet also records the eventual departure of the sh'khinah from Israel. It is in progressive stages in his day that the Glory first leaves the Temple through the

Eastern Gate (Ezek. 10:18–19, 11:22–25). As far as Jewish history is concerned, this departure of the sh'khinah was so complete that it would only be restored in the messianic age:

> *When Israel is dispersed, the Sh'khinah is with them, as it is said, "The Lord shall return your captivity" (Deut. 30:3). It is not said, "Will bring back" but "will come back"; that is, He will come back with you."* [Deuteronomy Rabah 7:10]

With this history in mind, the Shavuot celebration in Acts 2 becomes even more spectacular. This is the *Shachrit* (morning) service (2:15), so we know the readings from Exodus and Ezekiel were on public display for all. Quite possibly the manifestation of God's Glory appeared to the crowds at the very moment of chanting about the departure of the sh'khinah. The Ruach was stirring as was the fire manifestation of the Glory right as the crowds were retelling the story! All this got the attention of the larger crowd of the *religious Jews* who were *staying in Yerushalayim* for the holy day, but there was more. The Messianic disciples *began to talk in different languages, as the Spirit enabled them.*

Some take this to mean the Jewish believers were speaking in a spiritual prayer language they alone could understand (I Cor. 14:1–2). But in context, it's clear that they were miraculously speaking in a foreign language (Greek *glossa*) they had not studied. That is why the writer points out that the international Jewish crowd, including some *proselytes*, could hear *the believers speak in their own language*, even in their exact dialect. This got the attention of the holiday crowd as they were from such far-flung areas of the diaspora as Babylon, Asia and North Africa. The crowd is clearly amazed and confused as this Messianic group is mostly from Galil. How could they speak about *the great things God has done* especially since they heard them in their own dialect? Some were sincerely asking, *"What can this mean?"* The skeptics mocked, *"They've just had too much wine!"*

At this key moment *Kefa stood up with the Eleven* to not only address the questions but to give one of the most amazing sermons ever delivered on the Temple Mount. He calls for their attention, first addressing the skeptics. Yeshua's disciples aren't drunk; *it's only nine in the morning*. It would be in the middle of the *Shacharit* morning prayer service for the holy day. This traditional Jewish service is still modeled in the modern synagogue structure between dawn (*shachar*, "morning star") and noon. There are the requisite prayers and the standard Torah and Haftorah readings, which still includes Ezekiel 1. Traditional Jews often follow a modified fast where they usually do not eat or drink until the prayers are over.

This in mind, Kefa continues: No, this is what was spoken about through the prophet Yo'el (Joel): "*ADONAI* says: 'In the Last Days, I will pour out from My Spirit upon everyone. Your sons and daughter will prophesy...'" He is quoting Joel 3:1–5, which also predicts a day of miracles in the sky and on the earth, a darkened sun, a blood moon—all a harbinger of the "great and fearful Day of ADONAI." He emphasizes that these signs are for the divine purpose of messianic redemption: "Whoever calls on the name of ADONAI will be saved."

After quoting this spectacular passage, Kefa makes a personal application to that first-century Shavuot service: "*Men of Isra'el! Listen to this! Yeshua from Natzeret was a man demonstrated to you to have been from God by the powerful works, miracles and signs that God performed through him in your presence. You yourselves know this. ... This man was arrested ... you nailed him up on a stake and killed him!*"

It is a strange connection between the Romans and some of the top Jewish leaders of the day, agents of both the pagan world and the chosen nation. Some leaders from both groups opposed Yeshua, if for very different reasons. We can understand some of the Jewish opposition to this rabbi who made messianic claims. The Romans did not understand or care about such religious issues but didn't welcome the political turmoil surrounding this "King of the Jews." Kefa acknowledges some of these religious and political reasons but asserts that all these things were "*in accordance with God's predetermined plan and foreknowledge.*" Tragically, we Jews are sometimes accused of being "Christ killers" and worse. But Yeshua's suffering and death was ultimately orchestrated by God. Yeshua himself testified that he was voluntarily giving his life for the messianic redemption of the entire world, both Jews and non-Jews (Jn. 10:18; Isa. 53).

Yeshua's death would not complete the prophetic picture if that was the end of the story. As Kefa proclaims, *God raised him up and freed him from the suffering of death,* fulfilling the prophecies given to David: *"You will not abandon me to Sh'ol or let your Holy One see decay"* (Ps. 16:8–11). While applying in some sense to David, he could not fulfill this passage; *he was buried, and his tomb is with us to this day.* He anticipated that *one of his descendants would sit on his throne.* The God of Israel *raised up Yeshua* for this purpose, and Kefa emphasizes that the messianic group were *all witnesses of it.*

In fact, the good news of Yeshua is that *he has been exalted to the right hand of God* and even *poured out the gift of the Ruach HaKodesh.* This too is a fulfillment of the Tanakh: Psalm 110:1 calls on *my Lord to sit at my right hand.* The Hebrew says *the LORD / ADONAI* is speaking to someone also with the title *my Lord / Adonee.* The Messiah must have a divine nature to fulfill these supernatural predictions. No wonder several rabbinic interpretations apply Psalm 110 to the Messiah (Midrash Tehillim 2:9, 18:29).

The famous medieval rabbi Saadiah Gaon touches on this as he explains his view of Daniel 7:13, which says Messiah will be brought to the Ancient of Days (a title for the Lord). The rabbi quotes the opening line of Psalm 110 as his proof text that "the Lord will be at the right hand of the Lord" (Brown, 143). Kefa quotes some of these Jewish ideas as he describes the life, death and resurrection of Yeshua. It is his hope that the *whole house of Isra'el know beyond doubt that God has made him both Lord and Messiah!*

The reaction to this radical message was mixed, as is often the case today. In that crowd of tens of thousands, many either rejected or were apathetic. But Luke focuses on the large Jewish contingency that responded favorably. He says many were *stung in their hearts* with conviction and asked Kefa, *"What should we do?"* This group could not deny the supernatural manifestations taking place, including the amazing reappearance of the sh'khinah. These signs gave credibility to the message about the arrival of the promised Messiah, Yeshua.

In response to their question, Kefa said they should *turn from sin and return to God*. Each step is vitally important. Turning from sin implies we all fall short of God's standard. In fact, the Hebrew *chet* ("sin") is also used in the context of a soldier using a slingshot and not missing the mark (Judg. 20:16; Rom. 3:23). Some people may be better than others and even closer to God than other people. But we all miss God's target. The Messiah was promised to bridge that gap and connect us in close relationship with our Father in Heaven.

But we must proactively turn from sin; that is repentance. Another word for repentance is *teshuvah*, "return." Though sometimes translated "convert," to many Jews this seems to imply that turning to Yeshua is changing our religion or even our Jewish heritage. The Hebrew terms are much more understandable; Jews are called to return, not convert. We do not need a new religion or a new God; we need to turn from sin and return to the God of our fathers! It is the Gentiles who must convert away from the pagan Greek and Roman religions and connect to the true God of Israel.

Kefa gives other steps for the Jewish crowd to follow. *Each should be immersed on the authority of Yeshua the Messiah into forgiveness of their sins.* Ritual immersion in water was commonly understood in first-century Judaism. Since the days of Moshe, *tevilah* was an immersion in a *mikveh*, a manmade or natural body of water. This ritual was for purification after any "impure" event. (Men and women may take a mikveh for purity before other events as well.) But Kefa's exhortation was to be immersed, or baptized, in the name of Yeshua, for the forgiveness of sin. Kefa was presenting a new mikveh. This immersion was to testify that the person trusted in Yeshua as the promised Messiah. In Matthew 28:19 he said to *"make disciples of all nations, baptizing them in the name of the Father, Messiah and of the Ruach HaKodesh"*; some people claim a contradiction, as Kefa says to be immersed *"in the name of Yeshua."* But Acts 2 is to *"all the house of Israel"*—Jews—who already understand the Father and the Ruach; their mikveh was to declare they received Yeshua as Messiah. Matthew 28:19 refers to bringing the Good News to *"all nations"*—i.e., Gentiles, who would have lacked even a basic understanding of one God and Holy Spirit.

As the crowd followed Kefa's admonition, he assured that they would also *receive the gift of the Ruach, the promise for you, for your children, and for those far away* (a hint of God's similar invitation to non-Jews). Kefa and the disciples presented *many other arguments*, implying even this beautiful sermon of Acts 2 is but a summary. Finally Kefa challenges them to *save themselves from this perverse generation*. Luke records that *about 3000 people were immersed and added* to this early Yeshua movement. These details also underline the fact that the dramatic events of that Shavuot could not have been in a small "upper room" but in *the house* of the Temple Mount (Acts 2:2). Not only was it a large crowd who heard Kefa's message, but they also faced the logistical challenge of having a *mikveh* for 3000 new Messianic Jews! Modern archaeology confirms that dozens of ritual baths surrounded the Temple Mount.

As that dramatic Shavuot ended, the early Yeshua followers faced a daunting challenge. What were they to do with 3000 new believers? How would they all connect to this nascent community? Who would lead these new spiritual sheep? Acts documents four general areas that were developed to address these needs. I use the acronym *HATS* to summarize four Hebrew concepts. ***H*** is for *Havurah* ("fellowship"); the believers *continued faithfully in fellowship* (2:42). Jews have always emphasized the value of community. We are not meant to be alone; you can't live the *mitzvot* (commandments) without other people. "Synergy" means the total (like of the community) is greater than the individual parts. It is good to meet in larger groups as they did in the Temple and synagogues. With such a large group, it was also beneficial to meet in *several homes where they shared their food in joy* (v. 46). The Messianic Jewish community was a place where they could be strengthened in their new faith and use their gifts to bless others. There are also references to the community in very practical terms, even *selling their extra property* and giving the *proceeds to all who were in need* (v. 45). The early believers aided any who were in need. It is still true today that we are not to forsake our assembly together (Greek *synagogue*; Heb. 10:25). The modern Messianic Jewish movement continues to grow, but there are still too many believers who are not plugged in as they are instructed to be.

The *A* in *HATS* is for *Avodah* ("worship, service"). Acts 2 documents several actions that speak to this. There were gatherings for lifting up God through music, *the prayers and even miracles* (vv. 42–43). They were *praising God in the Temple courts daily*, convening in the "messianic corner" of *Shlomo's Colonnade* (Solomon's Porch; 2:46, 3:11). Likely they worshiped in the only form they knew—Jewish tradition from the Temple and synagogues, including music, psalms, prayers, and the Torah service with its readings. The reference to "*the* prayers" (v. 42) refers to specific liturgical prayers in the *Siddur* (prayer book). Many foundational prayers were already in place in the first century. Many psalms were highlighted from the times of King David (Ps. 95–100) and the *Shema/V'ahavta* from Moshe's time (Deut. 6:4–9). There were also such ancient prayers as the *Amidah* and the reading of the Torah, all incorporated in first-century worship. "Avodah" means both "worship" and "work"! Too many today believe they have worshiped by sitting in a pew. In Jewish thought, we have not truly worshiped until we do some work for God's Kingdom!

The letter *T* is for *Torah*, which summarizes another vital part of the early Yeshua community. When we say "Torah," most think of the 5 Books of Moshe, or Law in general. But the Hebrew root, from *morah*, "teacher," is far broader. Clearly the early Yeshua believers also had a strong focus on teaching; Torah, the larger Tanakh and surely the more-recent New Covenant ideas as expressed by *the teaching of the emissaries* (v. 42). This no doubt included the ongoing Jewish tradition of reading (actually chanting) the traditional *Parasha* portion of the weekly synagogue service. Much of the rest of the Tanakh would be reviewed in the Prophets, which is also coordinated throughout the Jewish world to this day.

As we will see many times in Acts, the early Jewish believers did not change long-standing traditions but added their newer messianic perspective. We even have indications that the early Yeshua movement added some of the messianic writings to congregational meetings (Col. 4:16). Messiah's modern followers can again glean some important lessons. Teaching must be the strong foundation of our contemporary messianic synagogues and churches of other communities. We do well to apply Sha'ul's focus to teach "the whole council of God" in a balanced diet of *Torah, Tanakh and Brit Chadashah* (20:27). Such teaching will help us know God's perspective on all the other areas of messianic life and practice.

The last letter, *S*, is for *Sh'lichut* ("outreach"), a major pillar of the early messianic community. This can be seen in the allusions to *helping those in need* and even *breaking bread in their homes* as they reached out to their local community (vv. 45–46). This *breaking of bread* is not about the Last Seder; it is literally sharing meals together. It was, and still is, quite common to literally "break bread" (*betziat lechem*) as seen in the Shabbat blessings over the challah.

Besides these practical outreach efforts, the early Messianic Jews were excited to share their faith in Yeshua as the greatest act of Sh'lichut. And *the Lord kept adding to them those who were being saved*. These outreach efforts must remain a core value of today's messianic movement. It is good to connect with our larger community through such efforts as food drives, homeless assistance and a variety of other *mitzvah* projects that bless others, Jews and non-Jews (Mt. 5:16). Yet the greatest outreach focus should be sharing the blessing of Yeshua with all peoples; to the Jew first (Mt. 28:19; Rom. 1:16).

As modeled in Acts 2, this does not mean a conversion campaign to take Jews away from their heritage but sharing Yeshua as the fulfillment of what we Jews should be looking for. These Jewish additions to the community did not see themselves as leaving the faith of their fathers but as receiving the wonderful reality that Messiah has come! The modern messianic synagogue model is a great way to show that our faith in Yeshua is compatible with our Jewish heritage.

These last few verses of Acts 2 give us an incredible snapshot into the early Yeshua movement and its structure. The acronym *HATS* is a summary of their core values. Many dynamic synagogues and churches have used this model over the centuries to try to capture the original vision and enthusiasm. If it succeeded in the first-century Jewish community, we modern Messianic Jews strongly believe it can be the key to our ongoing strength and growth!

All whom the Holy One, blessed be He, smote in this world He will heal in the World to Come. The lame will be cured; as it is said, "Then the lame man will leap as a deer." (Isa. 35:6) (Beresheet Raba 95.1)

V. Miracle on the Temple Mount – 3:1–4:4

It had been a spectacular few weeks since Yeshua's Last Pesach. Roman leaders thought they'd rid themselves of a political agitator. Some Jewish leaders hoped this renegade rabbi would be just a passing memory. Yeshua's resurrection on Bikkurim not only sustained but intensified the Jewish religious movement. It was clear from the Shavuot service at the Temple that this was merely the first fruits of a revitalized messianic movement. By the power of the Ruach, Kefa proclaimed the risen Yeshua as the promised Messiah.

With the addition of 3000 new Jewish believers, the Yeshua movement was rapidly growing. It didn't take long for the continuation of some amazing events. Yochanan and Kefa (part of Yeshua's inner circle) were *going up to the Temple one afternoon*. Though they were part of the new messianic community, they stayed connected to the Temple as the gathering place for the larger Jewish community. They still saw themselves as fellow Jews and could participate in their long-standing tradition. Luke's phrasing again reveals his knowledge of Judaism as he speaks of *"going up"* to the Temple. Though Yerushalayim is in the hill country of Judea, it is not geographically the highest point. But they say that going to the Holy City is always an ascent (*aliyah*). Even if you come from the Himalayas, you must "go up" to Yerushalayim because it is a journey to a higher spiritual level!

Luke says it was precisely *three o'clock, the hour of Minchah prayers*. Since the earliest days of the Temple and later synagogue, the Jewish prayer service has been structured around the daily offerings. Between the morning prayers (*Shacharit*) and the evening prayers (*Ma'ariv*) were the mid-afternoon *Minchah* prayers (Dan. 6:11). These services were originally the times of the animal sacrifices at the Temple, but after its destruction in 70 C.E., the services were adjusted to the local synagogues as a replacement of the sacrifices (Donin 13). Kefa and Yochanan were coming to the Temple for the afternoon service when they saw *a man crippled since birth being carried in. … Every day people used to put him at the Beautiful Gate so he could beg*. The concept of *tzedakah* (charity) has long been a key value in Judaism. We are to help all in need and with a good attitude; a secondary meaning of tzedakah is justice (Deut. 15:9–11; II Cor. 9:7). So important is this mitzvah that even a person who receives tzedakah must himself give tzedakah (Tractate Gittin 7b)! As Kefa and Yochanan were about to enter, the man asked them for some money.

Kefa, seeing the man's deeper needs, replies with a powerful exhortation. Instead of silver or gold, he offers the beggar to *walk in the name of the Messiah Yeshua*. Kefa does not see himself as a miracle worker in his own power; he invokes Yeshua's authority. Not long before, Kefa had revealed his personal weakness as he denied his rabbi. These bold, miraculous events testify to the life-changing power of the Ruach that was now upon the messianic believers.

At that moment, Kefa *pulled up* the beggar as *his feet and ankles became strong*. Doctor Luke uses a medical term that connotes a long-term healing process, but here it was instant (*Linguistic Key* 268). This all occurred to a man who was lame from birth! With this instantaneous healing, he could not contain himself and began *walking and leaping* for the first time *and praising God*. As everyone in the Temple courtyard witnessed his excitement, they were *utterly amazed and confounded*. Since the restored man *clung to Kefa and Yochanan, all the people came running* to meet them in Shlomo's Colonnade, which seems to be the messianic meeting-place at the Temple area.

With another Jewish crowd assembling on the Temple Mount, Kefa saw a chance to again declare the Good News of Messiah's arrival. His message has some parallel themes of the earlier Shavuot sermon, but with more details. He starts with some questions for his fellow Israelites. Why are they *amazed*, and *why do they stare* at them as if this man could now *walk through some power* of the disciples? *The God of Avraham, Yitz'chak and Ya'akov* has shown his power. Kefa emphasizes the continuing connection between this new Yeshua group and the larger Jewish community, noting it is *the God of our fathers* (not "*your* fathers") who is at work. The Jewish believers still did not believe they were propagating a new religion but sharing the fulfillment of the Torah promises with the coming of Yeshua, *who was handed over and disowned before Pilate.*

Kefa emphasizes both sides of Yeshua's rejection and says, *you denied the innocent one* and *asked for a murderer (Bar-abbas).* Kefa says "you," but in the historical context, the rejection was clearly led by some of the Jewish leaders. Anti-Semites sometimes invoke such statements to justify their hatred of the Jews, but a close study of the New Testament does not reveal a uniform rejection of Yeshua. In fact, in Acts we find thousands of Jews who approved of him and still appreciated their people and heritage (21:20).

But Kefa doesn't gloss over the reality that many Jewish leaders gave Yeshua to Pilate and the Romans for execution. Kefa points out that *God has raised Yeshua from the dead*—and many of them were *witnesses*! By referring to the famous "Suffering Servant" passage, he again shows that Yeshua of Nazareth is the predicted Messiah ben Joseph (Isa. 52:13–53:12). The living Messiah has given *strength to this man whom you see and know.* It is not just the historical facts of Yeshua's death and resurrection that are key. Personal faith and *trust* has unleashed the power of *this perfect healing.*

Kefa now redirects his message away from the tragic rejection of Messiah to the positive promises of what it would accomplish. First, he addresses the Jewish group as *brothers*, affirming they remain connected despite differences. He points out that they did not grasp the significance of what they did. Many of the crowd likely weren't even present at Yeshua's actual rejection; still others disagreed with the majority verdict. Even some of the *leaders* didn't know what they were doing; hence Yeshua's prayer of forgiveness for those in that category (Lk. 23:34). Through all the twists and turns, Yeshua's death fulfills what *God had announced through all the prophets.*

Having summarized the recent amazing events in the Holy City, Kefa calls on his Jewish brothers to *repent and turn to God.* The Greek *metanoia* literally means "a change of mind." This is a good start, but the older Hebrew word is much deeper. The equivalent Hebrew term *shuv* means "return." In Jewish thought, one has not truly repented until there is an authentic change of direction. It is not just changing one's thoughts or feelings but actually turning around one's actions.

The concept to *shuv* or *making teshuvah* is also quite apt for the Jewish audience. Everyone needs to repent, but for us Jews it's a return to where we should have always been. Too often we turn from our Father in Heaven. Kefa points out that he is not advocating a new religion or a new god but a return to the God of Israel.

This act of teshuvah is said to have wonderful benefits. Kefa explains that as anyone returns to God in this way, their *sins will be erased.* The wording is significant. In the Temple-period Judaism where these events are occurring, God provided a way of covering the sins of corporate Israel and the individual Jew. The various *korbonot* (sacrifices) were given in the Torah as a way for our sins to be covered. The greatest picture of this was the annual observance of Yom Kippur, where the sins of Israel were covered symbolically by the sacrifices. The wording in Kefa's message speaks of a different level, not just covering but *erasing* the sins.

This was always the promise of the Tanakh, that there would come a new covenant era where we would no longer need the annual sacrifices because Messiah would erase our sins in a final way (Jer. 31:31–34). To Kefa and the early Messianic Jews, that day had come through the work of Yeshua! Another benefit of returning to God is that the *times of refreshing may come* to Israel and the nations. This is descriptive of the long-awaited Kingdom of God where there will be peace and blessing upon all. Since the days of our father Abraham, Jews have longed for the Kingdom where Israel will enter its full potential. But this is not only in the distant future; a beautiful refreshment comes as one opens their life to the presence of Messiah. We can deduce that Yeshua actually offered the promised Kingdom to Israel in the first century. Hypothetically, had all Israel received him and his offer, the Kingdom of God would have come at that time. It was not to be, as most of the nation, especially many leaders, rejected him as the promised Messiah. Though the wait continues, the promise of the Messianic Age is still a bright hope for those who believe.

Because of the national rejection of Yeshua, he has to *remain in heaven until the time comes for restoring everything*. We again see an allusion to the rabbinic concept to the Messiah's twofold mission. Though Yeshua fulfilled the work of ben Yosef by his suffering, he still awaits the proper time to return as King Messiah, ben David. These things are confirmed by *what God said long ago through the prophets*. The Jews on the Temple Mount would have respected these words as Kefa alludes to the greatest Jewish prophet, *Moshe himself*. By invoking the words of the Torah, the emissary focuses on one of the most amazing prophecies ever given. In Deuteronomy, Moshe tells his people to watch for a *prophet like* himself and, in some ways, greater than him. He will come *from among your brothers* (as a Jew), and they must *listen to everything* he will tell them. Those who disregard him or *fail to listen will be destroyed*.

Kefa ends his Temple Mount message by encouraging the people that they are in fact *the sons of the prophets* and *included in the covenant which God made with our fathers*. This Good News of Yeshua is the final piece of the puzzle regarding the promises given to Abraham, Moses and Isaiah. He calls this message a wonderful gift to the whole world: *By your seed that all the families of the earth will be blessed* (Gen. 12:3). Since these promises were made to the Jewish people first, it is natural that *God first sent his servant to them*. Through the power of the risen Messiah, *he might bless* them as they turn from their *evil ways*. Yeshua fulfilled all the necessary work for our redemption, but the choice is ours: receive, or turn a deaf ear.

As in the earlier Shavuot service, there was a mixed response from the crowd. As the emissaries were still telling about Yeshua, some of the Temple *leaders came upon them*. This included *cohanim* (priests), the *Temple police* and even some *Tz'dukim* (Sadducees). The latter were *very annoyed* that the Messianic believers were *teaching the doctrine of the resurrection*, especially that the risen *Yeshua* was the ultimate *proof*. This is understandable in light of the Sadducee rejection of this core teaching of the Tanakh (Dan. 12:1–2; Mt. 22:23ff). With this turmoil disrupting the Temple Mount, the *Temple police* arrested the messianic leaders and *put them in custody overnight*. But even amidst this open opposition, many Jewish seekers were curious about, even positive toward the message. Luke estimates that *about five thousand* trusted in the message and became part of the growing first-century Yeshua movement.

The Temple Mount miracle had a dynamic impact on first-century Israel and still reverberates today. With the growth of the modern Messianic movement, Jews from all backgrounds continue to be intrigued by the message of the new covenant. Estimates vary, but some say there are at least 100,000 Jews who trust in Yeshua today. The growth of the messianic synagogue movement (some 200 such groups in the U.S. and Israel) is also testimony of the power of the risen Messiah. As was the case in the first century, there were certainly those opposed to the idea of Yeshua as Messiah. But as we see in Acts 3, multitudes of traditional Jews welcomed Yeshua as part of their faith. Acts will continue to document the growth of the early movement. We modern Messianic Jews are witnesses today of God's move among our people as the *times of refreshing* draw ever closer!

VI. The Jewish Controversy After Bikkurim – 4:5–31

With such a big public display on the Temple Mount, the local authorities quickly responded. Yerushalayim was increasingly taking note of this messianic community. The miraculous healing of the man born lame got the attention of many. The subsequent teaching of Kefa and the other messianic leaders no doubt stirred many questions, especially the focus on the resurrected Messiah Yeshua. So, *the next day that the people's rulers, elders, and Torah-teachers assembled.* This could be the entire body of the Sanhedrin, which included 70 religious leaders and the High Priest. It is also possible this meeting was not of the larger body but a legal quorum of 23 (Tosefta Sanhedrin VII.I). Luke notes some of the representatives present. Chanan (Annas) was High Priest from 6–14 C.E. and was influential even after his retirement. Kayafa (Ciaphas) was appointed reigning High Priest by the Romans from 18–36 C.E.

The name *Yochanan* gets scholars' attention, as it could refer to two men. The High Priest who succeeded Kayafa was Yonatan; this name is very different in Hebrew. There was also a famous rabbi, Yochanan ben Zakkai, the most influential leader of rabbinic Judaism in that day. Alexander is also mentioned; we know little of him, but he is mentioned in Josephus as a ruler in Yerushalayim (Bruce 98; Lightfoot 44). Luke notes the emissaries stood *"in the midst"* of the Sanhedrin. The Sanhedrin was always seated in a semi-circle so the members could have a full view of their colleagues, to encourage the transparency of legal proceedings (Tractate Sanhedrin 4.3).

The board has one overarching question: *"By what power or in what name* did you heal this lame man?" Given the phrasing, the religious authorities clearly were not casting doubt on the event itself. They wanted to know by what means it was accomplished—by the power of the God of Israel, or some other source. Some of the rabbis reflect the same view in the Talmud. A classic creative story recounts how a later rabbi, Yehoshua ben Perachyah, had a fictitious encounter with Yeshua where he repelled him because he "practiced magic and led astray and deceived Israel" (Tractate Sanhedrin 107b; Herford 52). The miraculous signs of the first-century Yeshua movement couldn't be denied, only their source called into question. It's an understandable concern and valid question by many sincere people even today.

Kefa gives a clear answer to the Sanhedrin representatives. The answer to how *this good deed was done for this disabled person* lies in the one the disciples call *the Messiah*. It is in the name of *Yeshua from Natzeret who was executed on a stake as a criminal*. But the healing miracle could only take place because *God has raised Yeshua from the dead*. Only a risen Messiah could do such things, not a dead rabbi! Kefa says Yeshua is a picture of King David's prophecies that *the stone rejected by the builders has become the cornerstone* of our Jewish faith (Ps. 118:22). Could it be that the builders / leaders at that time failed to acknowledge the very foundation of Messiah?

Kefa continues to uphold the importance of Messiah by emphasizing that *there is salvation in no one else*. This is wordplay in Hebrew: There is *yeshuah* ("salvation") in no one but the one called *Yeshua* (a personal name meaning "salvation"). To emphasize his point, Kefa says *there is no other name under heaven given to mankind by whom we must be saved*. This statement is inclusive of the whole world (mankind). There are many world religions with great moral values. But they all lack one thing: the promise of a divine Messiah who has come to pay for our sins and shortcomings.

It is not arrogant to say the Bible has a unique revelation from the true God. The fact is that the message of the Bible is a unique message of redemption as a gift from God through his Anointed One. Note, Kefa is addressing a totally Jewish crowd at this Sanhedrin hearing, and he highlights that there is no other name given for the spiritual salvation of us Jews as well. It is through embracing Yeshua that *we (Jews) must be likewise saved*. In fact, Yeshua came as a Jew to our people first! In short, no amount of religiosity (Jewish or Gentile) can take away our sins except for the work of this risen Yeshua. Of course, God alone is the ultimate Judge of every person, and he alone knows each person intimately. With that assurance, it is a message that is just as vital today as ever in the Jewish community and to the ends of the earth.

This was a challenging declaration amid this august committee. They were *amazed when they saw how bold* the emissaries were. This was magnified in their minds as they realized these disciples were *untrained 'am ha'aretz*—common people of the Jewish community. They would have been educated, orthodox Jews who participated daily in the synagogue and Jewish culture. But standing before some of the top rabbis in the Sanhedrin, one can see how these Galileans would be looked upon as ultra-orthodox or as not attending a Yerushalayim rabbinical yeshiva. It was almost hilarious if it weren't so serious— Galilean fishermen explaining themselves to the rabbinical board! The scholars detected something unusual about this group as *having been with Yeshua*. More than just a historical reference to their being disciples of the rabbi from Galil, it also hints at some spiritual quality that stood out as these disciples reflected the character of their rabbi.

The committee could *not discredit the healing* of the Temple beggar; he was *standing there beside them*. All this gave them a conundrum as to how to respond. They could *not possibly deny* the confirmed events, so they sought an alternate route. They decided it would suffice if the messianic disciples would *not speak any more to anyone in this name*. Sometimes even modern Messianic Jews call this an acceptable compromise: Maybe we can just fit in with the larger Jewish community by not making Yeshua an issue. But the solution was not acceptable to the early Jewish believers.

Kefa and Yochanan answered with a challenge: *"Should we listen to you rather than God?"* They couldn't stop sharing *what they have actually seen and heard*. These were not zealots but eyewitnesses to a resurrected Yeshua and miracles in his name. This is one of the greatest encouragements to believers in every age. The boldness and love for their community testifies to the reality of their encounter with God through his Messiah Yeshua. This is not just ignorant men's wishful thinking. They lived this faith with conviction, many to the point of death. They actually experienced that which they boldly testify. Luke says the Sanhedrin did not have an adequate answer for this messianic group. They *couldn't punish them* because of their popularity with many people in light of the healing on the Temple Mount. So they *let them go back to their friends*.

There was likely much anxiety in the larger group regarding the Sanhedrin hearing for their key leaders. But when they heard Kefa and Yochanan's positive report, they couldn't help but *raise their voices* in a prayer of thanks. This an important insight into the early Messianic Jews' faith and spiritual perspective. Addressing their request to *Adon* ("Master") itself reflects a common Jewish term for God. Their first thought affirms their appreciation for the One who *made heaven, earth, the sea and everything in them* (Ps. 121). With such a Master, everything is under control, even in the face of adversity. As is common in the Siddur, they reflect also on David's inspired words. They ask in prayer, *"Why did the nations rage and the peoples devise useless plans?"* It is an interesting application of Psalm 2, which certainly applies to the Gentiles and pagans of the world, but they infer that the principle also applies to these particular Jewish authorities who are opposing God's perfect plan in Yeshua. Such people are *"against ADONAI and against his Anointed One."*

Again we see a common method of Jewish interpretation of Scripture: *gezerah shava*, a word connection between two different ideas. Though the original context of Psalm 2 speaks of the nations coming against the anointed King David, the disciples see a natural connection also to the opposition to the greater anointed one, the Messiah. However, this prayer of the disciples expands the culpability to several parties. It is in fact many different groups *assembled against God's holy servant Yeshua including Herod and Pontius Pilate, with Gentiles and the peoples of Isra'el.*

"The Jews killed Christ" has been an inaccurate charge through history. Crucifixion is illegal in Jewish law. Historians and scholars (Jewish and other) do not deny Yeshua's rejection by most of the first-century Jewish leadership. That same group turned him over to the Roman authorities for execution. But the disciples' prayer here offers a balanced view that many groups participated in the rejection of the Messiah. Herod and Pilate are held responsible before God and even listed first here. Pilate's washing of his hands didn't fool the disciples or God. Along with this list of earthly accomplices, the prayer acknowledges that the larger reality of *God's power and plan [had] already determined beforehand what should happen*. Not only is it inaccurate and anti-Semitic to blame the Jews for Yeshua's death, it was all part of God's design for universal redemption through the death of the Messiah. It seems fitting that many groups representing the entire world participated in this plan that would ultimately benefit the entire world!

The messianic disciples close their group prayer beseeching God to *take note of the threats* of the secular public while enabling the believers *to speak the message with boldness*. They likewise ask him to continue *the signs and miracles through the name of Yeshua* as a confirmation to all that Messiah has come. Before they even stopped praying, *the place was shaken*. God answered their request as they were *all filled with the Ruach and spoke God's message with boldness*. The Jewish controversy after Bikkurim would continue with a renewed sense of purpose and steadfastness on the part of Yeshua's Jewish followers.

VII. Tzedakah in the Yeshua Community – 4:32–5:16

There were many blessings in this new Messianic Jewish community in those early months after the death and resurrection of Yeshua. Several tests came upon the group as they proclaimed this risen Messiah. While many of the challenges came from the external local community, Acts now turns to some of the internal dynamics of the first-century Yeshua movement. Luke says the large group in Yerushalayim was strongly unified, *one in heart and soul*. This is quite a statement for such a large, diverse entity. Though most of these Yeshua believers came from the Jewish community, there were still many ways that could potentially divide them—political parties (Zealots or Rome sympathizers) or religious differences (Pharisee, Sadducee, Essene, etc). Yet this diverse group had a strong focus on unity since they had a more important bond of the Ruach and their personal encounter with the living Yeshua. It is a good reminder for all Yeshua followers today. Even with the many differences among believers, the most important things in common must be our focus.

As we saw in Acts 2, the unity of the messianic community led many to share their possessions. There was surely a beautiful aspect of their community life; they watched out for each other and shared with those in need, even as their Torah background would encourage (Lev. 19:9–10, leaving the corner of the field for the poor). This was quite natural in light of all the blessings they had received through their new faith. It is also very understandable when we consider tzedakah, the focus on helping those in need. The word itself means "charity" or more directly "righteousness, justice." In Jewish tradition, helping the needy is the right thing to do. The medieval scholar Rambam (Rabbi Moshe ben Maimon) elaborated on eight degrees of tzedakah, starting with the lowest level:

1. When donations are given grudgingly.
2. When one gives less than he should but does so cheerfully.
3. When one gives directly to the poor upon being asked.
4. When one gives directly to the poor without being asked.
5. Donations where the recipient is aware of the donor's identity, but the donor still doesn't know the specific identity of the recipient.
6. Donations where the donor is aware to whom the charity is being given, but the recipient is unaware of the source.
7. Giving assistance in such a way that the giver and recipient are unknown to each other. Communal funds, administered by responsible people, are also in this category.
8. The highest form of charity is to help sustain a person *before* they become impoverished by offering a substantial gift in a dignified manner, or by extending a suitable loan, or by helping them find employment or establish themselves in business so as to make it unnecessary for them to become dependent on others. [*Mishneh Torah, Matanot Ani'im* 10]

These guidelines are helpful as we look at this Yeshua community. In such a large group, there were certainly some in need, including those who lost jobs or were otherwise persecuted for their faith. But *no one was poor*; the tzedakah funds were *distributed to each according to his need. Yosef ... called Bar-Nabba* ("the Exhorter"), *a Levi from Cyprus*, sold some of his real estate and *brought the money to the emissaries*. He will play a special role among them, especially as Sha'ul's assistant in ministry to the Gentiles. *With great power*, Luke says, *the emissaries continued testifying to the resurrection of the Lord Yeshua*. Evidently because of the positive testimony and lifestyle, the community was *held in high regard* by even the general public. All this was a wonderful testimony of the love of Yeshua in the first century and is still a great model for Messianics even today. The Good News certainly must be shared verbally today, but a picture is also worth a thousand words.

But Luke is clear that this growing community was far from perfect. Acts 5 gets our attention by starting with an abrupt *but*. In contrast to the sincere sharing of many in the Yeshua community, we now hear of a very different situation: *Hananyah and Shappirah* (Ananias and Sapphira). The names mean "God is gracious" and "beautiful," but their actions are ugly. Hananyah *sold some property* but, *with his wife's knowledge, withheld some of the proceeds for himself*.

On the surface, this looks like another example of tzedakah; they bring a sizable donation *to the emissaries*. But it becomes clear something is amiss. *"Why has the Adversary so filled your heart that you lie to the Ruach?"* Kefa asks. He affirms that *"the property was yours, and after you sold it, the money was yours to use as you pleased."* But they *withheld some of the money* pledged and *lied* about the true amount. They lied not just to the emissaries but *to God* himself.

These verses affirm another truth: The Ruach is the same essence as God. Add to this the Messiah Yeshua's divine essence, and the logical conclusion is that the one God is revealed in three entities, *Father, Yeshua and Ruach HaKodesh*. It's consistent with the ancient declaration, *"Shema Yisrael ADONAI Eloheinu, ADONAI Echad"*

("Hear, O Israel: the LORD our God, the LORD is One" (Deut. 6:4). Many scholars hold to the impossibility of God being revealed in multitudinous ways, but *echad* implies as much. Biblical Hebrew uses it to describe a unity of multiple entities. (In Gen. 1:5, *yom echad*; "evening ... and morning, one day. In Gen. 2:24, *basar echad*; "man ... and wife ... one flesh.") Other rabbinic sources debate that that God's mysterious nature could include the unity of various revelations. An intriguing quote from Jewish mystical literature:

> *Come and see the mystery of the word YHVH: there are three steps, each existing by itself: nevertheless, they are One, and so united that one cannot be separated from the other. The Ancient Holy One is revealed with three heads, which are untied into one.* (*Zohar* Vol. III, 288; Vol. II, 43)

This evidence reminds us of an overarching truth: God cannot be fully defined by mere human definitions. His tri-unity in no way compromises his uniqueness but in fact supports it! There are some mysteries around God's nature, but the bottom line is, if the Tanakh teaches such truth, it must stand as the ultimate authority. Acts 5 with the situation around Hananyah and Shappirah powerfully reaffirms that the Ruach is a direct manifestation of God.

Because of the gravity of this deception, especially in this new Yeshua community, there are grave consequences. *Hananyah fell down dead* as an immediate act of judgment. We are not told details, but perhaps this public confrontation of lying to God brought a heart attack. Some *young men*, fulfilling the duties of a *chevra kaddisha* (Jewish burial society), prepared his *body in a shroud and buried him*. People unfamiliar with Jewish tradition might find this swift burial odd or insensitive. It actually confirms the Jewish background of Acts. All this is a brief but accurate description of Jewish burial customs based on the biblical principle of Genesis 3:19 (dust to dust). As there is no embalming or tampering with the body, burial often takes place 24 hours after death (*Customs* 76).

Three hours later Shappirah *came in, unaware of what had happened*. Kefa tests her to see if she'll continue the scam. She lies about the donation, and Kefa accuses her of also *testing the Spirit of the Lord. Instantly she also collapsed and died.* She was buried *beside her husband.* Not surprisingly, great fear came over the messianic community. Some commentators question the intense judgment for lying. But it recalls Achan's deception and judgment (Josh. 7). Surely more-grievous sins have been committed by other believers. But God in his wisdom singled out this couple for this very-public judgment. In this new community, it was an early lesson as to the seriousness of discipleship. Not only did the lesson impact the first-century believers, but here we are contemplating its meaning even today. God is not looking for perfection but sincerity—which is good news for us!

With the leaven removed from their midst, a new door opens; *many new signs and miracles were done among the people.* They manifest *unity* as they continue to publicly gather in the Temple, especially at Solomon's Porch (3:11). Luke somberly observes that *no one else dared to join* the messianic community, no doubt as word spread of the seriousness of this commitment. But the disciples were *highly regarded* by others and there were many *new believers, both men and women*; the Lord was drawing people in despite their initial fears. Word spread that as the public came under Kefa's shadow, they would experience God's healing power. The Scripture does not encourage this expression but merely records the sentiments of the crowds. Nonetheless, throngs of Jewish people *gathered from the towns around Yerushalayim* to seek the healing power of God that was manifested in the work of the messianic disciples.

Some people see these great works and ask why this is missing or not emphasized in the modern Yeshua community. But many real miracles do happen today. Many Jewish believers are in the faith precisely because of events only God could orchestrate. But beware "false signs" that could take us away from the true God (Mt. 24:4–11). For discernment, Scripture says to not just naïvely accept any manifestation but test all things to verify they are from God (I John 4:1). Throughout the Bible, when God is about to powerfully move, there's usually a special outpouring of Holy Spirit activity (days of

Moshe, Joshua, Elijah, etc). So when the Messiah comes to earth, there will surely be testifying signs and miracles. We see this in Yeshua's ministry. It also explains the dramatic occurrences in Acts.

God is doing his work today, but recall that first-century Israel was in a unique time of history with the revelation of Messiah and the spread of the Good News. We should expect such spectacular signs to verify that Yeshua and his followers indeed have a message from the God of our Fathers (Heb. 1:1–4). We are blessed today to have the written history of the Tanakh and New Covenant to verify our faith in this age. Likewise, the God of our Fathers is still performing miracles in our midst as he sees fit. Whether God chooses to show a miracle or not today, we should let God be God.

VIII. The Second Arrest in Yerushalayim – 5:17–42

The booming Yeshua movement continued to dramatically impact Yerushalayim and its environs. As the emissaries shared their first-hand accounts of Yeshua, their Jewish brothers' responses varied. Multitudes were thrilled with this Good News and embraced the faith—not as converts but as those adding to their Jewish faith the final link of Messiah. We have seen, though, that some leaders in Yerushalayim had a different view. Because of the messianic fervor, the *cohen hagadol* (High Priest) and other members of the *Tz'dukim* (Sadducees) *were filled with jealousy*, having the messianic leaders *arrested* again (4:3). But this time, God had other plans. *During the night, an angel of ADONAI opened the doors of the prison and let them out.* The angel said to *stand in the Temple court and keep telling the people all about the new life* in the risen Yeshua. This they promptly did at the crowded early-morning service on the Temple Mount. This all came as quite a surprise to the High Priest and the Sanhedrin. What was expected to be a preliminary hearing of the messianic leaders soon turned to anxiety when *they did not find them in the prison*. In fact, *the jail was securely locked and the guards were still standing at the doors!*

Amidst the confusion, they learned the emissaries were *teaching the people in the Temple court*. The messianic leaders were taken to the Sanhedrin hearing and strongly rebuked. They had been told *not to teach in this name* but were *filling Yerushalayim* with the New Covenant teaching. Worse, by their message of Yeshua being the true Messiah, they were implicating the Temple leaders of *his death*. To these charges Kefa quotes the familiar refrain: *"We must obey God, not men"* (4:19). The emissaries reiterate a summary of the messianic message: *The God of our fathers raised up Yeshua.* Even at this emotional juncture, Kefa reminds the Sanhedrin that the message is not of a new religion but a fulfillment of the ancient promises. The Messianics saw themselves as still connected with the larger Jewish community, stressing that it is a message from the God of *our* fathers.

There is no doubt a basic disagreement between the Yeshua community and the rabbinic one, but it is between fellow Jews. Again Kefa recounts the recent history of their rejection of Yeshua, *having him hanged on a stake.* But the undeniable events did not stop there. *God exalted this man at his right hand as Ruler and Savior.* All this seems to be a reference to some of the ancient prophecies in the Tanakh about crucifixion (Deut. 21:22–23) and the exaltation of Messiah (Ps. 110:1). These recent events are not without purpose. It is *to enable Isra'el to do t'shuvah (repentance) and have her sins forgiven.* Recall that the root word *shuv* means "to return" to where we should have always been. This faith in Yeshua, according to the Jewish apostles, is a return to the God of Israel through the Messiah. The emissaries proclaim they *are witnesses to these things as well as the Ruach HaKodesh.*

The message of this encounter was not well-received by all. Some in the Sanhedrin were *infuriated and even wanted to put the emissaries to death.* Others were more sympathetic, particularly Rabban Gamli'el, a highly respected teacher of the Torah and the grandson of Rabbi Hillel. The Talmud shows great regard for Gamli'el: "Since Rabban Gamli'el HaZaken died, there has been no more reverence for the Torah, and purity and abstinence died out at the same time" (Tractate Sotah 9). As a top representative in the Sanhedrin, his view of this dynamic Yeshua movement differed.

After they put the messianic leaders outside, Gamli'el warned his colleagues to *take care of what they do to these men*. They should not rush to judgment because of some recent events in Israel, like the Jewish rebel named Todah / Theudas. The historian Josephus records how a charismatic leader by this name acquired several hundred followers with the promise that they would soon expel the Roman occupiers. To rally the Jewish troops, Todah took them to the edge of the Jordan and asserted they would cross it completely dry. The Romans were not too excited about these developments and seized the Jewish group while executing Todah, thus quelling a rebellion (*Antiquities* 20.5.1; 17:10.4; see also Bock 250).

The rabbi brings up another important example in the recent rebellion led by Y'hudah HaG'lili (Judah the Galilean), who led a revolt against the oppressive taxes being levied on the Jewish state. This example probably got the attention of the leaders especially since it was a rebellion started in the Galil, the home base of this Yeshua movement. This Judah *was also killed* by the Romans and his tax revolt came to naught (*Antiquities* 18.1.6; 20.5.2).

Gamli'el's point was, the leaders should *not interfere* with this Yeshua movement; *leave them alone*. The prior Jewish rebellions ended in defeat. His wisdom of the situation is: *If this movement has a human origin, it will collapse* like the other recent ones. *But if it is from God, they will not be able to stop them* and may even find themselves *fighting God!* The original Greek manuscript uses two different forms of the word "if." The first, about the human origin of this religious movement, implies an answer of "maybe." The second, about the possible connection to the God of Israel, implies "probably." So Gamli'el was at the least a sympathizer with this messianic movement and possibly a believer himself! It's a startling thought, but there were other first-century rabbis and leaders in the same category (Nicodemus and Yosef of Arimithea, who both served in the chevra kaddisha that aided in Yeshua's burial; Jn. 19:38–40).

The Sanhedrin members saw the wisdom in such an approach and *heeded Gamli'el's advice*. They voted for a lighter judgment of *flogging, commanded the emissaries not to speak in the name of Yeshua, and let them go.* The emissaries *were overjoyed at having been considered worthy of suffering disgrace on account of God.* They quickly returned to *teaching and proclaiming Yeshua as Messiah both in the Temple courts and in private homes.*

There are lessons for us who follow Yeshua. Most of us don't live in areas of intense persecution, but there is vocal opposition to our faith. Whatever the situation, are we willing to stand for Yeshua even when it is not popular? If he is the true Messiah, then we, like our early messianic forefathers, can take a stand for him even in joy!

> *As the first Redeemer [Moses], so the last Redeemer [Messiah]. Just as the first Redeemer was revealed [to the children of Israel] and then again hidden from them ... for three months ... so the last Redeemer will be revealed and then again hidden from them.* (Numbers Rabah 11:2)

IX. Leadership in the Yeshua Community – 6:1–7:60

After several chapters describing the complex relationship between the Yeshua movement and the larger Jewish community, Luke now focuses on some of the group's internal dynamics. By all accounts, the *disciples were growing* rapidly from all the diverse branches in first-century Judaism. There were new Jewish believers from Yerushalayim and greater Israel and all over the diaspora (2:5–11). Their unity was striking but not without its challenges. *Around this time, the Greek-speaking Jews began complaining against those who spoke Hebrew.* This situation highlights two of the main groups in the Jewish community at the time: Hellenistic Jews and Hebrew Israelis. Hellenists were those born and living primarily outside the land of Israel. Because of their location and history, they spoke the common language of the diaspora, Greek.

Many Jews found themselves in the midst of the Greek Empire and pervasive Greek culture after the rise of Alexander the Great (356–323 B.C.E.). While the Maccabean Revolt was a successful battle (celebrated every year at Hanukkah) against this Greek influence, most Jews outside Israel assimilated much of this Hellenistic influence into their daily lives. They were still strong in their identity as Jews, but they lived their Judaism within the culture of Greek Hellenism (not unlike how many American Jews today live within the American influences).

By contrast, the Hebrews were Jews born and living in Israel who retained the cultural focus of the land and their mother tongue. Most first-century Jews were fluent in several languages that permeated the Roman Empire, but it was a matter of emphasis. An analogy would be the parallels and differences between modern Askenazi (European) Jews versus Sephardic (Mediterranean) Jews.

What was the Hellenistic Jews' complaint? Amid this Yeshua movement's explosive growth, many of *their widows were being overlooked* in the daily benevolence support. The focus on community tzedakah was an essential work (4:32). To address this need, *the Twelve Sh'likhim called a general meeting.* They saw they were overwhelmed with their expanding responsibilities as spiritual shepherds. Though servants at heart, they did not feel it was a task consistent with their God-given job descriptions and giftings. They would be remiss if they were to *neglect the word of God in order to serve tables.* There were thousands of potential servants in the growing community, so they recommend the community itself *choose seven men* from among the group who were *known to be full of the Spirit and wisdom.* The servants must have strong spiritual maturity as well. Sha'ul later gives expanded details into the nature and qualifications for New Covenant *shamashim* (servants), including good character, trustworthiness and a good track record (I Tim. 3:8–13). The Twelve call this practical work an *important matter* though they themselves are to serve in the other important areas of *prayer and the Word.*

This proposal was *agreeable to the whole gathering.* It is hard to believe every person in the large meeting agreed (2 Jews, 3 opinions?), but there was strong unity on moving forward together with the plan. There are important lessons here for us. With a larger group (be it a congregation or ministry organization), there must be a broader perspective of the greater good. This makes things easier within the organization as it seeks to accomplish important goals.

Within the Body of Yeshua, we have extra motivation. The Yeshua movement is not just an "organization." It is a living organism of true believers seeking to accomplish our Messiah's will in his world. There will certainly be human disagreements even among good people, but we do well if we graciously see God at work through the consensus of the sincere group. This is one of the keys in Acts explaining the dynamic success of the early movement, and it is ongoing wisdom for ministry today.

These core values in mind, the community chose seven men who fit the qualifications. Top of the list is *Stephen*, a man *full of faith and the Ruach*. Likewise chosen were *Philip, Prochoros, Nikanor, Timon, Parmenas and Nicholas*. They all have Greek names. How fitting that when the need came up in the Hellenistic branch of the community, they appoint Hellenistic workers. Today when people might complain about a need, they likely should be the very ones to volunteer to meet it! Even with the diligent work of the larger group, *these men were then presented to the emissaries* for their approval. They did so through *prayer* and as they *laid their hands on them*.

Laying on of hands has long been a sign of connection between two parties. In the Torah, the connection can be between humanity and the Temple sacrifices as in the case of the High Priest laying hands on the goat of Yom Kippur (Lev. 16:20–22). The ceremony was also used in ministry ordination for spiritual leaders as well as a sign of imparting power for their task (Moshe/Joshua in Deut. 34:9). Even today, the Hebrew word for "ordination" of a rabbi or Jewish leader is *smikhah*, from the root word "connection." The symbolic gesture is striking, as it publicly illustrates the approval and connection of the recipient with the ordaining body, in this case the commissioning of these new servants by the existing apostles.

Though Luke focuses on the inner dynamics of congregational leadership, he notes its impact on those outside. With the spiritual leadership structured this way, the word of God continued to spread around Israel. The number of disciples in Yerushalayim grew rapidly. Perhaps it was because the spiritual infrastructure was healthy that the Ruach could draw even more new believers. Seekers likely were drawn to the community because they could see the beautiful interactions and healthy environment of the Yeshua group.

The impact was great as even *a large crowd of cohanim were becoming obedient to the faith.* Undoubtedly many common people continued to be drawn to the appealing message of Yeshua and his community. Sometimes people today wonder today why "the rabbis" and other leaders don't follow Yeshua as the Messiah. Acts gives a balanced view of the real history. There were many in Israel who did not receive Yeshua as the Messiah, but this verse simply yet profoundly attests that Jews from all strata of society were drawn by the words and works of this Messiah, as is still true today!

In a dramatic transition, the rest of Acts 6–7 centers on Stephen's work and ministry. One of the appointed Hellenistic Jewish servants, Stephen is a leading shamash and *a man full of faith and the Ruach HaKodesh.* As he is about to become the center of attention, Stephen is also called a man *full of grace and power who performed great miracles and signs among the people.* This was a dynamic combination of attributes that describes some powerful works of this Jewish disciple but also his beautiful personal spirit. Both the miracles and the graciousness with which they were performed got the attention of many in Yerushalayim.

As we've seen, along with the positive response from the multitudes is some pushback. Here it was *opposition from members of the Synagogue of Freedmen,* Jews formerly enslaved to Rome. This synagogue consisted of *Cyrenians, Alexandrians and people from Cilicia and the province of Asia.* These too were Hellenistic Jews from the diaspora who'd heard Stephen's message of Yeshua as Messiah. The synagogue members *argued with Stephen, but they could not stand up against his wisdom.* He was not only performing powerful signs but also articulating Yeshua's message in a way that connected with his Jewish brothers. The Hellenists had a hard time refuting his wisdom, so they secretly persuaded some men to accuse him of speaking *blasphemously against Moshe and against God.*

Of all the possible accusations, these were the gravest. A long-held tenet of Judaism is that no true prophet or message can be from God if it contradicts Moshe, the greatest prophet. This is reflected in 13 Principles of the Faith summarized by Maimonides (Rabbi Moshe ben Maimon), contained in the Jewish prayer book even today:

> *"I believe with perfect faith that this Law will not be changed, and that there will never be any other law from the Creator, blessed be His Name."*

It is commonly understood that there will be many later prophets and Scriptures, but if they contradict Moshe, they aren't of God. *"I have not come to abolish but to complete"* the Torah, Yeshua stressed (Mt. 5:17). Sadly, some Christian theologies confuse the issue, saying the Law is somehow annulled. For most Jews, this would make belief in Yeshua a non-starter as evidently the New Testament is changing the Law. For too long this one issue has caused a huge chasm between many Jews and Christians and kept many Jews from considering faith in Yeshua. A right understanding of Yeshua's teaching can do much to create a clearer appreciation how the Tanakh and New Covenant are in fact one consistent message from the one true God.

Still, these false accusations *stirred up the people as well as the elders and the Torah-teachers* to such a degree that they had Stephen *arrested and brought before the Sanhedrin.* It was there that *false witnesses* claimed he was *speaking against the Torah* and that *we have heard him say that Yeshua ... will destroy this place.* These were emotional charges at a tense judicial hearing, yet at that very moment the Sanhedrin members *saw that Stephen's face looked like the face of an angel,* aglow with the presence of the Sh'khinah glory.

Most English versions now start chapter 7, but the original scroll format of the New Covenant continues with Stephen's reply. The High Priest asks but one question: *"Are these accusations true?"* Stephen gives a lengthy response to prove his point. His message can be divided into three parts: the patriarch Yosef, the prophet Moshe, and the Temple service. These may seem arbitrary, but on closer inspection, they answer his accusers and even proactively address the idea of Yeshua being the Jewish Messiah.

He starts by addressing the council as *brothers and fathers*. Having been accused of speaking against the Torah, Stephen affirms he is speaking of an approach to Judaism where he still considers himself part of the Jewish family. He is talking about a vital part of historical Judaism, not a new religion. He affirms this by referencing Abraham our father as the starting point of his understanding and quotes at least four references to the Tanakh as he retells the journey and calling of this father of the Jewish people (Gen. 12:1, 7; 15:13–16; Deut. 2:5). Such impromptu quotes also show Stephen was a well-educated Hellenistic Jew of his day and is using this knowledge to challenge any accusation that he was somehow no longer a Jew.

After his statements about the father of Judaism, Stephen focuses on the patriarch Yosef—his rejection by his brothers and his miraculous *rescue* to the house of Pharaoh. Not only was he rescued, he was elevated to one of the highest positions as *chief administrator over Egypt*. Every Torah-educated Jew knew of the subsequent famine in Canaan and how Ya'akov sent our fathers there. The Jewish family first interacted with this Egyptian official without realizing he was their long-lost brother. On the second visit *Yosef revealed his identity to his brothers*. After that, the family settles in Egypt until the Exodus some 400 years later. Again Stephen has ready access in his spirit to many Torah sections about these historical events (Gen. 37:11, 28; 39:1–3; 41:37–44; 42:5; 45:1).

But there seems to be more to this extended reference to Yosef than even the history of Genesis. In the development of the Talmud, there are many stories and discussions that predate the New Testament era. One such discussion revolves around the idea that there may be coming a suffering Messiah called "son of Yosef."

"And the land shall mourn" (Zech. 12:12). *What is the reason of this mourning? Rabbi Dosa and the rabbis differ about it. Rabbi Dosa says: "They will mourn over the Messiah who will be slain, and the rabbis say: "they will mourn over the Evil Inclination which will be killed in the days of the Messiah..."* (Patai 167, quoting Tractate Sukkah 52a; see also Tractate Sanhedrin 98a, which connects the suffering Messiah with the servant of Isaiah 53 who is broken for our iniquities.)

The name Yosef is fitting; this Messiah is said to suffer much the same fate. As Yosef was rejected by his brothers and ultimately becomes their savior, so too will Messiah ben Joseph. He will be rejected by his own Jewish brothers but become their savior. And as Yosef was not recognized at the first visit, neither will this Messiah be recognized at first. Interestingly, Yosef didn't look like a Hebrew when his brothers saw him. So too with Yeshua, who often is portrayed as anything but a Jew, even beyond the point of Jewish recognition! Yet the beautiful truth of the connection between Yosef and Yeshua is, both are recognized and there is a big family reconciliation at the end. Stephen centers on the life of Yosef so his first-century brothers will consider the connection. We too live in a day when more and more of us Jews are recognizing Yeshua for who he really is: Messiah ben Joseph, who has come for us the first time as the suffering servant. Happily, many Christians are recognizing their Jesus as a traditional Jew!

Stephen moves on to the major portion of his *d'var Torah* (Torah message), which centers on the greatest prophet of Judaism, Moshe Rabbeynu (Moses our Teacher). This is to be expected; one of the accusations was that Stephen was against Moshe and the Torah. He invokes the long history of this time of Israel, recalling Moshe's childhood survival of Pharaoh's persecution only to end up in his court! Stephen divides his teaching into the traditional manner of looking at the life of Moshe in the scroll of Exodus: 40 years upbringing in Egypt, 40 years in the wilderness, and 40 years of deliverance.

Stephen covers such details as Moshe's adoption by Pharaoh's daughter, *striking down an Egyptian* and fleeing to the wilderness. He notes the *burning bush*, his calling by God, and the miraculous Pesach deliverance. He recounts the trials in the wilderness, the *golden calf* debacle and the building of the true Tabernacle *according to the pattern Moshe had seen*. Stephen quotes many Scriptures from the Torah and Prophets (Ex. 1:7–8; 2:14; 3:1–10; 32:1, 23; Jer. 19:13; Amos 5:25–27). For one supposedly against Moshe, he has much knowledge and affirmation. If anything, he shows the committee that the real problem is the crowd who rebelled against him.

Most informative is Stephen's citation of the famous Torah verse where Moshe tells the people, *"God will raise up a prophet like me from among your brothers"* (Deut. 18:15). According to Jewish tradition, Moshe (like Yosef) would also be a type of the coming Messiah, with several intriguing parallels connecting the two.

> *"As the first Redeemer [Moses], so the last Redeemer [Messiah]. Just as the first Redeemer was revealed [to the children of Israel] and then again hidden from them ... for three months ... so the last Redeemer will be revealed and then again hidden from them.* (Numbers Rabah 11:2)

Moshe himself seems to make this connection with his call for Israel to always be on the lookout for a future prophet who will closely resemble him. As the above quote interprets, only the Messiah could be such a future prophet for Israel. Moshe was called to redeem the people from their bondage in Egypt, yet there was controversy and a 40-year delay. Yeshua as the Messiah was also called to redeem the people spiritually, yet there was controversy and delay. Moshe did many miraculous signs as part of the deliverance; so too Yeshua in his offer of redemption. Moshe seemingly did not complete the redemptive work as he died before entering the Land. Likewise, many interpreted Yeshua's death as a failure. But both Moshe and Yeshua ultimately succeed in completing their work. Some rabbinic sources conclude that Messiah will in some ways even succeed Moshe.

> *A Prophet from the midst of thee. ... In fact, the Messiah is such a Prophet as it is stated in the Midrash of the verse, "Behold my Servant shall prosper"* (Isa. 52:13) *... Moses, by the miracles*

*which he wrought, brought a single nation to the worship of God,
but the Messiah will draw all peoples to the worship of God.*
(Ralbag, Rabbi Levi ben Gershon commentary on Deut. 18:15)

Stephen ends his remarks on Moshe with a penetrating statement that
our fathers did not want to obey him. He draws a parallel between the
early rejection of Moshe and the response to Yeshua. According to
Stephen, the problem is not the messianic rejection of Moshe, as he
sees faith in Yeshua as consistent with the promise of Moshe himself.
Much of Israel's history is laced with some rejection of Moshe and *the
Prophets* and the resultant truth that *God turned away from them.*

Having dealt with the lie that his faith was anti-Moshe, Stephen
turns to the charge that he is against the House of God. Addressing the
Council, he uses the relational term *"our fathers."* He is still trying to
affirm that this Yeshua movement is consistent with Judaism and the
promise of the Torah. He highlights the construction of the *Mishkan
(Tabernacle) in the wilderness which was assembled according to the
pattern Moshe had seen.* This temporary house of worship continued
through the *days of Joshua and King David.* It is well-known that
Solomon built a house even though God *does not live in places made by
hand.* While Stephen is not against the Tabernacle or Temple in
Yerushalayim, he does remind the Council that such places are
temporary at best, invoking the prophet Isaiah, *"'Heaven is my throne,'
says ADONAI. 'What kind of house could you build for me?'"* (66:1–2)

After this long message, Stephen strongly exhorted the Sanhedrin
leaders. Comparing them to the *stiff-necked people* of the days of
Moshe was a forceful way to make his point. God himself used the
term to describe those who refuse to listen to his voice (Ex. 32:9, 33:3).
Stephen is implying a pointed question: If Yeshua is the true Messiah
as described by Moshe, then who is it that is against Moshe? He
admonishes the leaders of having *uncircumcised hearts and ears.*
Again, these terms aren't new or anti-Semitic; the Tanakh uses them to
describe those who are closed to the things of God (Lev. 26:41; Jer.
6:10). Sadly, anti-Semites use such verses to try to justify their hatred.

Stephen's words, while strong, are addressed to a small group, the Sanhedrin. Some were even sympathizers toward the Yeshua movement, as in the case of Rabban Gamliel (5:33ff). There is no place for hate for any Bible believer as "love fulfills the Torah" in the New Testament (Rom. 13:10). But love also speaks the truth, and Stephen continues to rebuke this group as *opposing the Ruach HaKodesh.* The leaders are in danger of following those who rebelled against God's prophets with persecution and even death. They clearly *receive the Torah, but they do not keep it!*

The leaders were *cut to their hearts and ground their teeth at him.* The rage was palpable, but Stephen, *full of the Ruach HaKodesh, looked up and saw God's Sh'kinah.* With this infusion of God's presence, he also saw *Yeshua standing at the right hand of God.* As he described this vision, the group grew even angrier, as this phrase directly quotes David's vision of "the Lord" speaking to "my Lord" at his Throne (Ps. 110:1). Yeshua is proclaimed as *the Son of Man standing at the right hand of God* (Dan. 7:13).

This was too much for the council to endure; *they began yelling at the top of their voices and threw him outside the city.* As punishment for such blasphemous statements, they *began stoning him, and the witnesses laid down their coats at the feet of a young man.* Some question if this was the response of a legitimate legal proceeding. It was more like a mob of radical zealots administering their own justice. Luke notes one zealot, Sha'ul, who would later have his own divine encounter with the risen Yeshua. Perhaps Stephen's zeal and death would make an indelible impression on this rabbinical student.

As he succumbed to the death by stoning, Stephen called out, *"Lord Yeshua! Receive my spirit!"* His final words are telling: *"Lord! Don't hold this sin against them!"* The stoning was a grievous sin, but he held no resentment. As with the example of Yeshua himself, Stephen knew many acted out of ignorance or fear. Even in the worst situation, God's grace and mercy can be extended. There is no place for hate. What is *our* response in the face of opposition?

Chapter Three

THE EARLY YESHUA
MOVEMENT BEYOND JERUSALEM

*The rabbis said: "[The Messiah's] name is 'leper scholar,' as it is
written, 'Surely he hath borne our griefs and carried our sorrows;
yet we did esteem him a leper, smitten of God and afflicted.'"*

[Tractate Sanhedrin 98b]

X. Outreach to Shomron – 8:1–25

Luke continues his narrative of the early messianic history after
Stephen's startling death. He makes special note of Sha'ul, a
young rabbinical student. It is evidently important that he was
present at Stephen's stoning death and even *gave his approval*
(7:58). Quite possibly Sha'ul had prior contact with the Yeshua
believers as he could have been part of the synagogue debaters from
Cilicia, his hometown (6:9). This tragedy seems to be a watershed
event with vast implications on the nascent Yeshua movement.

*Starting from that day there arose an intense persecution against the
messianic community in Yerushalayim.* Until now, it was virtually the
sole center of messianic activity. With this new wave of persecution,

59

most Jewish believers were *scattered throughout the regions of* Y'hudah and Shomron, also called the "West Bank" (Gen. 15:18). These areas made up the historic land promised to Abraham and are the traditional parts of Israel beyond Yerushalayim. Though contested today, the Tanakh and New Covenant promise this area will be just a small part of the entire land of Israel in the days of Messiah (Rom. 11:25–29). After Stephen's martyrdom, the other Jewish believers (except the emissaries) were pressured to leave the Holy City.

Despite the intense opposition, *some godly men buried Stephen and mourned him deeply.* In Jewish context, this is not just a generic reference but seems to confirm that a chevra kaddisha was involved in the last rites. This group would be responsible for details like same-day burial and no embalming (Kasdan, *God's Appointed Customs*). Likewise, the seven-day mourning period would begin after proper burial. This tells us Stephen's death was cheered by many but hardly unanimously. There were traditional Jews of Yerushalayim who had high regard for this disciple of Yeshua.

This seems a tragic turn of events. Sha'ul even intensifies the troubling situation, as he *set out to destroy the messianic community.* As a zealous rabbinical student, he was not opposing Gentile Christians (there were none!). But within his fiery spirit, he saw the Jewish Yeshua sect as a threat to his understanding of traditional Judaism, so he *handed over both men and women to be put in prison.* He would later admit that many of his actions were "out of ignorance" and he was truly sorry (I Tim. 1:13). We wonder how many people react out of ignorance even today.

Yet from God's perspective, all the *tzuris* (trouble) still had a divine purpose. *Those who were scattered announced the Good News of the Word wherever they went.* Luke uses the technical term *diaspora* to describe this scattering. Of course, throughout history there have been several Jewish diasporas (e.g., 586 B.C.E., 70 C.E., 1492). Interestingly, Jewish scholars have speculated that those scatterings were actually to facilitate the spread of the Torah to all the nations where Jews have been dispersed. This may very well be.

Luke makes a similar application to this scattering of Messianic Jews outside Yerushalayim to facilitate the spread of the Good News of Yeshua! Acts 8 also provides one of the major transitions in the Yeshua movement from Yerushalayim to Y'hudah and Shomron, following Luke's stated theme for the entire Book of Acts (1:8).

After giving some background as to why there was a new wave of persecution, Luke focuses on a key leader of this new outreach, Philip, a disciple listed among the Hellenistic Jewish believers chosen to be a servant in the growing community (6:5). He *went down to a city in Shomron and was proclaiming the Messiah*. It was always considered a vital part of greater Israel, but it was often a place of tumultuous change. As early as 722 B.C.E., this northern area was captured by the Assyrian army, who forced the Israelites to assimilate. Through this assimilation and intermarriage, a new people resulted: the Samaritans. Though they had some similarities, the Samaritans ultimately created their own religion and culture, even insisting God's holy mountain was not Mount Moriah but Mount Gerizim. There was an uneasy relationship between Jews and Samaritans over the years with a mutual distrust and disagreement. Yet the Samaritans kept some key elements Judaism, such as respect for the Torah and the coming Messiah.

Luke says the crowds were paying close attention to what Philip was sharing about Yeshua, especially since they saw the miraculous signs he was doing. Many paralytics with unclean spirits were being healed. There was great joy in that city. But as was often true, some negative elements also manifested. In this case, it revolved around a man named Shim'on, who was also astonishing those of Shomron. But in his case, it was by pagan magic. Many of his fellow Samaritans were giving heed to him, even calling him "the Great Power." However, these two religious groups met in a head-on collision as many men and women believed in the name of Yeshua the Messiah and were immersed in messianic mikveh (2:41). Astoundingly, Shim'on himself came to believe and attached himself closely to Philip, amazed by the great works of power through Yeshua's name. All this is a reminder that just because someone witnesses a miracle or great work, it is not automatically guaranteed to be from the true God of Israel. The Jewish disciple Yochanan said it well: "Test the spirits to see whether they are from God" (I John 4:1). A true sign will be consistent with the Scriptures, which God himself gave.

Philip's amazing outreach journey to Shomron got the attention of the Jewish leaders still in Yerushalayim. As a result, *they sent Kefa and Yochanan* to specifically pray for the new Samaritan believers, that they too *might receive the Ruach HaKodesh*. This action is consistent with Yeshua's promise to Kefa that he would be given the "keys of the Kingdom" (Mt. 16:13–20). Keys open new doors; in this case, a new door of the Good News going to those outside Yerushalayim. It makes sense—in fact, it is essential—that Kefa be sent to Shomron to verify this new open door was a work of God. Though the Samaritan believers were *immersed into the name of Yeshua, Kefa and Yochanan also placed their hands on them to receive the Ruach*. As this took place, it was confirmed to all that this was indeed a move of God upon this new people.

Again with a movement of the true God, there was some reaction from those on the fringe of the messianic movement. As Shim'on witnessed these events, it is said *he offered money* to acquire this power of the Ruach. While it is commendable that he expresses faith in Yeshua, this is a troubling turn into syncretism, combining true faith with worldly systems. It is quite popular even today.

Many people, both Jews and non-Jews, are actually pro-Yeshua and greatly appreciate his teaching. The problem is when they try to combine the confusion of the world with the light of Yeshua and make it their own pluralistic philosophy. It never succeeds. Kefa rebukes him: *"Go to ruin ... for thinking the free gift of God can be bought! ... Repent of this wickedness of yours, and pray to the Lord. Perhaps you will yet be forgiven. ... You are extremely bitter and completely under the control of sin!"* As strange as this situation may sound, there are always those who try to buy or sell an encounter with the Spirit, be it with Tarot cards, astrology, etc. We expect this from the larger pagan world (like Shim'on), but it is especially tragic when it comes from within the Jewish or Christian world. But too many people are seeking some kind of spiritual experience from outside sources when the answer lies within our very own dynamic tradition of Torah and Messiah! Shim'on seems to realize this and asks Kefa to pray for him to have proper understanding. With that, Kefa and Yochanan finished the fruitful outreach in Shomron. As they headed back for Yerushalayim, they continued *announcing the Good News of Yeshua to many villages.* A new dramatic door was indeed now open to those beyond the Jewish community.

XI. An Ethiopian Jew Finds the Messiah – 8:26–40

Having ended his part in the outreach in Shomron, Philip gets a surprising visit. *An angel of ADONAI* appears and says to *get up and go southward on the road that goes down from Yerushalayim.* He is to take *the desert road that leads to 'Azah* (Gaza). This coastal area was part of the first-century state of Israel, though it has been juggled back and forth over centuries of political turmoil. In modern Israel, Gaza was reincorporated into the Jewish state after the victory of the 1967 Six-Day War, only to be surrendered to the Palestinian Authority in 2005. The Gaza Strip remains a significant challenge to Israel as rocket fire and terrorist attacks are common under Hamas' current control. It is to this area Philip goes, not knowing what awaits him.

The reason for the angel's message quickly becomes apparent as he encounters *an Ethiopian eunuch, a minister of the queen.* "This man is a government official who had worshiped at the Temple. We can even conclude that he was Jewish! Also, Luke tells that the leader is *in his royal chariot, reading the prophet Isaiah.* Some speculate that this man may have been a Gentile God-fearer or perhaps a convert to first-century Judaism. But many overlook the amazing history of the Jewish tribe in Ethiopia!

The story of the Beta Yisrael Jews has been documented over the last 3000 years of Jewish history, tracing their Jewish connection to the story of the Queen of Sheba and her visit to Israel (I Kgs. 10).

She traveled from Seva (ancient Ethiopia) to Yerushalayim to experience firsthand King Solomon's accomplishments and famous wisdom. That is where the biblical account ends. But other sources give more details (*Antiquities* viii.6; "Ethiopia" in *Encyclopedia Judaica*). Tradition says Solomon took the queen as another wife (he had 700; what's one more?) Of course, these were not necessarily personal marriage relationships but often, in the ancient world, a good basis for political alliances. Jewish tradition says the Queen and Solomon produced a son, Menelik, and that this mother and son (and other Jews from Y'hudah) ultimately returned to Ethiopia as the foundation of a whole new group of Jewish people.

Over the centuries there have been rumors of the existence of the Beta Yisrael Jews, but because of their geographic seclusion, they were not connected to the other Jewish tribes. It wasn't until the exploration of the Christian missionary journeys to Africa that the Ethiopian Jews were rediscovered. How strange to find, among all the pagan African tribes, one with a hut with a Star of David along with Torah scrolls in the native language of Ge'ez! Likewise, this tribe observed such Jewish customs as Shabbat, eighth-day circumcision and kosher dietary laws. So different was their culture from the other Ethiopians that they were also called "Falasha" Jews, which means strangers or exiles. It was so long ago that when the Beta Yisrael returned to Ethiopia, their version of ancient Judaism had not been influenced by the development of the Talmud.

In 1991, "Operation Solomon" airlifted tens of thousands of Ethiopian Jews to modern Israel. Many of their brothers and family members were left behind. It was discovered that many actually believe in Yeshua as the Messiah! Their fate is still unfolding as the debate continues about the Israeli law of return and who is a Jew.

With this background, it is far more logical to see the eunuch of Acts 8 not as a pagan but as a Beta Yisrael Jew coming to Yerushalayim to worship, likely on one of the Shalosh Regalim. At this crucial time, as he is *returning home riding in his chariot*, he is *reading the prophet Isaiah*. In classic divine appointment, *the Ruach* tells Philip to *go over to this chariot.* As he approached the chariot, he *heard the Ethiopian reading*; he was likely chanting the *haftarah* portion according to Jewish custom (Tractate Avot 6.5). Philip asks poignantly: *"Do you understand what you're reading?"* The official humbly admits he needs some help and invites Philip *to explain* this Isaiah passage. This is the exact *portion of the Tanakh*:

> *He was like a sheep led to be slaughtered; like a lamb silent before the shearer, he does not open his mouth. He was humiliated and denied justice. Who will tell about his descendants since his life has been taken from the earth?* (Isa. 53:7–8)

Scholars note the translation varies noticeably from the Masoretic Hebrew text of the Tanakh but aligns well with the Ethiopian Ge'ez translation. The official has one overriding question to these verses: *"Is the prophet talking about himself or someone else?"* This is a relevant question regarding possible Jewish interpretations of Isaiah 53. The medieval rabbi Rashi was the first to apply this passage to the Jewish people in general reflecting on the suffering and trials of our history. At first this seems a valid interpretation, but there are grammatical issues. In fact, the verse immediately preceding the Acts 8 quotation makes clear, through the uses of two different pronouns, that it is not just the Jewish people referred to:

> *We all (Israel), like sheep, went astray; we (Israel) turned, each one, to his own way; yet ADONAI laid on him (second person) the guilt of all of us.* (Isa. 53:6; emphases added)

This can be confusing. Why two different pronouns? Who's taking Israel's sins? Not Isaiah; he never claimed to erase Israel's sins. The most natural interpretation is also the oldest as reflected in the Talmud. Rabbinic discussions of the possible names for Messiah surmise that he will be called "the leper scholar" as he is either despised like a leper or heals them. All this because "it was our diseases he bore, our pains from which he suffered; yet we regarded him as punished, stricken and afflicted by God" (Isa. 53:4, quoted in

Tractate Sanhedrin 98b). Little wonder that we are told that Philip *went on to tell* the Ethiopian Jew *the Good News about Yeshua!*

This official's true faith became clear from his reaction. *As they were going down the road, they came to some water* that would serve as a natural mikveh. At his request, this messianic brother is immersed in traditional fashion. That he already knows the meaning of ritual immersion underscores his Jewish knowledge and identity. There are many such immersions in Judaism illustrating the ritual cleansing needed before Shabbat, before a wedding ceremony, even after a personal healing. After Yeshua's resurrection, he gave his followers one more mikveh: be immersed in his name to illustrate the spiritual healing found in him (Mt. 28:19–20; Acts 2:38).

So *Philip and the official went down into the water* to confirm the man's newfound faith in Messiah. Some manuscripts have Philip saying, "If you believe with all your heart, you may have the mikveh," and the man answers, "I believe that Yeshua the Messiah is the Son of God." With or without the verse, it is clear this official has faith in Yeshua and is ready for the sign of mikveh. *When they came up out of the water, the Spirit of the Lord snatched Philip away* (recall Elijah in II Kgs. 2). The official *continued on his way—full of joy.* Significantly, both the Messianic Jews of Ethiopia and the Coptic Church trace their spiritual roots to this man's encounter here. As for Philip, he *continued proclaiming the Good News as he went through all the coastal towns from Ashdod to Caesarea.*

> *Rabbi Alexandri said: "Rabbi Yehoshua ben Levi cast together two verses: It is written: 'And, behold, one like a son of man came with the clouds of heaven' [Dan. 7:13] and it is written: 'Humble, and riding on a donkey' [Zech. 9:9]! If they merit, [Messiah] will come 'with the clouds of heaven'; if they do not merit, [Messiah] will come 'humble and riding on a donkey.'"* [Tractate Sanhedrin 98a]

XII. A Rabbi Encounters Messiah – 9:1–31

Luke returns to some of the challenges in the early Yeshua movement. We've already met a zealous rabbinical student, Sha'ul of Tarsus, a strong opponent to this nascent religious group. He was part of the angry mob at the stoning of the Stephen, and he continued his opposition against these perceived heretics. Unsurprisingly, he is *still breathing murderous threats against the Lord's talmidim*. As a disciple of the top Pharisee of the day, he certainly had the connections and zeal to protect what he considered kosher Judaism. Sha'ul must have stood out from his fellow students as he takes the lead in his sincere but misguided opposition to the Yeshua movement. He has the gravitas to approach *the High Priest to get letters to the synagogues all the way in Damascus authorizing him to arrest* any Messianic Jews and *bring them back to Yerushalayim.*

Sha'ul wasn't interested in any Gentile converts to this faith (there weren't many) but he, and many others, was quite concerned about Jews turning away from the ancient faith of our fathers. Hence the involvement of the High Priest and the search in the synagogue community are highlighted. Luke delineates that the concern was for those Jews who belonged to *ha-Derekh* ("The Way"), an early term descriptive of Jews who follow Yeshua. Interestingly, the term "Christian" does not appear until there is a description of Gentile followers of Yeshua in Antioch (11:26).

As Sha'ul was *on the road and nearing Dammesek* (Damascus), *suddenly a light from heaven flashed all around him.* It must have been exceedingly bright, as this occurred at noon (22:6). The only thing that could outshine the midday sun is the glory of God! As the rabbi was knocked *to the ground,* he heard a voice say, in Hebrew, *"Sha'ul! Sha'ul! Why are you persecuting me?"* The manifestation of a voice from heaven is not unknown in Jewish experience. After the last of the prophets around 400 B.C.E., it was believed that God sometimes spoke through a *bat kol* ("daughter of the voice or echo") at times to give guidance to his people [Tractate Yoma 9b). Sha'ul's response indicates he is not surprised at the voice from heaven, but he questions the true source by answering the question with his own: *"Sir, who are you?"* This could simply be a generic way of addressing an individual, but it is also the root for how a traditional

Jew also addresses God. It seems to indicate this young rabbi suspects the voice is God's but humbly asks for confirmation. To his inquiry the voice says, *"I am Yeshua, and you are persecuting me."*

In addition to this startling revelation, Sha'ul is told to *go to the city*, where he will be given further instructions. Luke says the *men traveling* with him heard *the voice* but saw *no one*. They helped him off the ground, as *he could see nothing*. Humbled physically by this divine encounter, this zealous rabbi is led *by the hand* into Damascus. This state of dependence lasted *three days* as he was *unable to see* and entered into a traditional Jewish fast as he *neither ate nor drank*. Sha'ul would never be the same as he sought God's next step for his life.

The word "conversion" is never used here, though today it is often used to describe Sha'ul's experience. Too many, Christians and Jews alike, see this as a rabbinical student "converting" to become a Christian, hence no longer a Jew. Modern terminology is often the biggest barrier for the Jewish community to understand the New Testament. As the text gives no hint of a "conversion," this is best seen as a rabbinical student encountering the true Messiah.

From the Scripture evidence, Sha'ul never stopped considering himself a Torah-observant Jew. Now he was a Jew who included belief in Yeshua as the capstone of his Judaism (Acts 21:20–24; 23:6; Rom. 11:1). This is also how most contemporary Messianic Jews live our lives today in the context of Messianic Judaism. It would greatly increase the understanding and dialogue if both Jews and Christians can see there is in fact a Jewish way to follow Yeshua as our Redeemer, and cultural "conversion" is not a requirement.

Luke stirs our attention to a larger Messianic Jewish community that this dramatic encounter will directly impact. One particular member of the Damascus Jewish community is used by God at this critical moment: Hananyah (Ananias); appropriately, it means "God is gracious." This disciple received a vision from the Lord calling him to service. Hearing his name, Hananyah replies in obedience, *"Here I am, Lord."* God directs him to *go to Straight Street, to Y'hudah's house, and ask for a man from Tarsus named Sha'ul.* God assures him all things are prearranged as Sha'ul has also seen *in a vision a man named Hananyah is coming* to pray for him.

All this would normally give the disciple great confidence, but he expresses grave concerns about *this man who has done much harm to your people in Yerushalayim*. God reassures him he must go on this mission because *this man is my chosen instrument to carry my name to the nations, even to their kings, and to the sons of Isra'el as well*. So Hananyah *went into the house* (which took incredible faith!) and, *placing his hands* on Sha'ul, even calling him *"brother,"* said: *"The Lord Yeshua has sent me so that you may see again and be filled with the Spirit."* Luke says that *in that moment Sha'ul could see again!* He proceeded to take a mikveh immersion as a symbol of his new calling and *ate some food to regain his strength*.

After these amazing events that confirmed the reality of Sha'ul's faith, all should be well. But there were still some doubters and no small controversy. As he spent *some days with the disciples in Damascus*, Sha'ul also was *proclaiming in the synagogues that Yeshua is the Son of God*. The new believer undoubtedly shared some key Tanakh verses that highlight Messiah as a unique Son of God (Ps. 2; Prov. 30). Perhaps a special focus was given to the passage that speaks of a "son" coming with the clouds of heaven, as this is reminiscent of Sha'ul's experience. In speaking of the prophetic passage in Genesis 49, the rabbis state:

> There was a tradition from our Father Jacob concerning all that would come to pass in the future to every tribe until the days of Messiah. ... From whence do we know this about King Messiah? Scripture says, "behold with the clouds of heaven came one like unto a son of man." (Numbers Rabbah 13:14 quoting Dan. 7:13)

The Jewish crowds *were amazed* for a couple of reasons. First, they wondered how this young man who *was trying to destroy the people who call on this name* could now be supportive of Yeshua. Second, it was evident Sha'ul was *being filled with more and more power* as he presented *his proofs that Yeshua is the Messiah*. It was both the

69

content of his message and the Ruach's presence in his life that spoke to so many about the reality of the risen Messiah. These lessons are still applicable today. Even a newer believer can share, both in word and deed, in ways that speak to those around us. Because of this religious turmoil, there even developed *a plot by some to kill Sha'ul*. Ironically, these radicals closely aligned with his earlier position. Even though the city gates of Damascus were being closely guarded, he was smuggled by some of his new Yeshua friends as they *lowered him in a large basket under cover of night*.

There were new challenges both from the external opponents and in the Yeshua community. Returning to Yerushalayim, Sha'ul tried to join the disciples there. *They were all afraid of him*, not convinced he was now a true believer. He was infamous for persecuting Jews! Fortunately, another Messianic Jew, Bar-Nabba (Barnabas, "son of consolation") had firsthand knowledge of Sha'ul's encounter. This believer *took Sha'ul to the emissaries* and affirmed both that Sha'ul was now a fellow Messianic Jew and *he had spoken out boldly in the name of Yeshua*. The leaders were convinced, and as he *went all over Yerushalayim continuing to speak out boldly in the name of the Lord*.

He also showed some early indications of his future work in the diaspora as he was especially effective among *the Greek-speaking Jews*. However, here too there was some radical opposition and even *attempts to kill* Sha'ul until he escaped to Caesarea and ultimately all the way back Tarsus, his hometown. The chronology indicates he spent eight years there preparing for his unique ministry among the nations, including a three-year personal "yeshiva class" in Arabia under the personal teaching of the Ruach HaKodesh (Gal. 1:17).

Luke summarizes that current situation in the Yeshua movement: There was a season of *shalom throughout Y'hudah, Galil and Shomron* as they continued to be *built up*. The growing number of Jewish followers *lived in the fear of the Lord* as they were convinced of the reality of the risen Yeshua. They also walked in the *counsel of the Ruach HaKodesh*. This new life in Messiah cannot be fulfilled on our own strength or even good intentions. It takes an outside source of power to fully engage in the work and abundant life of God's Kingdom (Acts 1:8; Eph. 5:18). Finally, it is not surprising that the *numbers of believers kept multiplying.* As the larger Jewish community witnessed the dynamic power and changed lives of their friends, many were eager to receive Yeshua as Messiah. As with so much of the content of Acts, the lessons are still applicable today. After the early decades of Acts, there were centuries of relative quiet, at least in the Jewish community. But something began to change in recent decades.

Many see a parallel between the physical rebirth of the modern State of Israel and the spiritual rebirth of the modern Messianic Jewish community. Till the 1960s, there were few Jewish communities for Yeshua. There are now hundreds of Yeshua synagogues and tens of thousands of Messianic Jews. Acts serves as a template for Jewish spiritual renewal. Like the early believers, may we continue to see the Jewish believers (and all believers) multiply as the world sees our shalom-filled lives in Yeshua!

Chapter Four

THE EARLY YESHUA
MOVEMENT FOR THE GENTILES

XIII. The Ministry of Kefa – 9:32–42

Luke turns to one of the foundational apostles of this growing movement. He says *Kefa traveled around the countryside* and eventually connected with *the messianic believers in Lud* (modern-day Lod, near Tel Aviv). Luke desires to focus on Yeshua's healing power as the risen Messiah and finds a perfect illustration in a bedridden man, *Aeneas*. This man, paralyzed for eight years, is approached by Kefa, who exhorts him to *get up and make your bed as Yeshua the Messiah is healing you!* This immediately happened, and unsurprisingly, *everyone in Lud and the Sharon* coastal plain turned to the Lord. There is no doubting Yeshua's healing power. It's especially important in these early decades of the Yeshua movement to be a clear confirmation that the true Messiah has finally arrived.

Yet there are questions today. Why is every sincere believer not healed? There are many cases of faithful disciples who are not healed. Sha'ul himself is an important balance to the biblical teaching on healing. Though he was often used in bringing the Lord's healing to others, he admits he did not always experience it himself. In his classic testimony, he confirms he prayed diligently many times, yet God's ultimate answer was not physical healing but an extra dose of his grace to walk through his challenge (II Cor. 12:7–10). Acts gives

73

many examples of Yeshua's healing power. It is the same Holy Spirit who tells us that sometimes God's answer will not be immediate healing, but he promises us a special grace to endure any trial. Of course, ultimately, we all will experience total healing with our promised resurrected bodies; they will not know illness, tears or death (Rev. 21:1–4). One way or the other, God assures us he will work all things for our good as we keep our trust in him!

After Aeneas' dramatic healing, we learn of an even more spectacular encounter: victory over death itself! This takes place as Kefa now travels to the nearby coastal town of Yafo, next to modern Tel Aviv. A righteous Jewish believer named Tavita (Dorcas, "gazelle") lived there; she was known for *doing tzedakah and other good deeds*. Sadly, *she took sick* at that time *and died*. Since *Yafo is near Lud*, the disciples *sent two men to urge Kefa to come without delay*. As he *arrived at the room*, he was met with a heart-wrenching scene of *widows sobbing and showing all the dresses Dorcas had made for them*. Discerning that God might want to do something unusual, Kefa *kneeled down and prayed*.

There are various postures for Jewish prayer. Many traditional prayers are said while standing, as before a king. One may be seated at other times. It is quite common for Jews to bend the knee and bow during some traditional blessings of prayer. In biblical times, Jews even knelt in prayer as a sign of humility (Dan. 6:10). Of course, the posture of prayer is not so important as the fact that we earnestly seek God. Here we find Kefa humbly seeking God's will in the case of this deceased sister. In this state of prayer he received a confident word from God; *he turned to the body and said, "Tavita, kumi!"* ("Get up!") Immediately she *opened her eyes and sat up* as Kefa *presented her to the crowd alive*. The resurrection of the dead is the ultimate miracle that should get everyone's attention. It has long been believed that the pinnacle of Messiah's ministry (when he comes) will be the victory over death. One rabbinic tradition says:

*Messiah ben David, Elijah, and Zerubbabel, peace be upon him,
will ascend the Mount of Olives. And Messiah will command
Elijah to blow the shofar ... and will make the dead rise. All will
come to the Messiah from the four corners of the earth. ... The
children of Israel will fly on the wings of eagles and come to the
Messiah.* [Ma'ase Daniel 225, quoted in Patai, 143]

With such a spectacular miracle, it is not surprising that *many people
put their trust in the Lord.* Perhaps it is significant that Luke does not
say that *everyone* trusted in Yeshua. Some people, even today, will
not believe even if they witness a great miracle. It is not for lack of
credible evidence. There have always been some who refuse to
believe even as they witness a split sea or multiplication of bread or,
in this case, life from the dead! God knows the heart of every person,
but sometimes it is not that we *cannot* but *will not* believe. The call
of Yeshua is a challenge to humble ourselves and make him Messiah
and the center of our life. Acts gives us plenty of trustworthy
evidence. Where do you stand today with him?

*The Holy One, blessed be He, looks to the peoples of the world,
hoping that they will repent and so bring them near beneath His
wings.* [Numbers Rabbah 10.1]

XIV. The Bizarre Vision for the Gentiles – 10:1–26

We come now to a major transition in Acts. Luke has been closely
following his prescribed outline for his work after Yeshua's words in
Acts 1:8. This Good News of the Messiah's arrival is to naturally start
in the home of the Jewish people, Yerushalayim. This was powerfully
accomplished through the events of Acts 1–7. At that point, Yeshua's
message was to expand to Y'hudah and Shomron (Acts 8). It is now
time to report on the expansion of the Yeshua movement beyond the
Jewish community and Samaritan cousins, as it was always predicted
to go *to the ends of the earth.* It is consistently noted that Kefa must be
an eyewitness to each of these expansions as a fulfillment of his

responsibility of holding the "keys of the Kingdom" (Mt. 16:19). Keys open doors, and the Jewish apostle shows up at each major transition of the growing Yeshua movement (Acts 2, 8, 10).

As we look at this first-century expansion of the Yeshua movement, too many people (both Jews and Christians) have forgotten this historical perspective, assuming Yeshua is for Gentiles who identify as "Christians." Some people find it oxymoronic to even imply that Jews might somehow fit into this Yeshua movement. The fact is, we often have it turned around! As Acts carefully chronicles, the messianic movement started quite naturally among Jews who were anticipating the coming of Messiah. And Yeshua of Nazareth, in their estimation, fulfilled the requirements. Acts now makes a major shift to show how (surprise!) this Messiah would also be offered to the non-Jews of the world. It should not be a surprise to anyone who knows the Tanakh. On numerous occasions God is clearly inclusive of all peoples (Gen. 12:3; Isa. 49:6; Zech. 14:16; etc). He is the only God, and he relates to all his creation. Though a careful study of the Torah clearly revealed this truth, it was not easy to grasp even in first-century Israel. For this reason, God will do some amazing (and controversial) things to expand this Yeshua movement from traditional Jews to the pagans and non-Jewish seekers of the world.

This new focus of the Yeshua story unfolds around a particular Roman Gentile named Cornelius. He proves a natural candidate for outreach beyond the Jewish community. As a centurion, he had great respect as an established leader of 100 soldiers. Luke calls Cornelius *a devout man, a "God-fearer," as was his whole household.* The term does not merely mean he was religious but that he was a special category of non-Jews known as the *yirey Ha-shamayim* ("one who fears Heaven")—true followers of the God of Israel. In first-century Judaism, there were Jews who were born into the tribes of Ya'akov. There were also Pagan Gentiles (non-Jews), including anyone not part of Israel. In Jewish theology, non-Jews were and are considered accepted by God if they followed the "Seven Laws of the Sons of Noah" (*Sheva Mitzvot B'nei Noach*; see Gen. 9).

This is why the Jewish community is usually not concerned with acquiring Gentile converts; there is no soteriological need. But it's always been understood that some Gentiles wish to connect more directly with the Jewish people through a conversion process. In the Talmud, this special category is called *gerim* ("converts"), former pagans who fully converted to join the Jewish people because they were disenchanted with the Roman Empire's paganism and drawn to biblical Judaism's values. To become a *ger*, one had to fill three requirements: all males would be circumcised; all would take a mikveh to illustrate their new life; and in Temple times they had to bring a sacrifice (Tractate Yevamot 47a).

A good example of a *ger* is Ruth. We don't have a record of her following the later rabbinic requirements, but there's no question she wholeheartedly joined herself to the Jewish people (Ruth 1:16–17). There were also former pagans who desired to draw close to the God of the Jews. Like the *gerim*, they were likely intrigued by the Torah's monotheism and moral values. However, they stopped short of full conversion or fulfilling the rabbinic requirements, so they were called *"God-fearers"* as they attended synagogue and embraced the values of Judaism without the full *gerim* commitment. Later we will see how these categories of people were an important issue in the furtherance of the Yeshua movement among the Gentiles (Acts 15).

So here we are introduced to Cornelius, who is specifically labeled a yirey Ha-shamayim. Thus it is not surprising that he is described as a person who *gave generously to help the Jewish poor and prayed regularly to God*. In fact, he did not just lift up generic personal prayers (though God listens to all prayer) but was praying during one of the three traditional Jewish service times (Dan. 6:10; Tractate Shabbat 9b). These include Shachrit in the morning (sunrise to noon), Mincha in the afternoon (between 12:30 and sunset) and Ma'ariv (starting in the evening when three stars are visible). For convenience, it became customary to combine Mincha with Ma'ariv so a minyan of ten people is only needed two times daily.

In this case, at Mincha Cornelius receives *a vision of an angel*, and he is *terrified*. As he inquires of the angel, he is reassured that his *prayers and acts of charity have gone up into God's presence.* The purpose of the angel's visit was to exhort Cornelius to *send some men to Yafo and bring back a man named Shim'on, also called Kefa.* They find him on the outskirts of town *by the sea* at the home of *Shim'on the leather-tanner*. While a valuable profession, leather tanning was a smelly job that often required animal dung for processing. Humorously, the Talmud says if someone becomes a tanner, it is legitimate grounds for divorce (Tractate Ketuvot 77a)! No wonder Shim'on's place was on the outskirts of Yafo! Still, Cornelius *sent his men* from Caesarea to connect with Kefa as the angel directed.

As the Gentile group was on their way *the next day*, Kefa *went up onto the roof of the house to pray*. (Now we also likely know why Kefa was on the roof!) As sometimes happens, his mind began to wander as he was *hungry and wanted something to eat*. It's evidently the perfect teachable moment as Kefa falls into *a trance* and has a startling vision of *something that looked like a large sheet*. It is further described as being *lowered to the ground by its four corners.* This depiction would instantly remind Jewish readers of the *arba kanafot* ("four-cornered") garment known as a *tallit* (prayer shawl).

Of course, this fits the context of Kefa's prayer time perfectly. But Kefa is shocked to see in the tallit *all kinds of four-footed animals, crawling creatures and wild birds*; things expressly forbidden in the Torah as non-kosher (Lev. 11). If it wasn't enough to see such *treif* (unkosher) things on a tallit, Kefa is told to *"get up, slaughter and eat!"* Now he felt obligated to object; he vehemently declares, *"Absolutely not! I have never eaten food that was unclean or treif."* He is still keeping kosher and is a Torah-observant Jew even after all the years spent with Yeshua personally, even post-resurrection! Too many people, both Jews and Christians, assume Yeshua and his disciples ate unkosher and broke the Torah in other ways. But this is very confusing in light of Yeshua's own words that he was not erasing even one iota of the Torah (Mt. 5:17–18). He certainly kept all the

Torah as the sinless Messiah, or he would be disqualified from being Messiah! His Messianic Jewish disciples, while not sinless, certainly sought to follow the example of their rabbi.

The voice in the vision makes a startling statement: *"Stop treating as unclean what God has made clean."* This no doubt added greatly to Kefa's confusion. To emphasize the point, the vision *happened three times before the sheet was taken back up into heaven. But Kefa was still puzzling over the meaning of the vision.* Some people are tempted to take a simplistic interpretation of the vision as meaning the dietary laws of the Torah are now null and void. But Kefa did not come to this conclusion. He doesn't call for a bacon burger or any other treif! In fact, there's no subsequent mention of food items, but a surprising interjection—*Cornelius' men calling out at the gate* of the property to meet with Kefa.

Immediately *the Ruach* tells Kefa to *go downstairs and have no misgivings about going with them because I myself have sent them.* Again, many people cannot begin to grasp the angst that must have been in Kefa's heart. A vision seemingly about food was confusing enough. But now he is told by the Ruach to go with this nice Gentile Roman group for a yet-undisclosed task? For a kosher Jew to even associate with pagan non-Jews could potentially render him defiled. The Talmud says even the dust of the Gentile's home is enough to make one ritually unkosher (Tractate Oholot 18.7). Not only did Kefa keep a kosher diet, but his religious life presented him some challenging questions about affiliating with non-Jews in general.

Despite these nagging questions, Kefa knows he must heed the Ruach's message and greets the men. With this they describe how their boss Cornelius is a *true God-fearer and highly regarded by the whole Jewish nation.* They invite Kefa to come with them to Cornelius' *house so they can listen* to the message the emissary might have for them. In a very symbolic act, Kefa invites these non-Jewish guests into the Jewish household. What a wonderful picture of God's intention to have Jew and Gentile stand together in Yeshua! It will be even more astounding when the Jewish Kefa enters

Cornelius' home. It is not surprising that Kefa brings some other Jewish *brothers* for support and as witnesses to this highly unusual meeting. This happens the next day as the mixed caravan traveled *from Yafo to Caesarea*. Cornelius was so excited that *he had called together his relatives and close friends. As Kefa entered the house, Cornelius met him and fell prostrate at his feet. But Kefa pulled him to his feet and said, "Stand up! I myself am just a man."* This meeting is about to bear some remarkable fruit.

XV. The Yeshua Movement Starts Among the Gentiles – 10:27–48

As *Kefa went inside* Cornelius' home, he addressed the *many people* who had gathered. He points out how unlikely it is for *a Jew to come and visit someone who belongs to another people*. In fact, this crowd of many God-fearers living in Israel would be *well aware* of some of these traditional laws. Rabbinic law often warns of the dangers of visiting a non-kosher home of a Gentile (Leviticus Rabbah on Lev. 20). But Kefa reveals that he grasps the meaning of the vision of the tallit. It has nothing to do with food. It was about kosher versus non-kosher *people*! Kefa says God has shown him not to call any person unclean. This is not about being xenophobic or anti-Gentile; it was a huge issue about ritual purity for a traditional Jew.

Kefa tells how he came *without raising any questions*. Though many today assume Kefa ate Cornelius' non-kosher food, there is no proof. But as a kosher Messianic Jew, Kefa now saw he could have table fellowship without breaking kosher. Table fellowship would continue to be a challenging issue in the early Yeshua movement as more non-Jews were added. Even today, modern Messianic Jews have table fellowship with Christian friends without compromising their convictions. It is one of those personal beliefs we are called to respect even if there is a difference between two believers (Rom. 14:1–4).

The spiritual drama continues as Kefa asks his Gentile guests the obvious question: *"Why did you send for me?"* Cornelius relates that during the *Mincha prayers in my house, a man in shining clothes stood in front of me.* The angel exhorted him *to send* for a Jewish man *named Kefa*, staying with *Shim'on a leather-tanner.* Cornelius humbly states, *"Now all of us are here in the presence of God to hear everything the Lord has ordered you to say."*

Not known for being shy in presenting the message of Yeshua, Kefa addressed the group forthrightly. Especially when it is so obvious God has set up this entire situation! He acknowledges the recent lessons that *God does not play favorites, but he accepts anyone who fears him.* Kefa proceeds to share *the message that was sent to the sons of Israel announcing shalom through Yeshua the Messiah.* Though the message was given to the Jewish people first, it would have international ramifications. Kefa tells how in recent years there was a messianic renewal *throughout Y'hudah and in the Galil through the immersion that Yochanan proclaimed.* In God's perfect timing, *Yeshua was anointed with the Ruach* as he began his ministry of *doing good and healing all the people.* Kefa boldly affirms (with his Jewish associates) that they are *all witnesses of everything he did both in Y'hudah and Yerushalayim.*

Despite these blessings, there was controversy as Yeshua was rejected by many of the Jewish leaders as well as the Romans who ultimately murdered him on a cross (Deut. 21:23). That would be another tragic story of a martyred rabbi, but God *raised him up on the third day.* To educated Jews and these Gentile God-fearers, even the timing of Yeshua's death and resurrection is striking. It is no coincidence that as the Messiah died exactly on the first day of Pesach (15 Nisan) as the Lamb of God. Like the first Pesach, the blood of the sacrificial Lamb would deliver all who applied it on their door (or life!). The third day of Pesach is also a notable holy day, Bikkurim, when the first grain of the spring harvest is taken from the ground and lifted up for all to see (Lev. 23:5–11).

Kefa points out the amazing fulfillment of these events through the life, death and resurrection of Yeshua. It is not just Kefa and a few Jewish brothers who saw these things; many can testify to them.

81

Some even ate and drank with Yeshua after he had risen from the dead (I Cor. 15:5–8)! These are spectacular claims in themselves, but they are substantiated by the fact that many of these eyewitnesses would later even give their lives for the cause of Yeshua. Many in first-century Israel became believers because of this reality. All these things should make us unwavering in our faith. We have amazing evidence and personal, eyewitness accounts (II Kefa 1:16). Kefa closes his teaching to these non-Jewish seekers with a reference to the Great Commission to take this Good News of Messiah to the Jewish people. Kefa says *all the prophets bear witness* to Yeshua, and *everyone*, even beyond the people of Israel, *who puts his trust in him receives forgiveness of sins through his name.*

Kefa had not even ended his message when the Ruach fell on all in the crowd. The Messianic Jews who had accompanied Kefa were amazed that the Ruach was also being poured out on the Gentiles. There was likely initial skepticism that any Gentile could embrace this Jewish Messiah without first converting to Judaism. But their doubts vanished as they witnessed some of the same manifestations from the Jewish believers as they heard them speaking in tongues and praising God. We could call this the "Gentile Shavuot" because of the similarities to the earlier Temple Mount Jewish experience.

Upon seeing all this, Kefa asked the Jewish witnesses if anyone would prohibit these people from being immersed in water. These God-fearing Gentiles had clearly received the same Ruach as the Messianic Jews. With the crowd in agreement, the new believers were immersed in the name of Yeshua the Messiah. It was official: The promises to the Gentiles were now also being fulfilled with this start of the Messianic Age. God's salvation (Yeshua) is spreading to the ends of the earth (Isa. 49:6). Though coming with some controversy, it seems to fulfill the hope of the Jewish sages as well:

> *The Holy One, blessed be He, looks to the peoples of the world, hoping that they will repent and so bring them near beneath His wings.* [Numbers Rabbah 10.1]

It took some doing, with the help of a bizarre, thoroughly un-kosher vision, but the Jewish believers learned to welcome the non-Jews into their midst. For their part, the new Gentile believers were exceedingly thankful to be invited to be grafted into the Olive Tree faith of Israel and the new life in Messiah (Rom. 11:17–18). The household of Cornelius also reminds us that there are many who are always seeking to draw closer to God. They may not have full understanding or complete faith yet, but God is working on them as he did with us. May we be as welcoming and sensitive as Kefa as we share the Good News of Yeshua with those around us.

XVI. The Gentile Outreach Expands Beyond Israel – 11:1–30

Luke gives more details of the Yeshua movement's expansion to the Gentiles of the Middle East. Acts 1–9 clearly documents the belief by many that the Messiah had come in the person of Yeshua. This of course was a thoroughly Jewish message that took hold within the Jewish community of Israel. But it became clear that it was now God's time to fulfill his promises that ultimately all the nations would be blessed with the coming of the Messiah (Gen. 12:3; Isa. 49:6). Through the vision of Acts 10 and subsequent actions, Kefa was key in opening the doors of the Kingdom for the God-fearers in Cornelius' home. Radical as this was, it all still took place in Caesarea, in Israel.

Luke records the next logical expansion of the Yeshua faith to those areas outside Israel but still in the Middle East. First, there was some explaining to do especially to the Jewish leaders in Yerushalayim! *The emissaries and the brothers throughout Y'hudah heard that the [Gentiles] had received the word of God; but when Kefa went up to Yerushalayim, the members of the Circumcision faction criticized him, saying, "You went into the homes of uncircumcised men and even ate with them!"* While broadly true, Kefa feels the need to tell *what actually happened*. He summarizes the salient points so his Jewish colleagues can evaluate for themselves.

He starts with his *Mincha prayer time in Yafo* and how he *had a vision while in a trance*. He saw *something like a large sheet being lowered by its four corners*. This would be reminiscent of the four-cornered tallit, especially as he was in prayer. And in this vision, it was filled with all sorts of treif: *four-footed animals, beasts of prey, crawling creatures and wild birds.* If that wasn't strange enough, he *heard a voice* saying, *"Get up, Kefa, slaughter and eat!"* Kefa reveals he has stayed Torah-observant and objected, *"Absolutely not! Nothing unclean has ever entered my mouth!"* Note how different this statement is from many modern interpretations regarding the Torah and Messianic Jews.

Even after living for over three years with his Rabbi Yeshua (even post-resurrection), Kefa still keeps kosher. His understanding of Yeshua's teachings did not sway him from being a Torah-observant Jew who embraced Yeshua as Messiah. It was not a matter of earning his salvation or relationship with God. In response to his confession, the voice from heaven spoke again, *"Stop treating as unclean what God has made clean."* This seems so bizarre to Kefa that the vision repeats itself *three times before it was pulled back up into heaven.*

He says that while he was perplexed, God gave him clarity. *At that very moment, three men* (Roman Gentiles) arrived at the house in Yafo. *The Ruach* said to *have no misgivings about going with them* to Cornelius' home. This surely assuaged some of the concerns of the Jewish group as they realized the vision was about people and not food, though some questions remained. This was highly unusual as a kosher Jew could not eat with such a group, much less go to the home of a non-Jew; that in itself would be unkosher. But Kefa obeyed by faith, especially when he heard that the Roman crowd was told in their own vision, *"Send to Yafo for Kefa because he has a message so your household may be saved."* It seems God is up to something when a Roman Gentile is asking a Jew to tell them about the faith of Israel!

Kefa continues to relay the details to his Jewish brothers as he shares that *quickly the Ruach HaKodesh fell* on the non-Jews *just as it did on* the Messianic Jews in Yerushalayim. This reminded Kefa of God's promise, *"Yochanan used to immerse people in water, but you will be immersed in the Ruach HaKodesh."* If God gave the *Gentiles the same gift* as he gave the Jews who trusted in Yeshua, Kefa asks, *"who was I to stand in God's way?"* With such a controversial idea being presented to a skeptical Jewish audience, it was best to frame all this as a question! It was the right response as guided by the Ruach. Kefa was convinced by the Ruach not to avoid "unkosher" people. As the crowd heard and better understood what took place, they *stopped objecting and began to praise God.*

They were thrilled and said, *"God has enabled the Gentiles as well to do t'shuvah and have life!"* While this report to the leaders was not easy, it is beautiful to see the Jewish believers listened to God's will and received their new Gentile brothers in Yeshua. They were even welcome to come to this Messiah without "converting" or any other conditions. It has been a long history over the last 2000 years, but often today it is the opposite situation. There are a great many Gentile believers in the Body of Messiah, and sometimes there are questions raised if a Jew wants to follow Yeshua and still live as a Jew. Many Gentile Christians reciprocate and praise God that many Jews are also finding spiritual life in Yeshua!

The simple truth is, no one has to "convert" to a different people or culture to find spiritual salvation. Too often today we find believers arguing over non-essentials. Kefa's experience reminds us that Gentiles and Jews may have differing cultures, but true believers are all united in Messiah. This sounds exactly like what the Messiah is supposed to do! Countless denominations all embrace Jesus / Hesus / Isa / Yeshua. Today there are myriad expressions of faith communities as well. We may not agree with or even understand some of the other religious communities' cultural expressions. Whether we attend a church or a messianic synagogue, whether in the U.S. or the Middle East, God is not requiring us to be *uniform* in expression but *unified* in our faith. Yeshua himself said the outside world will know he is Messiah when they see the unity of his true followers (Jn. 17:21). The early Jewish believers praised God for this realization.

Having resolved the controversy of Gentile inclusion (for now), Acts pushes on to describe a new extension of the messianic revival. Luke reflects on *those who had been scattered because of the persecution related to the death of Stephen*. Many of those Jewish believers had been forced out of Israel to various places like *Phoenicia, Cyprus, and Antioch*. This "messianic diaspora" did not curb their enthusiasm for sharing the Good News of Yeshua in their new communities, though Luke notes *they spoke God's word only to Jews*. On the surface, this forced dispersion did not seem like a good thing. But like the later diaspora of 70 C.E., these events were God's way of spreading the light of Torah plus the Good News of Messiah to lands outside Israel. As Luke consistently shares, this messianic message is always taken to the local Jewish community first since they were the first to receive the promise through the prophets (Rom. 1:1–4; 16).

In this transitional time, some of these believers from *Cyprus and Cyrene came to Antioch and began proclaiming the Good News to the Greeks* as well. Antioch (southeastern Turkey) had to be an attractive focus for potential messianic outreach. In that day it was the third-largest city in the Roman Empire (population 500,000), surpassed only by Rome and Alexandria. Of course, in such a large metropolis, there was a significant Jewish community. But Antioch was also known as a great center of the Gentile world boasting pagan culture and religion.

Even with the new emphasis of outreach to the Gentiles, it's only fair that the Jewish community has a priority to hear the fulfillment of the hope of Messiah. I venture that this has not changed and that there is still wisdom in sharing with our Jewish family and friends first. It does not mean to the exclusion of our non-Jewish friends, but as Romans 1:16 says, *"to the Jew first and also to the Greek."* As you share the Yeshua message with the Jewish community, also share it with the non-Jewish community. This way, all people will hear.

Sadly, many people and churches forget this mandate and seem to go to everyone *except* our Jewish people! Luke is careful to note that *the hand of the Lord* was with these outreach workers in Antioch and *a great number of people turned to the Lord.* Maybe it was because of obedience to the scriptural policy that we see such an explosive growth of the Yeshua movement among Jews and non-Jews together? It seems there is a connection between the philosophy of outreach and God's blessing on their broader efforts. This resulted in the first larger group among the Gentiles outside of Israel who embrace Yeshua.

As *news of this* outreach reached Yerushalayim, the *messianic community sent Bar-Nabba* to check it out. This believer had already lived up to his name ("son of encouragement"); he mentored Sha'ul in his new faith (9:27). He was a natural choice to go to Antioch to evaluate the situation and mentor the new believers; he is *a good man, full of the Ruach and trust in God.* He also is from the island of Cyprus, one of the new areas in the expanded outreach. *On arriving, he was glad and encouraged them to remain true* to God.

This is an important reminder for us. It's wonderful to witness the new spiritual birth of those who put their trust in Messiah. But there's also a vital need for those new believers to be mentored and cared for. A birth is quick, but raising the baby takes time and dedication. We need more Bar-Nabbas today! We should all obey Yeshua's mandate to make disciples. One of the true measurements of our own discipleship is if we ourselves are mentoring another disciple! Opportunities are all around us.

Bar-Nabba now goes off to Tarsus to seek his old disciple *Sha'ul*, who spent eight years in his hometown after his encounter on the Damascus road. No doubt for Sha'ul this was a time of study, spiritual growth and seeking God's plan for his life. That time had come as *Bar-Nabba brought him to Antioch and they met with the messianic congregation, teaching the sizable crowd.* We again see an important principle of spiritual growth. Sha'ul needs his time of growth and input. But true growth will not happen if we simply continue to soak in God's truth. There comes a point where we must step out and let the spiritual blessings flow from us. Think of the Dead Sea. It receives plenty of fresh, good water from the Jordan River and Sea of Galil. But being the lowest spot on earth, its water has nowhere to flow. We don't want to be a spiritual Dead Sea! Are we taking in the good waters of Yeshua and letting them flow as we serve our community? Do a mitzvah. It's good for the soul!

Luke makes an important note: *It was in Antioch that the talmidim for the first time were called "Messianic."* There are now tens of thousands of new followers of Yeshua as Messiah, mostly from the Jewish community but now breaking forth in the Gentile world as well. In the Jewish world, these believers were called by different names such as "believers" (4:32) or followers of "the Way" (9:2). Even in later stages of Acts, Messianic Jews are known by their Jewish brothers as *"the sect of the Natzratim"* (Nazarenes; 24:5). There was disagreement between the Jews who embraced Yeshua and those who did not, but they were clearly perceived as a sect within first-century Judaism. The term "believers" simply shows this group had faith in Yeshua as the Messiah, unlike the other Jewish denominations.

Ha-Derekh is a good Jewish term to describe this group that followed Yeshua's distinctive path. The title "sect of the Natzratim" clearly shows that, though their Messiah beliefs were different, they were still considered Jews. The term in 11:26 clearly seems to be used of a different group entirely. Our CJB translation uses "Messianic"; most other versions use "Christian." Why is this term used for the first time at this point in Acts? Acts 11 records the first large Gentile salvation group. This takes place, for the first time, outside the Jewish community in Antioch, Syria.

As all the prior situations took place in the heart of the Jewish world, we see the various Jewish terms used to describe the messianic sect. Now, at a transitional time where non-Jews are the primary focus, for the first time there's a new term used to describe them. They are not Jewish, so there is need for another term; also, these were Gentiles in the Greek-speaking world, hence the new use of the Greek *Christianous*. Interestingly, it was the Antioch larger community that was using this term and not the believers themselves.

Are modern Messianic Jews "Christians"? Yes and no. The term means "follower of Messiah," so in that sense, yes. But many

Messianics prefer not to use "Christian" as it sounds like we are no longer Jewish. Add to this the mistaken belief that a Jew must convert to become a Christian / non-Jew. It seems some of these dynamics already existed in the first century, as Jewish believers were distinguished from the Gentile believers by these terms. In our translation, "Messianic" is a good alternative for "Christian." In fact, many non-Jews in the Yeshua movement today prefer "Messianic" to best describe their connection to the Jewish Yeshua and his people. Terminology is important to clearly express our faith and identity. It is confusing for Jewish followers of Yeshua to use the term "Christian" as, in modern use, it implies they are no longer Jewish. Of course, the terminology and even varying cultures are not the biggest issue; all true believers are united in the one Messiah!

The current ministry in Antioch ends on an informative note. Some prophets came from Yerushalayim to Antioch and foretold a severe famine throughout the land. The office of prophet (*navi*) always held an important place in the life of Israel. The Hebrew root means "to declare or proclaim" as it is often associated with proclaiming the revealed word of God (Jer. 1:1–2; Jon. 1:1, etc). There are several times where it also includes telling a future event only God could know (Isa. 7:13–14; 53, etc). The rabbis of the Talmud believed the spirit of prophecy ceased sometime before the destruction of the Second Temple. "When the latter prophets Haggai, Zechariah and Malachi died, the Holy Spirit departed from Israel" (Tractate Sanhedrin 11a). So serious was this ministry that a Hebrew prophet must be 100% correct or be stoned as a false prophet (Deut. 18:20–22). A true prophet of the God of Israel will not only be 100% correct, but his prophecy can be verified. The false prophets of the pagan world and today do not even pretend to be held to this high standard.

The New Testament lists prophecy as one of the gifts of the Ruach, and we find such a person here named Agav (Agabus). He does not delve into a scriptural exhortation but predicts a famine that will impact all Israel. Agav proves to be a true prophet; his words are verified during Claudius' reign and confirmed by secular historians

(*Antiquities* iii.15.3; Tacitus, *Annals* xii.43). This was not just an exercise in spiritual gifts; it also had a practical application. In light of the impeding famine, the Gentile disciples decided to provide relief to the brothers living in Y'hudah. What a beautiful picture of the unity between the Messianic Jews and the Messianic Gentiles!

The latter clearly understood they had been blessed in spiritual ways from their Jewish brothers. It seemed only right to respond with a financial love-gift to return a blessing to them. This is the first mention of the love offering the congregations of the Gentiles collected and send back to Israel (Rom. 15:25–27; I Cor. 16:1–4). More and more churches are recalling the spiritual debt they owe the Jewish people. Every spiritual blessing they now enjoy came through the conduit of Israel. It is a blessing to see more and more churches doing something tangible today to help the people of Israel and the Messianic Jewish community in particular. It speaks well of the growing understanding and unity today in the Body of Messiah!

> *"'Love the Lord your God and serve Him with all your heart'
> (Deut. 11:13)—which is the service in the heart? Prayer."*
> [Tractate Taanit 2b]

XVII. The Power of Prayer – 12:1–25

Having spent much time on the Gentile expansion, Luke focuses again on the Messianic Jews of Israel: *It was around this time that King Herod began arresting certain members of the Messianic community.* The House of Herod was a powerful ruling family during the Roman occupation of Israel. The New Testament records some of the activities of Herod the Great (ruled 37–4 B.C.E.). He was born in neighboring Idumea to a family of converts to Judaism of the day. In the Roman estimation, he was an ideal ruler; he had a Jewish connection but politically was fully Roman. He was known for magnificent building projects such as Herodian, the fortress of Masada and the remodeled Second Temple.

Yet Herod was also known for his paranoia and brutality, once murdering family members he suspected of disloyalty. This led Emperor Augustus to mockingly say of his pseudo-Jewish colleague, "It is better to be Herod's pig (Greek *hus*) than his son (*huios*)." It is sadly consistent that this Herod also murdered the Jewish infant boys in Y'hudah after rumors of a newborn "King of the Jews" (Mt. 2:13–18). After Herod's death, his kingdom was split among remaining family. Acts 12 describes some of the activities of a later grandson named Herod Agrippa I who was in charge of Y'hudah around 44 C.E.

Perhaps Agrippa inherited some of his grandfather's paranoia and, for whatever reason, struck against the local Yeshua movement. The Romans did not care about religious movements within their empire but took political threats seriously. They could not afford for any subjugated people to rebel against their authority, and too often such rebellion manifested in tiny Y'hudah. Perhaps this is why Agrippa took strong action against the Messianic Jews, even having *Ya'akov, Yochanan's brother, put to death by the sword.* These brothers, as early disciples of Yeshua, were called *b'nei-regesh* ("sons of thunder") and seem to represent the kind of threat that worried the Roman establishment (Mk. 3:17). *When Herod saw how much this pleased the Judeans, he went on to arrest Kefa as well.*

Many translations generalize the Greek term *tois Houdaiois* as "the Jews," but it is better rendered "the Judeans." This current situation takes place in Yerushalayim, so it references some of the city' Jewish leaders of the city. It is not every leader in the city and certainly could not be every Jew in the Roman Empire! Sadly, many misread verses like this to mean the latter. Even more tragic is when anti-Semites use such twisted information to try to justify their animus toward all Jews. There is a dire need for a close study of the Bible today, especially from its original Jewish context, to clearly understand the Good News of Messiah. We contemporary Messianic believers, both Jews and non-Jews, also have an important calling to educate and build some bridges of healing and love between Jews and Christians as we regain the historical story of Yeshua.

91

Luke notes that the *arrest of Kefa* took place *during the Days of Matzah* (unleavened bread). This is a reference to the holy time connected to Pesach. Technically, it is a separate holiday season of seven days after the first night Seder. Herod had Kefa thrown in a high-security prison, *guarded by four squads of four solders each.* From past experience, the Roman governor didn't feel it wise to start a trial of a Jewish defendant during the holy days, so he intended to start the *public trial after Pesach.* It is interesting that Luke uses a Jewish holiday as his time of reference instead of anything Roman or even Christian. Some Bibles translate the original word *Pascha* as "Easter." This patently wrong anachronism ignores the Jewish context of Acts 12. It's as if the translators had a hard time imagining the Jewish believers still celebrating Pesach! This is especially odd as one realizes the same translators interpret "Pascha" as "Passover" in every other context (Mt. 26:2). So it is not an issue of translation but misunderstood culture, 1600 years after the fact.

While Kefa is under high-security confinement, the messianic believers break out another surprising weapon. Luke succinctly summarizes that *intense prayer* was lifted up. Prayer has great power in the Scriptures yet too often is under-utilized. There are great promises that prayer can change things around us as in the case of *Eliyahu* (Elijah; Jas. 5:16). Things can happen through prayer that won't happen if prayer is ignored.

Another important Jewish perspective of prayer is gleaned when one looks at the commonly used Hebrew word *hitpalel.* The root word *palel* means "to judge" because prayer is a form of judgment or arbitration as we lift up requests to God. However, *hitpaal* is to be translated as *"to judge yourself."*

It is true that prayer can change things, but many times, prayer is meant to change *us*! The Jewish model of prayer (which of course includes the Bible and the Siddur) is more often than not about taking an honest look at oneself rather than trying to tell God what to do. We are better served when we align ourselves with God's plan through humble prayer in the spirit of hitpalel, seeking his plan and not our own (Ps. 37:4; Mt. 6:10; etc).

It is with that understanding that the *intense prayer was being made to God*. This kind of situation called for concerted, dedicated prayer (the tense indicates continuous action). Too often we pray with a half-hearted attitude, hoping God might answer. The best answers often come through hard labor. Maybe this is why the least-attended weekly meeting at the local church or *shul* (synagogue) is usually the prayer group. It is hard work that many people are not willing to put in.

Yerushalayim's messianic community knew the danger of Kefa's situation and called on God as the only one who could deliver. Many times, it is God himself who purposely puts us in a situation beyond our control. Sooner or later, we realize we must pray for his help and not rely on our own solutions or false gods. This minyan specifically prayed *on Kefa's behalf*. We are reminded here that the most effective prayers are specific. It is always good to "pray for Israel" or "the outreach workers." But God seems to answer specific requests with specific answers. How much better to pray for some detailed needs in Israel or for a Messianic Jewish ministry that you know? Sometimes, we have not because we ask not (Jas. 4:2)!

As the messianic community of Israel prayed with such focus, some amazing answers were about to be revealed. In jail the night before his trial, *Kefa was sleeping between two soldiers* and *bound with two chains*, with *guards at the door*. Evidently he was so secure in his trust that he could rest no matter the answer. Even with this heightened security, *an angel of ADONAI* appeared, and a *light shone in the cell*. He woke Kefa: *"Hurry! Get up!"* *The chains fell off his hands*. Kefa put on his clothes and *followed* the angel. Humorously, Luke says Kefa thought it was all just a *vision* (he's had those before!) but obeyed. As Kefa and his angelic assistant passed two guards, *they arrived at the iron gate leading to the city*. The *gate opened to them by itself* (Greek *automatay*) and, as they *made their exit*, Kefa began to realize all this was actually taking place! Though he doubted at first, Kefa now has enlightened faith to *know it is the Lord who sent his angel to rescue me from Herod's power.*

On obtaining his freedom, Kefa went to Miryam's house, where many had gathered to pray. He *knocked at the outside door,* and in another humorous twist, the minyan don't believe their prayers have been answered! Rhoda *recognized Kefa's voice at the door and was so happy that she ran back in without opening the door.* She said Kefa was there, but the group said, *"You're out of your mind!"* They thought it was *his angel,* a common belief (Genesis Rabbah on 33:10). As he *kept knocking,* they finally *opened the door* and were *amazed.* Quieting down the minyan, Kefa told *how the Lord had brought him out of the prison.* He said to share this miracle with Ya'akov (not the man in 12:2), the leader of the local believers in Yerushalayim, and *the messianic brothers.* Perhaps the group, even while believing in God, had been praying for a different outcome. The community was greatly encouraged, having learned some lessons about prayer. The dire circumstances had changed for the better, as did the believers' outlook. The same God of our fathers is available today, offering the same resources. May we offer the service of our heart through prayer in the powerful name of Yeshua!

Luke tells what transpired in the Roman community because of these events. *There was no small commotion among the soldiers over what had become of Kefa.* They *could not locate* the emissary, so Herod *cross-examined the guards and ordered them put to death.* This was not surprising; standard Roman policy was that any negligent personnel received the penalty meant for their inmate (Code of Justinian 9.4). It was a stressful time for Herod, and he *went down from Y'hudah to Caesarea and spent some time there.* It didn't take Herod long to distract himself with other kingdom matters. For some reason he was *very angry with the people of Tzor and Tzidon* (Tyre and Sidon) in northern Phoenicia (now Lebanon). Historically this area relied on Israel as a major food supplier. After negotiations, a reconciliation meeting was set up between Herod and the northern neighbors. With great fanfare, Herod, *in his royal robes,* gave a *speech from his throne*. The zealous pagan crowd yelled, *"This is the voice of a god, not a man!"* At once, because Herod did not give the glory to God, an angel of ADONAI struck him down. The powerful governor was gruesomely *eaten away by worms and died*.

The accuracy of Luke's account is verified in a parallel account by the Roman-Jewish historian Josephus. He relates how this meeting took place with Herod attired in "a robe made of silver … that shone and glittered wonderfully as the sun's first rays fell on it." He also tells how the crowd "addressed him as a god" and, more disturbing, Herod "did not repudiate their impious flattery." At that moment, Herod looked up and saw an owl sitting on a rope above his head, which he interpreted as a "messenger of evil." Significantly, the Greek word "messenger" is the same word Luke used to describe the "angel" (*angelos*). Josephus ends by sharing that Herod was seized by a severe pain in his belly and died five days later at age 54 (*Antiquities* 19.8.2).

Luke adds a final word to these dramatic events. Focusing again on the Messianic Jewish community of Y'hudah, he says *the word of the Lord went on growing and being multiplied.* This did not come easily; we've seen persecution and even incarceration on death row. Yet God also brought deliverance and an explosion of new Yeshua faith. At this juncture, *Bar-Nabba and Sha'ul returned to Yerushalayim, having completed their errand* and delivering the love gift from the Gentile believers to their needy Messianic Jewish brothers. Also, a young Jewish believer named *Yochanan (surnamed Mark)* accompanied them on the trip. The spiritual lessons for us today are clear. Sometimes God blesses his children even amid their *tzuris* (troubles). In fact, often it is actually *because* of our tzuris that we experience some unusual blessings of the Kingdom of Messiah! May we, Yeshua's modern disciples, stand strong no matter what our experiences. Either way, our Father in heaven promises to work all things for good as we keep our trust in him (Rom. 8:28).

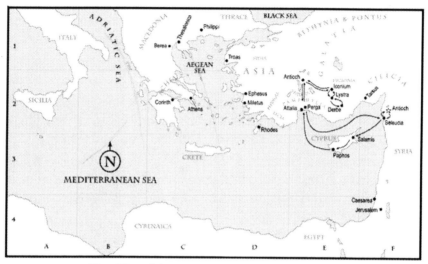

The First Missionary Journey – 13:1–52

Chapter Five

THE FIRST MESSIANIC
OUTREACH JOURNEY

A shaliach is the same as the one who sends him.

(Tractate Berakhot 34)

XVIII. The First Missionary Journey – 13:1–52

Luke makes a major transition in his account of the early Yeshua movement. As summarized in Acts 1:8, he has reviewed the dramatic events that took place in the Holy City within the Jewish community (1:1–8:4). From that point, we learn of the spread of the Good News to Y'hudah and Shomron, including the surprising encounter with the new Jewish believer Sha'ul (8:5–9:31). Luke goes into significant detail to describe the breakthrough into the Gentile community through the main personalities of Kefa and Cornelius (9:32–11:30). After Kefa's deliverance from Herod Agrippa (12:1–25), God is ready for his next big move for his messianic community. Luke sets the stage by describing the ministry team that will take these dramatic steps. It all starts *in the Antioch messianic congregation*, where specific *prophets and teachers* are listed. We have seen from the earlier account that some of the Jewish believers were scattered to this city of Syria and found great success as they shared the Good News of Yeshua with many non-Jews (11:19). It is logical that from this nucleus is birthed a new messianic congregation in the heart of this important crossroads of the Gentile world. Antioch would thus be the logical center of what would become the mission outreach to the Gentiles of the Roman Empire.

Some of Antioch's key leaders listed include some intriguing new names. *Bar-Nabba* is first noted, which is not surprising as he has already played a vital role as a Messianic Jewish leader in the preceding ministry (4:36; 9:27; 11:23–30). Next is *Shim'on (known as "the Black")*. The next one is intriguing: *Lucius (from Cyrene)*. The name Lukios is very similar to Lukos (Luke), and some scholars believe this man is the author of Acts, though this is debated (Bruce 260). *Menachem*, the next team member, is especially noteworthy: *he had been brought up with Herod (Antipas) the governor*. The final person is Sha'ul, who is already known as a great missionary to the Gentile world. All these outreach team members are Jewish believers in Yeshua who are poised to take this Good News to the non-Jewish world. This is confirmed as they were *worshiping the Lord and fasting when the Ruach said to the group, "Set aside for me Bar-Nabba and Sha'ul for the work to which I have called them."* Luke uses *leitourgeo* to describe the worship; this could be translated "liturgy," perhaps a further indication that the Jewish believers continued in the ancient prayer forms (2:42, "the prayers").

After fasting and praying, they placed their hands on them and sent them off. All these elements are common Jewish tradition. Observant Jews pray thrice daily, even fasting until the end of the morning Shachrit service on Mondays and Thursdays. The laying on of hands often symbolizes the ordaining of others (Hebrew *s'mikha*) for an important ministry or task. In this case, Bar-Nabba and Sha'ul are ordained for the new outreach ministry. This is no mere formality; in Jewish tradition it is considered one of the highest callings. The Greek idea of *apostolos* ("sent") is one sent out as a messenger. The original Jewish term "shaliach" has a much deeper connotation as reflected in the Talmud: *"A shaliach is the same as the one who sends him"* (Tractate Berakhot 34). The Jewish leaders understood that these representatives were being sent out not just as messengers but as direct spokesmen of Yeshua himself. This is also why modern Messianic Jews receive the later writings of Sha'ul and the first apostles as the inspired word of God, as they are called shl'chim in this technical Jewish sense (Rom. 1:1; I Kefa 1:1).

Luke recounts the early travels of these two apostles. They start at Seleucia, Antioch's nearby seaport, and set sail for Cyprus, the strategic and third-largest Mediterranean island. It was inhabited by a variety of peoples and cultures. The team lands on the east side of the island at the major town of Salamis, the Jewish center of the island (*Antiquities* 13.10.4). They *began proclaiming the word of God in the synagogues.* Some readers may be confused; this was to be a new mission to the Gentiles. But many times through the Sh'likhim's travels, even as they arrive in a predominantly non-Jewish area, they first seek to share their message with their Jewish brothers. This should not be confusing given the stated outreach philosophy of the New Covenant, to the Jew first and then also to the non-Jew (1:8; Rom. 1:16). It is not about favoritism; it is logical as the Good News of Messiah should be shared first with the people who were told to expect him! So Bar-Nabba and Sha'ul, *with Yochanan (Mark) as an assistant,* shared in the local Jewish community as *they made their way throughout the whole island.*

Not surprisingly, this new venture had some negative encounters. At Paphos (west side of the island), *they found a Jewish sorcerer and pseudo-prophet named Bar-Yeshua.* While Yeshua isn't an uncommon name, it's striking here as the ministry team is proclaiming the divine Yeshua. From early days, Israel was told to beware false prophets or those who use pagan means to conjure a religious experience (Deut. 18:9–13). How tragic that a fellow Jew is doing such evil practices. Still today some Jews forsake their God-given inheritance for the confusion of pagan practice! In this case, Bar-Yeshua had gained popularity and was well-received *by the Roman governor, Sergius Paulus.* He *called for Bar-Nabba and Sha'ul* so he *might hear the message about God.*

The sorcerer, also called Elymas or Chaloma ("interpreter of dreams"), showed his true colors and *opposed* the messengers, and tried to *turn the governor away from the faith* in Yeshua.

He was rebuked by *Sha'ul, also known as Paul.* This note has caused some theologians to believe Sha'ul "converted" and changed his name to prove he was no longer Jewish. In reality, like all first-century Jews, he always had both a Hebrew and a Greek name. It is no coincidence that this first mention of his other name comes as he is starting the mission outreach in the non-Jewish community. He did not convert or change his name; he was simply using his Greek name in this new setting. As this is a Messianic Jewish commentary, I will continue using his Hebrew name to remind us of his Jewish identity, which he always appreciated (Rom. 9:1–5; 11:1–5).

Sha'ul's rebuke of Elymas is forceful: *You son of Satan, full of fraud and evil!* (The word could be translated "con artist.") He is *making crooked the straight paths of the Lord.* This has been Satan's motive ever since his fall (Ezek. 28; Isa. 14). What God reveals, Satan opposes. God is love; Satan hates. God brings shalom; Satan makes turmoil. This also explains why there is still such strong opposition to the things of God even today! Sadly, this false prophet is making God's straight path confusing. Within the pagan culture of Cyprus, this false teacher was guilty of the worse kind of syncretism, trying to combine his knowledge of Judaism with the paganism of the heathen world. Some people still try to do this! As an immediate sign of judgment, Sha'ul proclaims Elymas will be *blind and unable to even see the sun.* Elymas was incapacitated, and *the governor was astounded and trusted in the message* of the messianic emissaries.

With this mixed reception, the team left Paphos and arrived at Perga. *Yochanan left them and returned to Yerushalayim.* This will be a source of controversy in later travels. The remaining group traveled *from Perga to Pisidian Antioch* (Turkey to Asia Minor / Galatia). This city was known to have a sizable Jewish population as well (*Antiquities* 12.3.4). Consistent with their outreach philosophy, the emissaries *went into the synagogue on Shabbat* to connect with their Jewish brothers first (Rom. 1:16). Luke records intricate details of a typical synagogue service. He notes the *reading from the Torah and from the Prophets* and the traditional *Parasha* Torah readings (Genesis to Deuteronomy) that are universally chanted in synagogue services every year. Added to this annual cycle are the Haftorah, readings based on parallel themes found in the Torah and restated in the Prophets (Joshua through Malachi). Modern Judaism follows an annual cycle of the readings, but in the first century there was also a three-year cycle that was much more expanded.

After the readings, *the synagogue leaders* invited the visiting emissaries *to share a word of exhortation* (*Devar Torah*). This tells us several things. The synagogue members didn't think it unusual to invite these Jewish guests to speak. Sha'ul and the team were Jewish and even looked it! The leaders never would have given pagan (or Christian) strangers such an important honor. The details substantiate that the Messianic Jews still looked like fellow Jews (called "brothers"), including tzitziyot and the customary head-coverings since they still identified as Jews. Often today there is a disconnect between messianic believers or Christians and the larger Jewish community, because it is often thought the message is a new religion that is not consistent with Judaism. The believers of Acts shared "as a Jew to the Jews" and saw many good responses as a result. This encounter tells us that Sha'ul and the team were willing and able to share the message of Yeshua in a Jewish way to this Jewish crowd.

What follows is a detailed message (vv. 16–43) of the Good News now revealed to Israel and all peoples. *Sha'ul stood up*, which is still customary today as one is called to the front of the synagogue for an Aliyah. Significantly, Sha'ul addresses both the *men of Israel* and any *God-fearers* in attendance. This would include born-Jews as well as those non-Jews who had such a respect for Judaism that they attended the local synagogue (10:1–2). His message contains a beautiful overview of the topics of the Tanakh.

The first main point (vv. 16–19) touches on a major historical event of the Torah—the Jewish experience in Egypt. Even though *the God of this people Israel chose our fathers*, they were subjected to over 400 years of oppressive slavery. With subtle detail, Sha'ul describes the ancestors as *"our fathers,"* emphasizing the common bond they all have as Jews, Messianic or not. At the right time, God led the Hebrews *out of that land* with the miraculous first Pesach. The miracles did not stop there; God faithfully *took care* of the crowd in the desert for the next *forty years*. Ultimately, the people were led into the *land of Kena'an* and received the land *as a promised inheritance*.

Sha'ul's second point (vv. 20–21) revolves around the period of the *Nevi'im* (prophets; Joshua through Malachi). In the time of the Judges, various leaders and warriors guided Israel until the anointing of *the prophet Sh'mu'el*. It is probably no coincidence that Sha'ul mentions his namesake, the first King of Israel, Sha'ul Ben-Kish, both men tracing their ancestry from *the tribe of Binyamin* (Rom. 11:1).

All this leads to the third point, which focuses on King David and references Psalm 2:7 as quoted in the *Ketuvim* ("The Writings" in Jewish tradition; Psalms through II Chronicles). David was raised up as king to replace the troubled King Sha'ul. God commends the young shepherd as *a man after my own heart*. Paul may have shared more details to the synagogue crowd, but these three main points represent all the sections of the Tanakh, an acronym from *Torah*, *Neviim* and **Ketuvim**. This last point becomes a natural transition for the message, as it is the greater descendent of King David who will someday rule as King Messiah.

Sha'ul insists that it is *in keeping with God's promise* that he sent *a deliverer* (*moshia*) of Davidic descendant named Yeshua. Note the wordplay: *moshia* and *Yeshua* are from the same Hebrew root. Right before the revelation of Yeshua, *Yochanan* prepared the way by proclaiming *an immersion in connection with turning to God from sin*. Yochanan openly stated that he himself was *not that anointed one* but that someone was coming whose sandals he felt *unworthy even to untie*. Sha'ul now connects all the historical dots to proclaim Yeshua as that promised one. Addressing the synagogue attendees as "brothers," the shaliach says, *"It is to us that the message of this deliverance has been sent!"* He adds that many in Yerushalayim *did not recognize who Yeshua was or understand the message of the Prophets*, so *they fulfilled that message by condemning him*. They asked Pilate to have Yeshua executed, actually fulfilling all the things written about him. This includes his death on a Roman stake and being placed in the tomb of a rich man (Isa. 53).

This would be a tragic story if left there, but Sha'ul shares the incredible news that *God raised Yeshua from the dead!* Not only that, the living Messiah *appeared for many days to those who had come from the Galil to Yerushalayim*, and hundreds of Jewish *eyewitnesses* affirm this spectacular reality (I Cor. 15:1–8). According to Sha'ul, Yeshua's death and resurrection is the Good News of *what God promised to the fathers*. Many other Scriptures confirm all this. God always spoke of having a special *Son* as written in Psalm 2. Though he will face an unusual death, there are other promises that affirm that the Holy One *will not see the decay* of the grave (Ps. 16:10). What King David predicts is also elaborated further in the rabbinic writings:

> *Our Rabbis taught: The Holy One, blessed by He, will say to the Messiah, son of David (may he reveal himself speedily in our days!), "Ask of Me anything, and I will give it to you," as it is said, "I will tell of the decree, etc., this day have I begotten you. Ask of me and I will give the nations for your inheritance" (Ps. 2:7–8). But when he will see that Messiah son of Joseph is slain, he will say to him, "Lord of the universe, I ask of You only the gift of life." "As to life," He would answer him, "Your father David has already prophesied this concerning you," as it is said, "He asked life of You and You gave it to him [even length of days forever and ever]." (Tractate Sukkah 52a)*

Sha'ul continues to drive his message home by noting that David could not be speaking of his own experience in the Psalms as he was *buried with his fathers and did see decay.* The evidence points conclusively to Yeshua, who is now *proclaimed for the forgiveness of sins.* Though the Torah revelation is good, it was not in itself a final solution for sin. It offered a way to temporarily *cover our sins* through many generations, but it is the Messiah who removes *the sins from everyone who puts his trust in Him.* A word of warning is now given. Like most references in Sha'ul's message, this is not new but a reflection on the past, where Habakkuk warned of impeding judgment on those in Israel *who will mock* the word of God, *even if someone explains it to you* (Hab. 1:5). With this strong message and exhortation, perhaps many expected a negative response. But *the people invited Sha'ul and Bar-Nabba to tell them more about these matters the following Shabbat.* In fact, after the meeting, *many of the born Jews and devout proselytes followed Sha'ul and Bar-Nabba, who urged them to keep holding fast to the love and kindness of God.*

The next Shabbat, nearly the whole city gathered to hear more of this messianic message. Evidently there were still many people, Jews and God-fearers, who were still receptive to this Good News, but it was not unanimous. Ironically, the positive reception antagonized some who did not receive the message of Yeshua. These skeptics were *filled with jealousy* and started *speaking against Sha'ul.* This divided multitude did not dissuade the emissaries from continuing their work in Antioch Pisidia, but it did slightly change their focus.

In keeping with their outreach philosophy, Sha'ul asserts this word of Messiah must go *to the Jewish community first.* But since many of them *have rejected* this message, they will now openly *turn to the Gentile* community of the city. They invoke a Tanakh verse that highlights Israel's call to be *a light for the nations* and for God's deliverance to go *to the ends of the earth* (Isa. 49:6).

The Gentiles were *very happy to hear this, and as many as had been appointed to eternal life came to trust.* Some Jews increased the pressure on the emissaries and their message. They tried to dissuade leaders (both *Jewish and God-fearers*), organized opposition against the Sh'likhim, and *expelled them from their district.* But the talmidim were not discouraged. In a symbolic act, *Sha'ul and Bar-Nabba shook the dust of their feet against them* as any Jew leaving an ungodly environment would. They *went on to Iconium, filled with joy and with the Ruach HaKodesh.* There would still be opportunities elsewhere for the Jewish community to respond to the message of Yeshua.

There are clear lessons from the first-century Yeshua movement. Yeshua is the fulfillment of the promises to our fathers concerning the coming Messiah. He came for Israel and died a sacrificial death for Israel (and all people). This is not a message of another martyred rabbi; Yeshua was resurrected from the dead! If all these things are predicted in the Tanakh, we too should be excited to share this Good News with those around us! (See Isa. 53 for the whole story.) But people will have different responses. Some oppose the message of the Jewish Yeshua out of ignorance of the Scriptures. Many, even among our Jewish brothers, have lost a real knowledge of the Tanakh. Rejection may even manifest in strong opposition to Yeshua and his people. It is not for us to judge; that is God's domain. Keep in mind that every person is on their own spiritual journey; some are seeking God and are only partly there. God is just, and he is patient. We do well to learn from the actions and attitudes of the early Yeshua believers as we represent Messiah to our generation. No matter the response, may we continue to lovingly share the good things that have come into our lives through faith in Yeshua!

XIX. Challenges of the First Missionary Journey – 14:1–28

The emissaries left Pisidian Antioch. There had been a great receptivity to their message of Messiah among both Jews and non-Jewish God-fearers, which led to multitudes of new believers. But there was also strong pushback from some Jewish leaders who were not convinced and strongly opposed this idea of the risen Yeshua. Moving on to another mixed community *in Iconium* (Asia

Minor / Turkey), *the same thing happened—they went into the synagogue and spoke in such a way that a large number of both Jews and Greeks came to trust.* That was the good news, but as before, there was much negative reaction to the Sh'likhim from some Jews *who would not be persuaded.* It didn't stop there. They *stirred up the Gentiles and poisoned their minds* against the messianic messengers. Despite this response of those opposed, all this again took place in the local synagogue. Some readers may be tempted to think that, based on the opposition, Sha'ul and team would give up on their Jewish brothers. But again we see the messianic team going first to the local synagogue to share the Good News of Messiah. Sha'ul believed the message of Yeshua is not only good for the Jewish community but a priority even in the face of rejection (Rom. 1:16).

Here in the Iconium Jewish community, the emissaries are not dissuaded by rejection but make an even stronger commitment to *remain for a long time, speaking boldly about the Lord.* The message of *God's love and kindness* was also confirmed with public *signs and miracles.* Some believers today think God must do a testifying miracle every week to confirm his presence. But this era of the Book of Acts (and Gospels) was a unique time in history. As the public would hear the spoken message, there was no other verifiable source to confirm this new idea of Yeshua being the Messiah.

Of course, there was no written New Testament to verify to facts. So it was vital in the first-century movement that the spoken message be verified with testifying signs and wonders, especially for the sake of the skeptical Jews (Heb. 2:1–4). It must have seemed odd for this team of itinerate Jews to speak of the coming of Messiah. There was surely a stronger need for confirming miracles in the early context. But God can and does do miracles today. There are many cases in the modern Messianic Jewish community, and it's enthusiastically welcomed. But there's additional testimony of the Jewish New Covenant Scriptures, which in many ways is better than a transitory event.

The bottom line is to have enough faith to let God be God, miracles or not. In this case even with dramatic wonders, *the people of the city were divided* (*eschisthe*, "schism") between those who followed the *unbelievers* and those who received the emissaries' testimony. Acts 14:14 is one of the references to Sha'ul and Yosef as "apostles" in the broad sense of the word. Spiritually, this is a sobering reminder that some people are disinclined to ever believe, even if they witness a miracle first-hand! It's not that they *cannot* believe (there is observable evidence); many *will not* believe because of other personal issues, like submitting our life to Yeshua's lordship. In Iconium, the pressure grew to the point that some of the unbelievers made *a move to mistreat the emissaries, even to stone them.* This growing opposition came from *both Jews and Gentiles.* It is not just strong emotions in the Jewish community; the pagan Gentile community has its own reasons for opposing this message, as we see even today. Because of this persecution, the team *escaped to Lystra and Derbe, towns in Lycaonia where they continued proclaiming the Good News.* Sometimes today we disciples of Yeshua face tough challenges. The emissaries at one point stand firm and stay engaged with the community. As we see, at one point the emissaries flee, the situation is so bad. Every situation is unique, and we too should seek God's wisdom if we are to stay with those who are receptive or to leave those who are strongly opposed.

As they began to minister *in Lystra*, the Sh'likhim were faced with an unusual situation. Within the public pagan community, they encountered *a man who could not use his feet.* He had *never been able to walk, being crippled from birth. Sha'ul, looking at the man, realized that he had faith to be healed* by the power of Yeshua. In a dramatic statement of mutual faith, Sha'ul said, *"Stand up on your feet!"* The lame man *jumped up and began to walk.* This miracle had a huge impact on the pagan crowd, but not in a way the disciples anticipated. Those present shouted, *"The gods have come down to us in the form of men!"* and called *Bar-Nabba "Zeus" and Sha'ul "Hermes."* It seems a logical reaction, as *a temple dedicated to Zeus was just outside the city*, and Hermes was a spokesperson for the other gods.

The Gentile pagans' response represented a different challenge than the response from the larger Jewish community. In some ways it was harder for these messengers to relate to the confused paganism rampant in the Roman Empire. At least in the Jewish community there was a commonality of belief in the Tanakh and the one God of Israel. Likewise, the concept of a Messiah is totally within the boundaries of Jewish theology. With pagans, they needed to start with Genesis 1:1, *"In the beginning, God!"* It is a similar dynamic today. We must discern where various individuals are coming from and relate to them according to their understanding. Sharing with a pagan was, and still is, very different from sharing with a Jew.

The emissaries' first reaction was striking: *They tore their clothes and ran into the crowd, shouting, "Men! Why are you doing this?"* Kria, the act of tearing one's clothes, represents the highest form of grief. It is often reserved for grieving at a funeral (Tractate Sanhedrin 7.5). Here it illustrates the grief over the pagans' blasphemy. Along with the graphic display of kria, the emissaries affirm what should have been obvious: *We're just men, human like you!* They turn the situation into a chance to tell the reason for their visit: *We are announcing Good News to you*, but first *turn from these worthless things to the living God.*

Unlike the corrupted pagan ideas, there is only one *God who made everything*, especially those things the pagan world worships. This one true God, the God of Israel, has been very patient with the peoples of the world. Even with this patience, he is seen in plenty of *evidence of his nature*. It is HaShem, the only God, *who does good things, giving rain from heaven and crops in their seasons, filling them with food and their hearts with happiness*. All good things come from above, not through mortals or false gods. With this pagan audience there is not even a mention of Yeshua as Redeemer; they must first turn from their religious ignorance. Even clarifying these eternal truths *barely kept the crowds from sacrificing to them.*

As if things weren't confusing enough, *some unbelieving Jews came from Antioch and Iconium!* This group, already opposed to the message of Yeshua, *won over the crowds* to their side, then *stoned Sha'ul and dragged him outside the city, thinking he was dead.* The pagans and Romans had many means of killing (like the torturous cross), but this was a Jewish way of execution; either by the witnesses hurling stones or casting the criminal off a cliff to land on jagged rocks. This is one of the situations Sha'ul recounts as his sufferings for Yeshua (II Cor. 11:25). Miraculously, *as the talmidim gathered around him, he got up and went back into the town! The next day, he left with Bar-Nabba for Derbe* (ancient Galatia / modern Turkey).

The apostles continued *proclaiming the Good News and making many new disciples* in this new town. Startlingly, they *returned to Lystra, Iconium and Antioch*, the very places of intense opposition. It was for this very reason that they felt the need to *strengthen the talmidim, encouraging them to remain true to the faith.* The young believers are told that it is often *through many hardships that we must enter the Kingdom of God.* This could be a reference to the teaching that there will be tribulations before the Kingdom of God comes. The rabbis graphically describe this time as the "birth pains of the Messiah" where the world will be in turmoil just before Messiah's return (Tractate Sanhedrin 98b; Rom. 8:12–25).

The term would apply to each new believer's personal trials as well. Knowing these new groups would need some continuing spiritual care, Sha'ul and Bar-Nabba *appointed elders* to take the lead as shepherds of the flock. Having done all within their power, the emissaries *committed the disciples to the Lord*, the greater Shepherd. This reminds us that the Yeshua community has a greater responsibility than making new believers. In the process of making a true disciple, new believers must be given additional attention. The same holds true today. We are always excited about a new birth, but who will continue the intense care of a new baby? This happens on a one-on-one level, but as we see here, it is also a byproduct of a healthy congregation and underlines the importance of a messianic synagogue in every Jewish community today.

With that, the emissaries departed *through Pisidia and arrived in Pamphylia*. They shared the same Good News of the Messiah *in Perga*, then traveled *down to Attalia*. Luke says the group then *sailed back to their original place of departure in Antioch*. There they had been commissioned for this first outreach journey and now returned, having completed this work of God. Now *they gathered the Messianic community together and reported what God had done through them*. What a huge step of faith it was for this band of believers to reach out *to the Gentile communities* of the Roman Empire! They excitedly share that *a door of faith had indeed opened* beyond the Jewish community and beyond the borders of Israel. It must have been a beautiful time as they *stayed in Antioch with the other talmidim*. But this successful outreach would also raise some strong questions among others within the Messianic Jewish community.

Today the shoe is on the other foot! The huge Gentile majority of today's church now face a similar challenge of reaching a group very different from themselves—Jewish friends and neighbors. Many in the church world today are rejoicing over what God is doing among the Jews. Something is stirring when there are some 100,000 Jewish believers in the U.S. and some 200 messianic synagogues scattered throughout the Jewish population centers of North America, Latin America, Russia and Israel. Yet it is not without some controversy in parts of the Christian community. The question is, will contemporary Christians see the significance and support the growing Jewish movement for Yeshua? An educated believer should certainly rejoice that the Jewish fig tree is blossoming once again (Mt. 24:32–35)!

Anyone who accepts upon himself the yoke of Torah removes from himself the yoke of the way of the world. (Pirkei Avot 3:5)

XX. Welcoming the Gentiles Into the Yeshua Movement – 15:1–35

There was no doubting the remarkable success of the First Missionary Journey to the Gentile world. It must have seemed daunting that a small group of Jewish followers of Yeshua would find a spiritual welcome in the pagan corners of the Roman Empire. As Luke has noted, many early Messianics welcomed this inclusion as a fulfillment of prophecy. As far back as Abraham, it was revealed that God's heart was to bless the entire world through the message of Messiah (Gen. 12:3; Isa. 49:6). But with this influx of new non-Jewish believers also arose some new spiritual questions. Chapter 15 starts with some of the controversial questions posed by some of the Jewish side who *came down from Y'hudah to Antioch.* These are not those opposed to Yeshua but Jewish believers from the Pharisee background.

These men *began teaching* Gentile believers they were not truly saved unless they were circumcised as Moshe had taught. The eight-day b'rit-milah has long been a sign of the covenant between God and the Jewish people since the days of the first Jew, Abraham (Gen. 17:9–14). This custom continued through the generations to this day and wasn't even a question for the first-century Messianic Jews. Sha'ul had his Jewish coworker Timothy circumcised, as his mother was a Jew (16:1–3), but didn't require it of his Gentile coworker Titus (Gal. 2:1–3). The Messianic Jewish community's early understanding was that b'rit-milah still applied as they were still Jewish sons of Abraham.

But the question here comes from a conservative Messianic Jewish branch that says all male followers of Yeshua are to submit to b'rit-milah. In their mind, the non-Jew was joining the Jewish people in every way, including all the ritual rites. Some today condemn these Pharisee Yeshua believers for even thinking such a thing, but it's a logical query given the new outreach to the Gentile world. Everyone seemed to agree that the Gentiles are grafted into the olive tree of Israel to share in the Jewish blessings (Rom. 11:17). But the question here is, must a Gentile convert to Judaism to follow Yeshua? It may sound strange today, but as we see in Acts, it was a sincere concern for the earliest community. It could be stated like this: How can Jewish believers and non-Jewish believers have table fellowship together? It is not a question of our *relationship with God*; that's settled through our shared faith in Yeshua. But it is a compelling question of *our relationship with one another* from our vastly different cultures.

Still, this controversial teaching caused *discord and dispute with Sha'ul and Bar-Nabba. So the congregation assigned Sha'ul, Bar-Nabba and some of themselves to go and put this sh'eilah* (question) *before the emissaries and the elders up in Yerushalayim.* The Antiochan community sent the emissaries to the Holy City to join what often is called the Jerusalem Council. On their way, they stopped in various areas of *Phoenicia and Shomron*, recounting how *the Gentiles had turned to God. This news brought great joy* to all. As the emissaries arrived in Yerushalayim, they gave a report of what God had done through them. Some of the Yeshua *believers from the P'rushim* objected. They raised some valid questions, and it is a reminder here that not all Pharisees were opposed to Yeshua.

In fact, it is precisely because of their staunch traditional beliefs that many would be inclined to be drawn to this growing messianic movement. From their traditional background, this group said it was *necessary to circumcise the Gentile men and direct them to observe the entire Torah.* In other words, circumcision is symbolic of a total Torah lifestyle including the 613 mitzvot required of Jews. These were weighty questions at the time and sometimes even today. Most modern Messianic Jews believe, like Sha'ul, that everyone is free to come to Yeshua's salvation within their own ethnic and cultural identity (Gal. 3:28). We all stand equal before God when we receive the Good News, and there is no need for anyone, Jew or non-Jew, to convert to a new ethnic status. It seems quite clear as one studies the Jerusalem Council's process and conclusions. Yet there are still some in both the Jewish and Christian realms who want to focus on a type of legalism that is clearly denounced in the New Testament.

The emissaries and the elders met look into this matter. After lengthy debate, Kefa addressed the meeting. This is to be expected given how important he was to the Yeshua movement's expansion. Yeshua gave him the keys of the Kingdom; thus, Kefa is present at every major open door; first to the Jewish community, then to the Samaritan population and finally to the larger non-Jewish world. He is certainly an important authority for the messianic community to consult on this question of the place of Gentile believers. Kefa prefaces his response by alluding to the fact that *God chose him to be the one by whose mouth the Gentiles should hear the message.*

Though it was well-known that God desired to ultimately bless all people with the message of Yeshua, it was still a bit controversial as to the details. To this, Kefa alludes to the fact that *God bore witness by giving the Ruach HaKodesh to them,* just as he did to the Jewish believers. With this body of evidence, Kefa poses an obvious question to the Council: *"Why are you putting a yoke on the [Gentile believers] which neither our fathers nor we have had the strength to bear?"* This is an interesting allusion to the common practice in ancient Israel of a pair of oxen connected by a yoke as they plow a field in unison. Though this passage is often read in a negative light, let's look at the meaning of "yoke" in Jewish thought. Instead of being a terrible burden, the yoke is used as a picture of our divine responsibility. The *Mishnah* uses the phrase *ol ha-Torah* to describe the Jewish responsibility to uphold Torah:

> *Rabbi Nechunia son of Hakanah said, "Anyone who accepts upon himself the yoke of Torah removes from himself the yoke of government duties and the yoke of the way of the world; but one who casts off the yoke of Torah accepts upon himself the yoke of government and the yoke of the way of the world."* (*Pirkei Avot* 3:5)

This blessing is said to be summarized by the Shema (Deut. 6:4; *Tractate Berakhot 2:5*). The phrase is also used to describe the acceptance of God's sovereignty, which would be especially appropriate of the Gentile who joins the Jewish people (Exodus Rabbah 30.5). As Kefa and the Messianic Jewish leaders would have had this understanding, we should not take his statement as a yoke or negative view of Torah. It rings true, though, that if our people have never completely fulfilled the obligations of Torah, then the Gentiles would have an even more difficult challenge. So Kefa summarizes his view: *It is through the love and kindness of the Lord Yeshua that we trust and are delivered—and it's the same with them.*

After explaining some of the theological reasons, *Bar-Nabba and Sha'ul shared what signs and miracles God had done through them among the Gentiles.* Then Ya'akov gave his reasoned response as the head *Zakeyn* (elder). Addressing the leadership, he points out it is consistent with the Tanakh that *God was taking from among the Gentiles a people to bear his name.* He quotes Amos, who has two important truths to consider. First, it is predicted that in the latter days *God will rebuild the fallen tent [sukkah] of David.* The "sukkah" reference recalls the temporal status of even David's great kingdom. That humble Sukkot hut is said to have fallen and lay in ruins. This is clearly a poetic picture of the status of Israel and the Jewish people during much of our challenging history.

But Ya'akov invokes the ancient prophet to declare that God is now beginning the restoration of the spiritual Jewish house with the arrival of Yeshua as Messiah. This was patently clear with the tens of thousands of first-century Jews who embraced this messianic faith. The second truth elucidated by the Amos prophecy connects to the first: Only after the rebuilding of the spiritual Jewish community *the rest of mankind may seek the Lord, that is, all the nations.* The lead elder says *all this has been known for ages* but is now occurring before their eyes!

Because of these fulfilled prophecies, Ya'akov proposes that the Jewish believers *should not put obstacles in the way of the Gentiles who are turning to God*. Though he would not require b'rit-milah, this is not to be without any conditions. He proposes four requirements for any new Gentile follow of Yeshua. They need not convert to become Jews as part of their Yeshua faith, but he suggests writing them a letter (now recorded in Acts) *telling them to abstain from things polluted by idols, from fornication, from what is strangled and from blood*. This has a strong Jewish precedent as seen in rabbinic Judaism, whose traditional stance is that Gentiles can be acceptable to God without needing to convert to Judaism.

Instead of taking the full yoke of the Torah (613 commandments), non-Jews do well to simply follow the Seven Laws of the Sons of Noah for all mankind (Tractate Sanhedrin 56a; Avodah Zara 8.4). Instead of requiring b'rit-milah and the other laws, these four areas are a logical summary of the 7 Laws given to Noah after the Flood. To follow Yeshua, a Gentile must turn from any kind of idolatry, a big challenge in the pagan Roman Empire. They must also repent of any immorality (Greek *pornea*), also rampant then. To abstain from what is strangled seems to refer to kosher sensitivities. This was often a pagan way to kill an animal in contrast to the more humane way of *sh'chitah* (ritual slaughter) in Judaism, which also lets the animal's blood be drained.

Abstaining from blood could refer to *kashrut* or even taking innocent blood (murder). A study of these recommendations shows they are parallel to the concepts in the Seven Laws. Ya'akov adds this justification for his proposal: As the words of Moshe (Torah) are read every Shabbat, the messianic Gentiles ought to be sensitive to the Jewish community. It could also be that these four areas would be a good starting point for the non-Jews, but they'd continue their education by their natural interaction with the Jewish community.

The Jerusalem Council received this counsel seriously and favorably. In short, the Gentiles didn't need to become Jews to receive Yeshua. They simply had to adhere to these four areas, which summarized well the *Sheva Mitzvot. The other emissaries and elders (along with the whole Messianic community)* decided to write such a letter and disseminate it throughout the Gentile messianic communities, starting with Antioch.

The apostolic letter makes these points: The Gentile believers had been *upset by some people who spoke without proper apostolic authorization.* So they *decided unanimously to select men of authority; namely, Sha'ul, Bar-Nabba as well as Y'hudah and Sila.* The letter affirms that all this *seemed good not only to the emissaries* as mortal leaders but *also to the Ruach HaKodesh.* The recommendations are not merely the ideas of men (though unanimous!) but confirmed as from God. With that confidence, *the messengers were sent off to Antioch and delivered the letter.* The non-Jewish recipients were *delighted by its encouragement.* When all was said and done, everyone in the messianic community was blessed by the decision of the Jerusalem Council, including the Jewish believers, the Gentile believers and even God himself!

This was a monumental Council in first-century Yerushalayim, but what are the implications today? One clear application is that Gentile believers can have faith in Messiah without converting to Judaism. Non-Jews are often pressured to convert to Judaism if they wish to join the Jewish community, especially through marriage. Yet these are all communities who do not believe the messianic era has arrived yet. Only Messianic Judaism currently believes Yeshua is that Messiah and, as such, he gives Jews and Gentiles equal access to God. There is some debate in Messianic Judaism about a conversion process for non-Jews, but the majority opposes such a process based on Yeshua's work, the Jerusalem Council, and New Testament principles to this effect (Gal. 3:26–29; I Cor. 7:17–20).

Having affirmed that beautiful truth, we also believe it is still important for Gentile believers to understand the guidance of the four principles of Acts 15 and their relationship to the 7 Laws. The message of the New Covenant is that sincere faith in Yeshua is all that is needed for justification before God. Yet too often the church has been ignorant of or ignored the Jerusalem Council's wisdom. While the admonitions have nothing to do with justification, they have everything to do with sensitivity to the Jewish culture of the messianic faith.

For example, Gentile Christians need not keep kosher, but they should be educated and sensitive to the Jewish roots of their faith. There is certainly no place for supersessionism or replacement theology! Had the Council's precepts been respected in church history, there might well have been a positive bridge of connection between the church and synagogue instead of the walls of separation and animosity.

It also becomes clear that Messianic Jews are to remain in their Jewish identity. Our standing before God is guaranteed by Yeshua's work while we are to understand that the gifts and callings of God, in this context to Israel, are irrevocable (Rom. 11:29). Jewish followers of Yeshua rest in Messiah's finished work. While there is much debate about what living within a Jewish identity means, the clear message of Acts and the New Testament is that Jewish believers are to retain a recognizable Jewish lifestyle within their messianic faith (Mt. 5:17–18; Acts 21:20; I Cor. 7:17–20). There can be myriad cultural faith expressions in Yeshua as Messiah yet a unity of all believers. This seems to be what Yeshua himself alluded to as he prayed that all his followers may be united so the world may believe He is the one sent from God (Jn. 17:20–21). With this proper balance today, all followers of Yeshua appreciate each other and stand together!

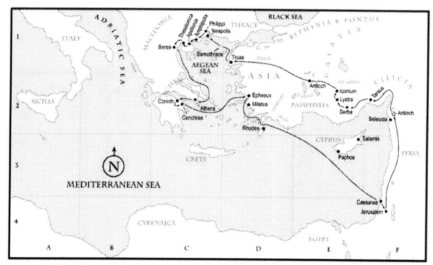

The Second Missionary Journey – 15:36–18:22

Chapter Six

THE SECOND AND THIRD
MESSIANIC
OUTREACH JOURNEYS

An idol appears to be near at hand but is in reality afar off. On the other hand, The Holy One, blessed be He, appears to be afar off, but in reality there is nothing closer than He.

(Tractate Berakhot 13a)

XXI. The Second Missionary Journey – 15:36–18:22

A. The Divine Plan – 15:36–16:15

fter some time, Sha'ul said to Bar-Nabba, "Let's go back and visit the brothers in all the towns where we proclaimed the message about the Lord, and see how they're doing." This visit, which will become the Second Missionary Journey, is commendable but presents a problem. Bar-Nabba wants to take Yochanan (Mark), but Sha'ul feels it unwise. Yochanan had left the teams in Pamphylia during the ministry outreach (13:13). We are never told why. Perhaps he felt the messianic outreach work was too dangerous. Sha'ul and Bar-Nabba disagree so sharply *that they separated from each other*. Bar-Nabba later reconciled with Yochanan and came to appreciate him, as he was later reinstalled in the messianic team (II Tim. 4:11). But currently, *Bar-Nabba took Mark and sailed off to Cyprus*, Bar-Nabba's home. *Sha'ul chose Sila and headed back to Cilicia*, Sha'ul's home province. Despite the *sharp disagreement* between the two leaders, some practical lessons can be gleaned. First, there can be major disagreements and even divisions between sincere believers. Often it can have a negative effect, but sometimes God uses the situation for his purposes.

Though Sha'ul and Bar-Nabba disagree and divide, it becomes the birth of two messianic outreach missions instead of one! We too will have disagreements and divisions. It can be handled in the flesh or in the Ruach. One who is guided by the Ruach can disagree without being disagreeable. We all have fallen human natures that contribute to such situations. Sometimes it is more about different people having different callings. Luke records openly and honestly the dispute as even the early leaders of the Yeshua movement were not perfect (good news for us!). Yet they seek to keep aligned with God's best plan and to treat all people with respect. This is a good model for us as we seek to walk with Yeshua.

With this compromise, the two Messianic Jewish teams set out on their respective journeys. This is the last we hear of Bar-Nabba and his ministry, but surely they had fruitful opportunities to share Messiah and encourage the believers. Luke focuses on the Second Missionary Journey led by *Sha'ul and Sila*; they made their first stops in *Derbe and Lystra*. In this area lived a promising young believer named Timothy. He came from a mixed "interfaith" family, *the son of a Jewish woman who had come to trust, and a Greek father*. Luke describes Timothy as highly regarded in the Yeshua community; as such, *Sha'ul wanted him to accompany* the team. But because of his family situation, Timothy had never received a b'rit-milah. This was not unusual, but Sha'ul feels it incumbent to follow this mitzvah *because of the Jewish community* in that area.

Some find it problematic that Sha'ul insists on this mitzvah, especially given the events of the prior chapter. Sha'ul would never have required a non-Jew to have an 8th-day circumcision, as this was clearly decided at the Jerusalem Council. But Timothy is a born Jew by virtue of his Jewish mother. He was not circumcised as a newborn, but it is deemed advantageous as he is still considered a Jew by the larger community. This situation, right after the Acts 15 Council, confirms that the decisions mainly addressed the place of Gentiles in the Yeshua community. It was clearly understood that Jews who follow Yeshua should continue in the Jewish customs and lifestyle.

Regrettably, even today some misapply the Jerusalem Council's edicts. Just because b'rit-milah was not enforced on Gentiles does not mean Messianic Jews should not follow the custom. At present, the Orthodox Jewish community (and the state of Israel) still holds to the matrilineal definition for Jewish identity. In recent years, though, other Jewish groups have also endorsed a patrilineal definition that includes the father's side of the family. This can be confirmed in the Tanakh with such cases as Yosef and even Moshe, who both had Jewish children through non-Jewish wives (Gen. 48; Ex. 2). As to the question of Jewish identity, most Messianic Jews follow both matrilineal and patrilineal lines. In our community, if one has a Jewish mother or father, one is considered a full Jew with the incumbent responsibilities. That Sha'ul has Timothy circumcised becomes even more significant given Luke's record that *they delivered the decisions reached by the elders in Yerushalayim for the people to observe.* Obviously, the b'rit-milah of Timothy was consistent with the elders' earlier decision. All this was received as good news by the congregations of Lystra as *they were strengthened in the faith and increased in number day by day.*

Sha'ul and his team continue their journey. They travel through the *region of Phrygia and Galatia* (central Asia Minor / modern Turkey). It would have seemed logical to revisit areas to the south like Ephesus, but they *were prevented by the Ruach HaKodesh.* The group also tried to move north *into Bithinia, but the Spirit of Yeshua would not let them.* The Spirit-directed path led the team to the far-flung city of Troas. This may have seemed odd, as they skipped over some prominent cities only to come to this dead-end port city facing the Aegean Sea. As the Sh'likhim were puzzling over this, *a vision appeared to Sha'ul at night. A man from Macedonia was standing and begging them, "Come over to Macedonia and help us!"*

So compelling was this event that the team lost no time getting ready to leave for this Greek province across the sea. For the first time, Luke actually mentions himself: *"**We** concluded that God had called us to proclaim the Good News to them."* Though he has been the historian on the details of the early Yeshua movement (Acts 1:1), possibly this is where he physically joins the outreach journeys. Some speculate that he was a doctor from Troas, a port city. It would have been wise to have a physician, especially given Sha'ul's health challenges (II Cor. 12:7–10; Gal. 6:11).

So, by a vision from the Ruach, the path forward is shown. There is much today about the ministry of the Ruach in the life of the messianic community. Some places claim to have a manifestation of the Spirit every day; others minimize his work. I believe the Spirit still ministers today, in miraculous ways. One of the great proofs is the testimonies of thousands of contemporary Jews who have had a dynamic encounter with Yeshua! Often this has involved visions or healings. While these can be documented, it still isn't the foundation of our faith walk. As Kefa reminds us, Messianic believers have the written revelation of the Tanakh and New Covenant as a more-certain source of revelation (II Kefa 1:19). It is good to let God be God in our experiences but to confirm all things through the Word he spoke. Here in Acts 16, the Sh'likhim show deference to the Ruach and the unexpected change of plans. It recalls the Jewish saying: "If you want to make God smile, tell him your plans!"

Convinced of the importance of the vision, the team *sailed from Troas* with an overnight stop at *Samothrace*, off the Macedonian coast. After a brief stop at Neapolis on the mainland, they went on about ten miles to the *Roman colony in this region called Philippi.* Luke says *we spent a few days in this city; then on Shabbat, we went by the riverside*, where they hoped to connect with a minyan. (This term usually refers to a gathering of at least ten Jewish men, the minimal requirement for the communal prayers. Of course, a minyan is not always possible in smaller communities, as seems to be the case in Philippi.) There was no synagogue in which to hold services, but per the Mishna, the next-best place would be by a body of water that could serve as a natural mikveh pool (Tractate Mikvaot 5.4).

A group of Jewish women had *gathered there* for Shabbat prayers. One was *a "God-fearer" by the name of Lydia*. She seems to be a traveling salesperson, as she was from Thyatira in Asia and is identified as a dealer in *fine purple cloth*. The colorful word used is often descriptive of the purple dye, derived from the special *techelet* sea snail, used for the *tzitzit* of the Jewish prayer shawl (Num. 15:37–41). As a *Yirey HaShamayim* (God-fearer), she already had a foundational knowledge of monotheism and the culture of Judaism and evidently was also a dealer in religious Judaica.

As we've seen before, it is often the God-fearing Gentile who gladly responds to the message of Yeshua. Such was the case here; *Lydia opened her heart* and became the first messianic believer in continental Europe. *She and the members of her household had a messianic mikveh* in Yeshua's name. Likewise, Lydia shows instant positive fruit in her life by inviting the Messianic Jews team to stay in her house. Sometimes today there are people who profess to have a new faith, but the fruit may be lacking. God is the ultimate judge, but if we are grafted into the vine of Yeshua, we cannot help but bear good fruit in our life (John 15:1–2).

B. The Spiritual Battle – 16:16–24

Luke records another dramatic encounter. Going down one day to the riverside minyan, they *were met by a slave girl who had in her a snake-spirit*. The literal term is "python spirit," which recalls the serpent slain by the Greek god Apollo. We are not told if she was Jewish or a Gentile God-fearer, but either way, she was dabbling in the forbidden occult world. She earned much money telling fortunes. She screamed, *"These men are servants of God HaElyon!"* It is a reminder of the spiritual battle in the first-century Roman Empire, whose confusing syncretism tried to mix various gods and religions. *Sha'ul, greatly disturbed, turned and said to the spirit, "In the name of Yeshua the Messiah, I order you to come out of her!" And the spirit did come out, at that very moment.*

Though this was a great spiritual victory, the girl's owners were angry, as her soothsaying business was over. *They seized Sha'ul and Sila and dragged them to the market square to face the authorities.* Their accusation includes some of the anti-Semitism of the day: *"These men are causing a lot of trouble in our city, since they are Jews."* Even these pagans recognize the Messianic Jewish emissaries as "Jews," not teachers of some new religion. The businessmen also say the emissaries are *"advocating customs that are against the law for us to accept or practice, since we are Romans,"* implying this new expression might be an unsanctioned religion that was a concern of the civil government (Tacitus, *Histories* 5.5).

It is ironic that the messianic message often gets pushback from the Jewish community as somehow breaking Torah and from the larger world as *too* Jewish! What began as a Roman judicial hearing got ugly; *the mob joined in the attack, and the judges tore [the emissaries'] clothes off* so they could be flogged. Roman law did not afford the protections found under Jewish law, where such treatment would be totally unjustifiable. One such protection is the proverbial "39 lashes" that could be administered to a guilty criminal. The sages came up with this number as a symbol of mercy, as the maximum sentence could include 40 lashes (Deut. 25:3). As the Romans had no such restriction, they administered a *severe beating* and threw the troublemaking Jews into *the inner cell* of the prison *and clamped their feet securely between heavy blocks of wood.*

C. The Remarkable Deliverance – 16:25–40

Amid this severe test, the emissaries' true character was revealed. This is often the case with God's children, even us today! It wouldn't have surprised anyone if Sha'ul and Sila cursed their situation. At the very least, one would expect them to have some doubt about God's plan. But around midnight, the two *were praying and singing hymns to God.* It would've been interesting to eavesdrop on the exact content of the prayers. We assume, from a Jewish group, that they relied on some of the memorized prayers of the Siddur. There are so many beautiful traditional prayers exalting God through the Amidah (18 Blessings) or the Shema (Deut. 6:4–9). Even embedded within the Amidah is a silent time to lift up our personal needs and requests. All the great men and women of faith in Jewish history also had a very personal relationship with God where they could bring prayers from the heart. No wonder one of the names for Jewish prayer is *Avodah She-balev*, "service of the heart."

Add to the emissaries' prayers the fact that they were singing hymns. Believers have penned many wonderful hymns, but *Amazing Grace* hadn't been written yet! There is also a long history of hymns composed in the Jewish community. In fact, the word *humnos* ("hymn") can be applied to Psalms, the greatest book of Jewish hymns. As the apostles were in a praise mode, perhaps they were chanting the *Hallel* (Praise Psalms; 113–118), sung at many Jewish holy days. Given their dire situation, maybe they were chanting this section:

> *My enemies pushed me hard to make me fall, but ADONAI helped me. God is my strength and my song, and he has become my salvation* [Hebrew root *"Yeshua"*]. (Ps. 118:13–14)

Whatever prayers and hymns were being expressed by Sha'ul and Sila, it got the other prisoners' attention. Many likely wondered how these incarcerated, beaten Jews could have any hope at all. Such is the case still today as unbelievers see the positive attitude of Yeshua's children amid strong trials. The faith walk with Messiah does not keep us from difficult situations. In fact, often those very situations become opportunities to let the hope of Messiah shine through! In this case, *a violent earthquake shook the prison to its foundations. All the doors flew open and everyone's chains came loose.* This incredible intervention was bad news for the jailer. As a Roman officer, he had strong accountability for his prisoners—so much so that the usual policy was if any prisoner escaped, the guard would pay their penalty himself even to the point of death (Justinian, *Code* 9.4). Understandably, when the officer awoke and *saw the doors open, he drew his sword and was about to kill himself.* But *Sha'ul shouted* from the cell, *"Don't harm yourself! We're all here!"*

The jailer began to tremble at the realization of what was taking place and asked urgently, *"What must I do to be saved?"* He may have meant physically, given the danger. But he likely asked it in a spiritual context as well, having witnessed some of the spiritual dynamics in his Jewish prisoners. The emissaries' straightforward response: *"Trust in the Lord Yeshua, and you will be saved—you and your household!"* The wordplay was obvious: You will be *saved* by the one called *Yeshua* ("salvation")—and perhaps more so had they just been singing the Hallel Psalm 118. The phrase also offers a contrast for this Roman employee: Caesar is no longer "lord"; Yeshua is his new boss! At this point, the statement became fulfilled prophecy as the emissaries *told him and everyone in his household the message about the Lord.* As proof of his new faith, the jailer *washed their wounds, and all submitted to the mikveh* in the name of Yeshua. Then he brought his new messianic friends *to his house and set food in front of them, and he and his entire household celebrated their having come to trust in God.*

The earthquake at the jail certainly got the attention of the authorities of Philippi. *The next morning, the judges sent police officers with the order, "Release those men."* The jailer told them they were free to go, but Sha'ul halted. He saw an opportunity to publicly correct a great injustice. He told the officers he and Sila were publicly flogged without being *convicted of any crime,* then pointed out the biggest thing: We *are Roman citizens*—i.e., with protected rights. *"Now they want to get rid of us secretly? Oh, no! Let them come and escort us out themselves!"* The emissaries insisted on an apology and official escort out of Philippi. The judges *became frightened when they heard that Sha'ul and Sila were Roman citizens.* Such mistreatment would have larger implications. So they apologized and escorted them out, and asked them to *leave the city.* Freed, they *went to Lydia's house, and after seeing and encouraging the brothers* they departed.

There are several lessons here. First, we can appreciate the need of people around us, and God's provision. As Sha'ul and Sila were set amid the people of the jail, we too are often strategically placed by God. We may not even realize it. It is often the people right around us in those situations who God is trying to reach with a message of encouragement and hope. Sometimes it's not our words but actions that speak loudly to others. Many were touched by the messianic praise service in that Philippian jail. People may also be touched by our attitudes in dire situations. How many around us might be wondering, "What must I do to be saved?"

Second, we are reminded that God is always about justice. Some people may misread Yeshua's teaching to "turn the other cheek" as meaning to always submit to any situation. Here is a classic example of ensuring justice and fairness when it's been ignored. God is love, and God is just. A key mitzvot of the Torah emphasizes, *"Tzedek, tzedek tirdof"* ("Justice, especially justice, you shall pursue"; Deut. 16:20). May we be attentive to maintaining a proper balance of love and justice as two important values of our faith in Messiah.

> *He who studies the Torah for its own sake merits many things ... he loves God, he loves mankind, he is a joy to God and a joy to man.* (Pirke Avot 6.1)

D. Messianic Dialogue in Thessalonica and Berea – 17:1–15

The Second Missionary Journey continues as the team travels deeper into Greece and the European continent. *Passing through Amphipolis and Apollonia, Sha'ul and Sila came to Thessalonica,* the capital of Macedonia, and stopped (where else?) at a *synagogue* (Rom. 1:16), *according to his usual practice. On three Shabbats* Sha'ul gave *drashes (teachings) from the Tanakh.* The word used is from the root *dialegomai* ("dialogue"), implying a logical discussion with questions and answers. Here the dialogue centered on the

127

Messianic Jews' message in a larger, philosophical sense and in a specific focal-point. The former point involved the concept *that the Messiah had to suffer and rise again from the dead*. This alludes to the prevalent rabbinic discussions around Mashiach ben Yosef (the suffering Messiah as in Isaiah 53) versus Mashiach ben David (the King Messiah as in Isaiah 11). These two missions of the Mashiach seem so contrasting that some speculate there may be two separate Messiahs to come (see Acts 1 comments).

The key, said the emissaries, is that *Yeshua is that Messiah*. He clearly suffered, with his death on the cross, yet he can also fulfill the prophecies of King Messiah through his resurrection. Instead of two messiahs to fulfill two missions, Yeshua is the one Messiah who will fulfill both. This was a respectful dialogue. No doubt many opinions and ideas were shared, but Sha'ul used the Tanakh as the arbiter of truth. These were certainly new thoughts discussed with the synagogue attendees, and *some were persuaded, including a great many Greek God-fearers as well as leading women*. This example of engaging dialogue is needed more today. We should all remember to listen to others and dialog in that spirit of mutual respect and kindness as we discuss these matters of the Messiah.

Again the Sh'likhim simultaneously find both opposition and success (see I Thes.). Along with the new Jewish followers of Yeshua, some *unbelieving Jews grew jealous* [or *zealous*] *and gathered a riffraff crowd to start a riot in the city*. They *attacked Jason's house*, the home of the new believers housing *Sha'ul and Sila*. When the mob did not find the apostles, they took *Jason and some other messianic brothers before the city authorities*. Their charge? *"These men have turned the whole world upside down, and they are defying the decrees of the Emperor by asserting that there is another king, Yeshua!"* These accusations threw the *crowd into a turmoil*, and they only calmed down after *Jason and the others had posted bond*. Still, the new messianic believers in Thessalonica saw it was expedient to *send Sha'ul and Sila off to the next town, Berea*.

Unsurprisingly, *as soon as they arrived*, they first stopped at the local *synagogue*. We are reminded again that even the rejection by some of the Jewish community did not curb their enthusiasm to keep taking the Good News of Messiah to the Jewish people. Nowhere do we see a hint of "replacement theology" or supersessionism, which says the Jews had their chance and have been replaced by the "Church." The rejection of Yeshua by some (even the majority) does not negate God's promises; it actually fulfills his long-term plan (Rom. 9–11)! That's how the first-century missionaries understood it, so they find themselves once again in the local shul.

Luke observes that the people of Berea *were of nobler character than the ones in Thessalonica; they eagerly welcomed the message* of Yeshua. This was no mere blind faith expressed by the Berean Jews. They *checked the Tanakh every day to see if these things were true*. Consequently, *many of them (along with prominent Greek women and men) came to trust.* Wouldn't it be wonderful if every person today also took their spiritual life so seriously that they would study the Hebrew Scriptures to see what God actually says?

On learning that that the Berean community had welcomed the message of Yeshua that Sha'ul preached, *the unbelieving Jews* did not consult the Tanakh with an open mind but went to *make trouble and agitate the crowds*. Again the team was forced to flee a perilous situation, with *Sha'ul going all the way to Athens* near the coast. He was likely singled out because he was clearly the ringleader. Sila and Timothy stayed behind for further underground ministry but then were told to *join Sha'ul in Athens as quickly as they could*. In sum, we see two different groups with two different responses to the Good News. We never know what response we might get as we share Messiah. That's likely why Yeshua said to go to all people and let them decide for themselves (Mt. 28:19–20).

E. Engaging the Pagan Philosophies of the World – 17:16–34

Having gone to the first two Jewish communities, Sha'ul and company are about to experience a totally different culture and

129

people-group. This occurred as he was *waiting for the team in Athens*. This metropolis was the highly regarded cultural capital of the Greek Empire, famed for its literary, artistic and philosophical innovations. But there was also a big challenge for any religious Jew. Sha'ul's *spirit was disturbed at the sight of the city full of idols*. There was a stark contrast between Judaism's monotheism and polytheistic Greek thought. Still, Sha'ul started in his usual fashion of *holding discussions in the synagogue with the Jews and the "God-fearers."*

The Athenian audience soon grew to include people *who happened to be in the market square* Sha'ul visited. *A group of Epicurean and Stoic philosophers* wanted to engage Sha'ul in an intellectual dialogue. These two schools of thought are classic representatives of the Greek first-century values. The Epicureans, founded by Epicurus ~307 B.C.E., held that life's greatest goal is to seek pleasure, avoid pain and "eat, drink and be merry!" The Stoics were founded by Zeno around the same time and took their name from the famous Stoa Porch in Athens. Their philosophy was the polar opposite of the Epicureans. Instead of seeking pleasure, Stoicism, emphasizing morality and self-discipline, said virtuous living was necessary for happiness.

As Sha'ul debated with these two diverse groups, they asked, *"What is this babbler trying to say?"* Others, because he proclaimed the Good News about Yeshua and the resurrection, said, *"He sounds like a propagandist for foreign gods."* The philosophers weren't impressed; the message wasn't flashy enough for their consideration. With this growing controversy, the Greeks *brought him before the High Council*. The Greek term for this group is *Areopagus* ("Hill of Ares"); it was the hill of judgment where a 12-member court would consider any new idea or philosophy. Ares' Roman counterpart is Mars; hence, this section of Acts is called the Mars Hill sermon. Though this educated pagan crowd presented a unique challenge, Sha'ul carefully considered their questions. They expressed interest in *what this new teaching is about*. *"Some of the things we are hearing from you are strange, and we would like to know what they mean."* The Athenians *used to spend their spare time talking or hearing about the latest intellectual fads*.

At this point *Sha'ul stood up in the Council meeting* and began to address the crowd. He began by establishing a common point between his message and the intellectuals. He commends them, *"I see how very religious you are in every way!"* Of course, their religious expression was reprehensible to any traditional Jew, but Sha'ul saw that many of the Greeks sincerely sought truth. He acknowledges looking at their shrines and noticing an altar inscribed *"To An Unknown God."* He makes a natural connection and declares, *"The one whom you are already worshiping in ignorance— this is the one I proclaim to you."* He builds on his message by proclaiming *the God who made the universe and everything in it.*

This was a necessary starting point for this idolatrous culture. With his Jewish brothers, there was no need to proclaim the creator God; that's how the Torah begins in Genesis! But with this group, the rabbi needed to establish that there is only one God. Here is a good example of Sha'ul living out his outreach philosophy of being "as a Jew to the Jews and as a Greek to the Greeks" (I Cor. 9:19–22). This God revealed to Israel *does not live in man-made temples nor does he lack anything*, unlike the Greek gods, who were constantly needy. In reality, it is this God of Israel who *gives life and breath and everything to everyone.*

From here, Sha'ul expands his discourse to describe how the true God made every nation on earth and let them flourish. He tells the crowd God did this so *people would look for him and perhaps reach out and find him although in fact, he is not far from each one of us.* Ultimately, it is in him we live and move and exist. Sensing the Greek intellectuals are skeptical of this new "Jewish religion," Sha'ul cleverly invokes some of the poets among them who spoke of mankind being *"children of God."* He could easily be referring to the poet Epimenides or even Aratus of Cilicia (his hometown!).

He says if humanity is in the image of this God, we shouldn't suppose that his essence *resembles gold, silver or stone shaped by human technique and imagination.* The Greek religions' pervasive idolatry was never right, but now a new day was dawning for the peoples of the world. Sha'ul says this God overlooked such human ignorance in the past but now *is commanding all people everywhere to turn to him from their sins*. With new awareness comes new responsibility. As our people have turned to God in the spirit of teshuvah, so too the pagan world is to turn from what is false and embrace the revelation of truth. The emissary alerts the crowd that a day is coming when God will judge the world justly. All this is *by means of a man whom he has designated* and, to confirm this fact, *given public proof by resurrecting this man from the dead*.

At this mention of the resurrection, some in the crowd *began to scoff*. Greek culture and mythology largely ignored this idea and adhered to other theories like immortality of the soul but destruction of the body. While most of the crowd evidently feel comfortable in their long-held beliefs, others want to hear more on this "Jewish" perspective. *Sha'ul left the meeting. But some men stayed with him and came to trust* in this message of Messiah. There were many new believers, including some high-profile members of the community. Among these was Dionysius, a member of the same High Council that was hearing Sha'ul's case. Also mentioned is a *woman named Damaris*. Though this new messianic community was encouraging, Athens proved an exceptional challenge overall.

There was a large crowd of skeptics with whom it was very difficult even to have a constructive dialogue. Significantly, there is no mention of a new congregation established, nor are there any future epistles to Athens. Yet even in this challenging environment, the emissaries focus not so much on their Greek debate skills but on the proclamation of the power of the Good News of Yeshua. Sha'ul summarizes: *"We go on proclaiming a Messiah executed on a stake as a criminal! To Jews this is an obstacle, and to Greeks it is nonsense; but to those who are called, both Jews and Greeks, this same Messiah is God's power and God's wisdom! For God's 'nonsense' is wiser than humanity's 'wisdom'"* (I Cor. 1:23–25).

In our complex, diverse society, there will be a variety of responses to the message of the B'rit Chadashah. Sha'ul's actions in

Athens reminds us that we too must not shy away from engaging modern society. Many believers bemoan the current darkness, but how much better it is to light a candle! May we too uphold the simplicity and the power of the Messiah who has conquered death and displayed the wisdom of God.

> The Holy One, blessed be He, will sit and expound the new Torah which He will give through the Messiah. "New Torah" means the secrets and the mysteries of the Torah which have remained hidden until now." (Midrash Talpiyot 58a)

F. Two Synagogue Presidents Stand with Yeshua – 18:1–22

After the diverse responses at Athens and Mars Hill, Sha'ul and the team sense it is time to move on in this missionary journey. The next natural stop was Corinth, another important cultural center of Greece. This vital port city, a crossroads between the east and west Mediterranean Sea, was more populous than Athens. While Athens was Greece's intellectual capital, Corinth was a party city known for its immorality. A temple to Aphrodite on its highest hill attested to its sexual idolatry. Here the emissaries encounter fellow Jews Aquila and Priscilla. This married couple lived in Italy under the oppressive governor Claudius. It was he who *expelled all Jews from Rome* in 49 C.E., evidently because of some turmoil from the Jewish community.

The Roman historian Suetonius references this event: "As the Jews were indulging in constant riots at the instigation of Chrestus, he banished them from Rome" (*Life of Claudius* xxv.4). *Chrestus* could have been any troublemaker in the Jewish community, but many have noted the similarities of this spelling to *Christos*, the Greek title for Messiah (Bruce 368). Given many of the events recorded in Acts, it is understandable that the turmoil in the Jewish community revolved around the controversial claims of early Messianic Judaism and its founder Yeshua. As usual, the Romans didn't distinguish between Judaism and this sect of Yeshua followers. Consequently, all Jews were expelled (or at least severely oppressed) from Rome, including

Aquila and Priscilla. Sha'ul desired to connect with them not just because of their common faith but also because of their common occupation. They are *"tent-makers"* (or leatherworkers in general), so unsurprisingly, *Sha'ul stayed with them as they worked together.* This is a reminder that most first-century rabbis and Torah teachers usually held an outside occupation to support themselves. They were not to derive profit from their study. The logic is reflected here: "Rabban Gamliel says: Splendid is the study of Torah when combined with a worldly occupation, for toil in them both puts sin out of mind" (Pirke Avot 2:2; I Thes. 2:9).

As Sha'ul settled into his new Corinthian community, he quickly *began carrying on discussions every Shabbat in the synagogue* (Rom. 1:16). *Dialegomai*, the word used, describes a respectful dialogue to discuss the issues of Yeshua and Messiah. With the arrival of *Sila and Timothy* in town, *Sha'ul felt an increased urgency* to share the message of Messiah. As the understanding of Yeshua increased, so did the opposition from many. As some set themselves against Sha'ul and the team, they responded with a symbolic gesture.

By *shaking off his clothes*, it was reminiscent of the traditional Jewish response as one encounters an unkosher environment. Usually this would be associated with contact in the Gentile pagan world, so it is quite ironic that here it is the unkosher response from many in the Jewish community that is the source of the action. Sha'ul makes this clear as he warns that their *blood will be on their own heads* for their personal choice to reject Yeshua. It is Sha'ul and his team who are *clean* and, because of this community rejection, they will *go to the Gentiles* of Corinth.

Too often, modern readers of such passages mistakenly conflate the local rejection by some first-century people to mean all Jews are against Yeshua today. Some also believe, based on this, that it is unfruitful and unnecessary to take the message of the Good News to the contemporary Jewish community. The modern Messianic Jewish movement is concrete proof that, despite the rejection of some, God is still doing amazing work as many of our Jewish people are coming to faith today. There are over 200 Messianic synagogues across the U.S., Russia, Ukraine, Latin America, and Israel, which testifies that God is still on his plan of world redemption centered in the Jewish covenants (Rom. 11:16–26). It is a blessing for all the Gentiles to understand this redemptive message as well. But the inclusion of the Gentiles does not mean the exclusion of the Jews. All believers in Yeshua are now sharers in the divine blessings through Messiah!

As has happened so often in the messianic outreaches, this closed door led to an amazing open window. Having left the spiritual blockade at the local synagogue, the team *went into the home of a God-fearer named Titius Justus*. This category of religious people included non-Jews who were drawn to Judaism's values and beliefs and attended synagogue to learn more. It is often the God-fearers who had a curiosity and openness for the messianic message as they were natural seekers (10:1–2). Interestingly, *Titius lived right next door to the synagogue.*

Despite the majority rejection at the synagogue, again some high-profile community members welcomed the message of Messiah. It seems Titius hosted a messianic Havurah for all those interested in knowing more about Messianic Judaism's philosophy. *Crispus, the president of the synagogue, came to trust in the Lord, along with his whole household; also many of the Corinthians who heard trusted and were immersed.* This is one of the earliest examples of the establishment of a messianic group outside the local synagogue.

A lot of us Messianic Jews would be content to stay in our local traditional synagogue if we could be entirely open about our faith in Yeshua as Messiah. But like this case in Corinth, Yeshua followers are not fully welcomed. The natural response is to start a synagogue (with all the beautiful history and culture) that embraces Yeshua as the promised Messiah. This explains the growth we are witnessing of the messianic synagogue movement.

This Corinthian situation likewise reminds us there are seekers and believers from all strata of Jewish society even today. Some come to Yeshua with a secular or weak Jewish education.

Sometimes that is held against them, as if they would not believe in Yeshua if they only had a better Jewish education. Yet there are also Jews from traditional and highly educated backgrounds, even a few former synagogue presidents! God is calling everyone today to seek God irrespective of the person's background. The more relevant question is, what are we doing now with our spiritual life?

This positive response in Corinth was no doubt very encouraging to the outreach team, but there are still dark clouds on the horizon. *In a vision, the Lord said to Sha'ul, "Don't be afraid, but speak right up, and don't stop, because I am with you. No one will succeed in harming you, for I have many people in this city."* Because of this encouraging word, Sha'ul and the team stand strong and end up staying in Corinth for *a year and a half, teaching them the word of God.* It's never been easy to be a disciple of Yeshua, much less a leader in the Messianic Jewish ministry. Trials and even opposition will come, but may we take the encouragement of this vision to strengthen our own walk!

The dark clouds increased. *The unbelieving Jews made a concerted attack on Sha'ul and took him to Roman court.* The charge was a familiar one, periodically put forth in Jewish circles: *"This man is trying to persuade people to worship God in ways that violate the Torah."* The Roman governor Gallio, who heard this case, made his opinion clear from the start: If this were a legal dispute or a serious crime, *he would hear them out patiently.* But it was *questions about words and names and their own Jewish law, they are the ones who must deal with it.* With that, he had the Jews *ejected from the court.* What transpires next is quite disconcerting: *They all grabbed Sosthenes, the president of the synagogue, and gave him a beating in full view of the bench; but Gallio showed no concern whatever.*

This raises some puzzling questions. Is it the Roman group who responds in an anti-Semitic attitude and attacks Sosthenes? Given Gallio's apathy, it seems more likely it was a group of Jewish leaders who administer a punishment within the Jewish context. This is especially true in light of the mention of Sosthenes becoming a leader of the Messianic Jewish community of Corinth (I Cor. 1:1).

Quite possibly he became the synagogue president after the beating and departure of Crispus. If that is so, we have a record here of not one but two synagogue presidents from Corinth who join the messianic community even under much duress!

From this tense encounter in Corinth, *Sha'ul said good-bye to the brothers and sailed off to Syria.* But first a rather unusual event took place in Cenchrea, the port of departure: Sha'ul had *his hair cut short because he had taken a vow.* Likely this is the famous vow in the Torah known as the *Nazir* (one who abstains; Num. 6). Among its curious details is abstinence from alcohol, grapes and hair cutting. This was most often a temporary vow of dedication for a person to focus on his higher calling from God. Most Nazarites (not to be confused with Nazarenes) ended their vow by cutting their hair and bringing the appropriate sacrifice to the Temple in Yerushalayim (Tractate Nazir 3.6; 5.4).

In a few notable cases the vow was a lifetime commitment, as with Samson and Yochanan the Immerser (Judg. 13:1–5; Lk. 1:15). Many times it was taken as an expression of thanksgiving to God for a special deliverance, which would be appropriate in Sha'ul's case. On leaving Corinth, he decides it is time to end his vow and fulfill the requisite details as he works his way *up to Yerushalayim.* On the trip home, the team stops in Ephesus. As usual *he went into the synagogue to dialogue* with his Jewish brothers. There was a spirit of receptivity among many in the Jewish community to the point that *they asked Sha'ul to stay with them longer.* But he was on a set religious schedule regarding his Nazir vow and had to get to the Holy City. So he *set sail from Ephesus* and promised to *do his best to come back to them.* With the team's return to Israel, the Second Missionary Journey through the Roman Empire was culminated, having successfully shared the Good News of Messiah's arrival with both Jews and non-Jews.

Some struggle with the idea that Sha'ul would enter a Torah vow or worry about a Temple sacrifice. This whole situation reaffirms that the early Messianic Jews continued to live within a strong expression of Judaism even as they embraced the Yeshua faith. This is not to say they followed every minute detail. But they saw no inconsistency with following the principles of the Tanakh as passed down to our forefathers. Yeshua himself said he was not advocating a new religion but fulfilling the ancient promises. Some of his followers often insisted on changes that blurred the Jewish connection of this New Covenant faith. If he is the promised Messiah for the Jewish people (and all people), then why the big surprise that his Jewish disciples continued to live a Jewish lifestyle? This situation in Acts illustrates why we modern Messianic Jews embrace Yeshua within the context of our beautiful Jewish heritage.

Let your house be a meeting place for the rabbis, and cover yourself in the dust of their feet, and drink in their words thirstily. (Pirke Avot 1.4)

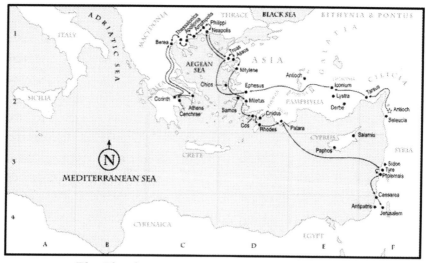

The Third Missionary Journey – 18:22–21:16

XXII. The Third Missionary Journey – 18:22–21:16

A. Equipping Workers for Yeshua – 18:22–28

With the culmination of the Second Missionary Journey, Sha'ul *arrived in Yerushalayim and greeted the messianic community.* This aliyah was for several reasons. First, it was important for the outreach team to report on their activities to the sending. Secondly, for Sha'ul to fulfill his Nazir vow, he had to bring a final sacrifice to the Temple. After fulfilling these duties, Sha'ul and the emissaries *came down to Antioch* and *spent some time there*. Antioch, though a vital city in the Gentile world, was the center of the early mission outreach to the Gentile communities of the Roman Empire (13:1–3). It is once again from Antioch of Syria that another messianic mission will commence. In the Third Missionary Journey, the outreach team sets off *through the region of Galatia and Phrygia to strengthen the talmidim* where they had previously ministered.

The important city of Ephesus was directly on this journey. Here the team met an educated Jew named *Apollos*, a messianic brother from Alexandria, an epicenter of education and scholarship both Jewish and secular. The thriving city was home to top-tier universities and such scholars as the philosopher Philo. So, it is not surprising that Apollos is described as an *eloquent speaker with a thorough knowledge of the Tanakh*. He also possesses *great spiritual fervor as he taught accurately the facts about Yeshua*. There was, though, a bit of a problem: Apollos *knew only the immersion of Yochanan*. He, and many other Jews of the diaspora, had heard of Yochanan the Immerser and his exhortations to prepare for the Messiah (Mt. 3:1–6). This exposure could have easily happened as dispersed Jews made pilgrimage to Israel to celebrate the Shalosh Regalim. It seems Apollos had made such a trip and heard the preparatory message of Yochanan. But there was a gap in knowledge as he evidently returned home to Ephesus before witnessing the coming of Yeshua. He was a strong teacher, but the truth he had was incomplete.

As Apollos spoke in the synagogue, Priscilla and Aquila realized this gap. They *explained to him the Way of God in fuller detail*. Of course, Yochanan's message was one of both repentance and preparing for Messiah's imminent arrival. Even with this, there would be a need to fill in some of the details like Yeshua's arrival, life, death and resurrection. On top of this would be the New

Covenant ministry of the Ruach in regeneration, immersing and empowering the believer for Messiah's work. Priscilla and Aquila mentored their fellow believer on these and other topics. No need to berate or embarrass him. So often today there are those who sincerely desire to walk with Yeshua but don't yet have the complete picture. This can be especially true for contemporary Jews who are open to the idea of Yeshua as Messiah but not quite sure what it really looks like. Patience and sensitivity are virtues when sharing the Good News of Yeshua, especially with to the Jewish community. On the other side, a true seeker will be open, as was Apollos, to humbly receive new information from those who are genuinely concerned about them. All this beautifully exemplifies what it means to make disciples and to be a growing disciple of Yeshua.

After Priscilla and Aquila spent time with Apollos, he was sent *to Achaia (Greece) where he greatly helped those who had come to trust* in Yeshua as Messiah. The brothers encouraged Apollos so he could encourage others. It was a powerful combination at work in his life. With his strong Jewish background, he could now *powerfully and conclusively refute unbelievers by the Tanakh that Yeshua is the Messiah.* His knowledge was strong and fortified by a loving spirit transmitted through his own personal life. Not surprisingly, we find other references to his fruitful ministry; Sha'ul says *I planted, Apollos watered, and God gave the increase* (I Cor. 3:5–9). This teamwork reminds us that believers have differing gifts and callings. In the first century, this was not a point of competition or pride but of complementing each other for the glory of God. May we reflect the same truth as we serve Yeshua with our varying abilities.

B. Outreach in Ephesus – 19:1–41

1. Questions About the Ruach – 19:1–7

Having established a solid messianic community in Corinth, Sha'ul felt it was time to continue his outreach and go to Ephesus. This is the emissaries' third journey through this strategic city of the ancient world. There will be some unusual spiritual encounters. On arrival, the team *found a few talmidim*. At first we assume these are strong followers of Yeshua and the revelation of the Good News of Messiah. But as with Apollos, this was not always so (18:24–28). The Jewish context of talmid is broad and could refer to anyone following any given first-century rabbi. It is common for a student to be so committed to his rabbi that he is covered with the dust from the rabbi's sandals (Pirke Avot 1.4). So, a simple reading of verse 1 should lead us to question whose disciples are these.

Evidently the same question crossed Sha'ul's mind as he asked this group if they *received the Ruach HaKodesh when they came to trust* Yeshua. His suspicions were justified: The group *had never even heard that there is such a thing as the Ruach*. Sha'ul knew rabbinic disciples were immersed in water to become talmidim, so he asked a logical follow-up: *"Into what were you immersed?"* When they responded *"the immersion of Yochanan,"* it became clear their experience was similar to that of Apollos. Sha'ul gave an overview of the recent messianic history that transpired in Israel, explaining that *Yochanan practiced an immersion in connection with the turning from sin to God; but also told the people to put their trust in the one who would come after him; that is, Yeshua*.

This was new information to this group living in the diaspora city of Ephesus; evidently they had been exposed to the message of Yochanan but had not witnessed the coming of Yeshua's ministry or the pouring out of the Ruach at Shavuot (Acts 2). Like Apollos, these disciples were open to this additional information and were gladly *immersed into the name of the Lord Yeshua*. They eagerly let Sha'ul *place his hands on them* so they could *receive the Ruach* for the first time, and they began *speaking in tongues and prophesying*.

This odd situation raises some questions. Some believe the doctrine of a "second" experience with the Ruach. After all, we seem to have real disciples here who have a delayed encounter. But a close study of this passage reminds us there can be many kinds of disciples following many different rabbis. What we have here is not a group of Yeshua

141

disciples missing a second blessing of the Ruach but a group of Yochanan's disciples who were unaware of the promise of the Ruach in the New Covenant. This was a first experience with the Ruach through Yeshua's redemptive work. This is consistent with Sha'ul's later teaching where he emphatically says one cannot be a true disciple of Yeshua as Messiah if they do not have the Ruach (Rom. 8:9). Likewise, one cannot be in a true talmid of Yeshua unless he or she is immersed by the Ruach into the one Body of Messiah (I Cor. 12:13).

But what of those who say one must have a deeper, second blessing of the Ruach? No doubt many experience a blessing of the Ruach in their life. I have. This wasn't a second "immersion" of the Ruach but a different "filling." This extra experience is also borne out in Sha'ul's teaching where he exhorts the believers (from Ephesus!) to *be filled with the Ruach* (Eph. 5:18). Two different words are used for these two different ministries of the Ruach: immersion (*baptidzo*), contrasted with filling (*pleirao*). The immersion of the Ruach (I Cor. 12:13) is in a completed, aorist tense, while the filling (Eph. 5:18) is a present-tense, ongoing action. These verses indicate all believers in Yeshua, at the point of their salvation, are spiritually immersed in the Ruach and join the messianic Body of Messiah. Every believer has 100% of the Ruach or else they are not a real disciple.

But there is another experience with the Spirit where believers are filled or empowered for their walk with God. The immersion of the Ruach is a one-time experience, whereas the filling of the Ruach is a daily (hourly!) challenge to let the Spirit control our lives. Some people use these terms interchangeably, but they're distinct for a reason. We don't need a "second" experience with the Ruach but a third, fifth, even thirtieth experience. When all is said and done, we do not need more of the Ruach, but the Ruach often needs more of us!

After this unusual encounter with the Ephesian disciples, *Sha'ul went into the synagogue; and for three months he spoke out boldly.* Luke carefully describes the interaction as a *dialogue* (*dialegomai*) as the emissary tries to *persuade people about the Kingdom of God.* As was often true, there were both positive and negative reactions to the message of Yeshua. Some were *hardening themselves* to the point of *defaming the Way before the whole synagogue*. They themselves brought on this attitude, paralleling Pharaoh's actions in Egypt (Ex. 9:35). In this Jewish context, even those in opposition did not call this movement "Christianity" (see notes on Acts 11:26). Despite the disagreements about Yeshua, the emissaries were still considered Jews who were talking about a *Way* (*derekh*, "path") as a sect within Judaism. This pushback caused Sha'ul and the other Messianics to move to a new location, *Tyrannus's yeshiva* (also a Jewish school)! For *two years the groups met* here to continue constructive dialogue with those who were open to the idea of Yeshua.

Inevitably, with the ongoing teaching ministry, there would be other spiritual dynamics manifested. As seen often in Acts, the proclamation of the Word was followed by *extraordinary miracles through Sha'ul*. This was common, especially in the first century, to substantiate this new message of Messiah (Heb. 2:1–4). Acts 19:12 says, *For instance, handkerchiefs and aprons that had touched him were brought to sick people; they would recover from their ailments, and the evil spirits would leave them.* All this is reminiscent of the woman who reached out to touch Yeshua's tallit and was healed (Mt. 9:20–22). It shows there are times when God uses various situations and objects as symbols of the healing that comes from him alone.

Now *some Jewish exorcists* tried to copy these manifestations. While there is a legitimate way of Jewish prayer and power, there are also fake substitutes. The Talmud reflects a little of both sides of this dichotomy. Dark magic was seen as thoroughly pagan: "Ten measures of sorcery descended to the world; Egypt took nine and the rest of the world one" (Tractate Kiddushin 49b). But the rabbis always believed in the existence of evil spirits, and the Talmud is replete with various incantations and formulas for deliverance. Sadly, some Jews trust in mysticism, numerology or Kabbalah, despite the warnings to rely solely on our relationship with God (Deut. 18). Egregious cases still exist today.

This situation shows a syncretism of religious beliefs originating from this diverse city of Ephesus. The mystics were especially impressed with *the power in the name of Yeshua that Sha'ul was proclaiming*. Luke highlights *seven sons of a Jewish high priest named Skeva* who tried to invoke *"the Yeshua that Saul is proclaiming."* But the evil spirit answered, *"Yeshua I know. And Sha'ul I recognize. But you? Who are you?"* At that instant, *the man with the evil spirit fell upon them, overpowered them, and gave them such a beating that they ran from the house, naked and bleeding.* This is a strong reminder that the spiritual world, both good and evil, is not to be underestimated. The light of God is especially not to be confused with the darkness of the pagan world or even our own human ideas.

When the residents of Ephesus heard of all this, *fear fell on all of them*, both Jews and Greeks, *and the name of the Lord Yeshua came to be held in high regard.* Many who had engaged in occult practices *threw their scrolls in a pile and burned them in public.* This response was evidence of repenting from evil and turning to the light of Messiah. Little wonder that the message of the Lord continued to powerfully grow through this region.

Luke notes Sha'ul's intention to go again to Yerushalayim, for several reasons. First, it is a religious requirement for any traditional male to attend the three major holy day celebrations (Pesach, Shavuot, Sukkot) in the Holy City (Deut. 16:16–17; Acts 20:16). Second, we know Sha'ul has been diligently collecting from the Gentile congregations a love offering to bless the Jewish brothers in Yerushalayim (Rom. 15:25–27). This was a beautiful, practical way for Gentile believers in the Roman Empire to show solidarity and gratitude now they were grafted into the olive tree of Israel (Rom. 11:17–18). It is heartening to see such expressions of appreciation today from some segments of the Gentile Church toward the Jewish community, especially Messianic Jews. The text also mentions Sha'ul's goal of visiting Rome, as he was Shaliach to the Gentiles. He can't overlook the capital of the Roman Empire as he thinks of his goals to reach the larger world with the Good News of Yeshua.

Rather unsurprisingly, *a major furor arose concerning the Way*. Though there was considerable pushback from some of the city's Jewish community, this turmoil emanated from the pagan Gentile population. Luke again uses "the Way" as a title for the early Yeshua movement; that is, not a new religion called "Christianity" but a different path or sect in first-century Judaism. Of course, the pagans of Ephesus didn't care about that; they objected for other reasons. *A silversmith named Demetrius* states he opposes the Messianic Jews because of the adverse financial impact on business. This man employed *many craftsmen* whose work centered on the idolatrous objects used in the *worship of the goddess Artemis*. So Demetrius, the "union leader," *called a meeting*.

He summarized the problem: *"This Sha'ul has convinced and turned away a considerable crowd by saying that man-made gods aren't gods at all."* The worry is that this is not only an attack on the local business economy but could adversely impact the entire *province of Asia*, and Artemis *could be brought down from her divine majesty!* This fear is not overstated, as the Temple of Artemis in Ephesus was one of the Seven Wonders of the Ancient World, and she was a highly revered goddess of sexual fertility (Bock 608). There were also legends about a meteorite-type stone associated with the goddess (Euripides, *Iphigenia at Tauris* 87–88).

At this dire warning, the pagan business crowd *was filled with rage and began bellowing, "Great is Artemis of the Ephesians!"* The mob scene intensifies as they grab two of the emissaries, Gaius and Aristarchus, and bring them into the Roman *theater* for interrogation (Col. 4:10; Phlm. 24). It was a perilous situation, but Sha'ul actually wanted to appear before the crowd. *The talmidim wouldn't let him*, nor would *some local Roman officials* who wanted to quell the situation. The unruly mob soon devolved into *complete confusion*. As Luke humorously notes, *the great majority of people didn't even know why they were there.* Sometimes today people vehemently oppose Yeshua or religion in general but don't know why!

145

At this point, the Jewish team tries to come up with a solution. A believer named *Alexander was pushed to the front of the crowd and motioned for silence, hoping to make a defense to the people.* But when the crowd saw *he was a Jew,* they repeated, *"Great is Artemis of the Ephesians!"* and continued unabated for two hours. Finally the city clerk quieted the crowd and reminded them, *"The city of Ephesus is the guardian of the temple of the great Artemis, and of the sacred stone which feel from the sky."* The officer wisely told the mob to *"calm down and not do anything rash. ... [These Jews] have neither robbed the temple nor insulted the goddess. So if Demetrius and his fellow craftsmen have a complaint against anyone, the courts are open and the judges are there."* Charges may be filed lawfully; otherwise, the higher authorities may accuse the people of an unlawful riot. The official convinces the crowd they have no *reasonable explanation for this disorderly gathering.* With that, the assembly disperses.

People can get very defensive when it comes to religion and their god. Yet a god that needs this kind of emotional defending is not much of a deity to begin with! Usually, such an attitude just shows the lack of security in a person's belief system. There are times to stand up and defend, with a humble spirit, that which we believe (I Kefa 3:15). In reality, the God of Israel and his Messiah need no other defenders. Often the best defense of our faith is the simple confidence we exude that the message of the Bible is true. Ultimately, we are not called to "convert" anyone but to sensitively share the message of the Messiah and leave the rest between God and that person.

> *Much have I learned from my rabbis, even more from my haverim, but from my talmidim, most of all.* (Tractate Taanit 7a)

C. Messianic Fellowship on the First Day of the Week – 20:1–12

If someone starts reading in Acts 20, they're in for a jolt! The first words of v. 1 remind us of the controversy of the early Yeshua movement as Luke picks up the story *after the furor died down.* This refers to the averted riot by the pagan Gentiles of Ephesus and the perceived cultural threat from the emissaries. We shouldn't be surprised that the message of the Jewish Yeshua often brings a furor, whether in the Jewish community, among agnostic non-Jews, or even from the church community. After the turmoil in Ephesus, Sha'ul and some of the team depart for Macedonia. Here and in larger Greece they spend *three months encouraging* the newer believers in Yeshua. Sha'ul had hoped to *set sail for Syria, but he discovered a plot against him, so he ... decided to return by way of Macedonia.*

Luke lists the emissaries who were in this vital stage of this Third Missionary Journey. Most names are Greek, delineating that they're either Hellenistic Jews or non-Jewish Greeks. The first, *Sopater son of Pyrrhus*, seems to be Jewish; his name is structured in a traditional Jewish manner. Also, he is a member of the Berean believing community that originated in the local synagogue (Acts 17:10; Rom. 16:21). Next is *Aristarchus*, also a Messianic Jew (Col. 4:10–11). *Secundus from Thessalonica* likely came from a place of great difficulties but is part of the fruitful ministry team (I Thes. 1:6). *Gaius*, whose name means "gladness," was no doubt a welcome member of the group. And *Timothy* would prove an important assistant to Sha'ul as a young messianic rabbi. *Tychius* appears often as Sha'ul's 'administrative assistant' of sorts, even delivering some of his important epistles to local congregations (Col. 4:7).

The one worker who appears to be a non-Jew is *Trophimus*, who later becomes the focus of Temple authorities who fear he was illegally brought into the Temple Mount (21:29). Luke says these co-laborers *waited for the rest of the team in Troas while **we** sailed from Philippi*. Luke uses the common designation to include himself in the team. Luke says they *departed from Philippi after the Days of Matzah*. Though a side note, it reminds us that the early Jewish believers (and grafted-in non-Jews) quite naturally continued to use the Jewish holy days and calendar as their frame of reference.

The emissaries reunited *in Troas for one week*. Luke records that they held a special meeting *on Motza-ei Shabbat* (the departing of the Sabbath). At this time the disciples were *gathered to break bread* and listen to a teaching from their leader, Sha'ul. Several important details here merit a closer look. Some interpreters assume the "breaking of bread" here is the ceremonial remembrance of the Lord's Supper. More likely, this is simply the common Jewish way of describing a shared meal as a time of fellowship. In fact, a breaking of bread (*botzey lechem*) is customary at Jewish meals as the bread is torn after the blessing, *"Hamotzi lechem min ha'aretz"* (Tractate Berakhot 46.1). Also, Luke uses the word *synago* to describe their gathering—a natural word for this Jewish-oriented time. Once again, we see Luke's Jewish understanding of minute details, which underlines his likely Jewish identity (Acts 1:1).

The exact time of this fellowship dinner is found in the term *Motza-ei Shabbat*. Many English translations render this "the first day of the week," but the original language is specific. The Greek phrase *mia ton sabbaton* means "the first from the Sabbath." Virtually all agree that this is the first day of the week. But many Christian interpreters assume this is a Sunday morning gathering, as they use the Roman calendar as their cultural source.

Jewish interpreters agree that this statement means the first day from Shabbat, but that leads us not to Sunday morning but to the start of the day in Jewish reckoning—Saturday night after sundown. In the Jewish context, this is an important time of starting a new week after the Shabbat ends. This transition time of the new week is celebrated with the beautiful *Havdalah* ("separation") ceremony including a braided candle, a mixed-spice container and cup of wine. With the accompanying prayers, we are to reflect on the light and sweetness of Shabbat with the hope of taking them with us into the next six days. The time of Motza-ei Shabbat is still today a joyous time of gathering with family and friends (especially in modern Israel) as we enjoy the afterglow of the holy day and enter *Yom Rishon* ("first day [of the week]") on Saturday night.

While this Jewish context seems the most natural understanding (as usual!), it does lead to some interesting questions. How is it that common Christian interpretation focuses so strongly on a Sunday morning meeting here instead of a Saturday night? Clearly some of the later non-Jewish Christians weren't always aware or appreciative of the Jewish calendar. It is clear the resurrection of Messiah took place sometime "on the first day of the week" (Mt. 28:1), similar to the language of Acts 20:7. Add to this some of the other references to Yeshua believers meeting on the first day of the week (I Cor. 16:2) or even conflating the phrase to mean "Lord's Day" (Rev. 1:10). All these Scriptures are of course accurate, but it is a mistake to just assume they refer to Sunday morning.

Some interpreters even try to connect the resurrection of Yeshua with Sunday morning; by Jewish reckoning, he could have been risen any time after sundown Saturday night. The Gospels clearly place the resurrection on the first day of the week, but a careful reading confirms it is daybreak on Sunday when the women discover the empty tomb. Yeshua could have been risen any time after sundown on Saturday, but the women wouldn't likely venture out to the burial ground in the middle of the night. Their early-morning discovery best confirms Messiah was already risen sometime shortly after Motza-ei Shabbat or Saturday night. It seems the Father would take the first opportune moment to raise his Son from the dead!

Along with the calendar differences, these varying interpretations took stronger hold in later centuries, when many encouraged non-Jewish Christians to meet on Sunday as a statement of their belief in Yeshua's resurrection. The earliest post-biblical mention is from the *Didache* (Teaching), a late first- or second-century document whose opening line reads, "The teaching of the Lord to the Gentiles by the twelve apostles." Sunday is specifically mentioned as the preferred day of worship for these believers outside of the Jewish community (*Didache* 14).

Eventually Emperor Constantine (Council of Nicea in 325 C.E.) enforced Sunday observance for the Western church (even for Jewish believers), in a largely political move to unify the Roman Empire and even create a separation between the Church of Yeshua and the Jewish people. How tragic that the Jewish roots were severed in those later eras when the New Testament encourages Gentile believers to always appreciate the fact that they are grafted into the Jewish blessings through Messiah!

All this certainly raises questions and even leads some to take the opposite extreme of being anti-Sunday. Most Messianic Jews do not take that perspective. Shabbat and much of the Jewish culture is a wonderful blessing and heritage for those of us who are born Jewish. This does not change when we enlarge our faith to include Yeshua as the promised Messiah. But the seventh-day Shabbat was always meant to be a distinctive covenant sign between God and the Jewish people, Messianic Jews included (Ex. 31:16–17; Rom. 11:26–29).

Of course, the Shabbat observance is freely open to anyone who desires it, just as some non-Jews have always joined the Jewish people (cf. Ruth). The New Covenant does not do away with Shabbat but expands the flexibility to worship God on other days. Ironically, that flexibility has led some Christians to denounce Messianic Jews who observe Shabbat! In Acts 15, the Gentiles were not told to keep Shabbat but to be culturally sensitive to their new relationship with the Jewish community. The bottom line is, there is freedom regarding days of worship. Messianic Jews and Christians are not to judge each other but to realize that, even with our diverse cultures, we are all united in the one faith of Yeshua (Rom. 14).

All this leads us back to that evening Havdalah meal in Troas. Sha'ul used the occasion *to address the group especially since he was going to leave the next day*. He *kept talking* all the way *until midnight* (not unlike some other messianic rabbis you may know). This detail is just another part of the evidence that this meeting took place on what we call Saturday night. If it started Sunday morning, this would be one of the lengthiest sermons in history! Still, it was a bit long for some in attendance. With *many oil lamps burning* (at night) affecting the air quality in the crowded room, *a young man named Eutychus grew sleepier and sleepier; until finally he went sound asleep and fell from the third story to the ground.*

The shocked crowd went *to pick him up*, but *he was dead*. Doctor Luke uses a term that confirms the man died in the fall. But this would prove another opportunity for God's power to be manifested in the early Yeshua movement. In a manner reminiscent of the Prophets Eliyahu and Elisha, Sha'ul *embraced the young man and said, "Don't be upset, he's alive!"* (I Kgs. 17; II Kgs. 4) This could be a divine combination of the Ruach and ancient CPR. With that statement of faith and trust in God, Sha'ul *went back upstairs and broke bread!* He continued with part two of his teaching ministry all the way *till daylight, then left*. The crowd was *greatly relieved* and strengthened in faith as *they brought the boy* (whose name means "lucky one") *home alive*. Add this miracle to the numerous supernatural events in Acts that testify to the power of the risen Messiah.

D. Shepherding the Messianic Flock – 20:13–38

After the miraculous resurrection of Eutychus, the Sh'likhim set sail from Troas to Assos. The aim was to arrive in Yerushalayim for Shavuot, as well as to bring the love offering to the Messianic Jews from their Gentile brothers in faith (Rom. 15:25–27). But curiously, Luke says this first part of the trip was for meeting with Sha'ul, who traveled to town by land. This land route is known to be difficult, so there must have been a good reason for his detour—likely security reasons after the intense opposition he met in the outreach in Greece (20:3). All the listed ports (Assos, Mitylene, Chios, Samos, Miletus) are off the coast of Asia Minor and are about a single day's sailing journey, which makes for a logical rest stop. It would have been convenient to pay another visit *to Ephesus*, but Sha'ul chose to *bypass the strategic city* as he was *hurrying to reach Yerushalayim, if possible in time to celebrate Shavuot*. This side-note is important to Luke and to us today, as it affirms the early Messianic Jews were not anti-Torah but still valued their Jewish heritage. Many of us today have found that our faith in Yeshua as Messiah actually gave us a greater appreciation for our rich Jewish heritage. Now we see the full picture of what the holidays and customs are all about!

Though Sha'ul felt he needed to bypass Ephesus, there was too much recent history he could not ignore. The *Shaliach summoned the elders of the Messianic community from Ephesus to meet him in Miletus*, 30 miles south. The office of an elder (Hebrew *zakeyn*) is well-known from ancient Jewish community and synagogue structures (Deut. 19–25; Lk. 7:1–3). Luke records Sha'ul's instructions to the Messianic leaders on how to shepherd this new community of believers. These instructions can also encourage contemporary leaders in Messianic Judaism and the Gentile Church.

The first vital point is the idea of feeding the flock (vv.17–27). Sha'ul says he *held back nothing that could be helpful, teaching them in public and from house to house.* Though there were various venues and formats, it was *the same message to Jews and Greeks alike*, to *turn from sin to God and put their trust in the Lord Yeshua the Messiah*. If the Yeshua community is like a flock of sheep, feeding is essential— including what food is given! According to Sha'ul, he *did not shrink from proclaiming to them the whole plan of God*. For an educated Jew, this would include God's revelation in the entire Bible. **Torah**, **Neviim** (Prophets) and **Ketuvim** (Writings) = the Jewish acronym **TaNaKh**.

Though there was no written New Testament at this time, it clearly included Yeshua's life and ministry as the final part of God's plan for Jews and non-Jews. Sheep need a balanced diet for physical health; it is no less important for the spiritual health of Yeshua's sheep. It is also a priority, says Sha'ul, to understand how the messianic ministry was carried. Among some of the details, the Ephesian *zekeynim* (elders) are reminded to serve the Lord with humility and even tears. Standing with Yeshua is not for the weak of heart. It only intensifies as one responds to the call to serve him in Messianic ministry.

Sha'ul senses he is going *up to Yerushalayim*, not sure what awaits him. He wonders *if he will see these friends ever again*. Even though his own life may be in peril, he is determined *to declare the Good News of God's love and kindness*. Whatever awaits him, he is confident he has fulfilled his shepherding duties as Messiah called him to. What a powerful synopsis of his service and important directive for spiritual leaders today! For modern-day Messianic rabbis, elders, Shamashim and other leaders, feeding the flock must be a top priority in the Messianic Jewish movement. Too often those around us reject the Good News. Could it be like the days of the prophets when our people were perishing for lack of knowledge (Hos. 4:6)?

Along with the primacy of teaching the entire Scriptures in a balanced way, Sha'ul also emphasizes other duties of a good shepherd. They are to be on guard for themselves. The messianic shepherd is only as effective as their own spiritual life. The shepherd of the Middle East had to be on guard against threats to the flock. The emissary warns the Ephesian leaders that *after he leaves, savage wolves will come in among them,* which has often been true in Israel's history too (Ezek. 22:27; Mt. 7:15). It's bad enough to fight off external threats to God's flock, but Sha'ul is especially concerned about *men who will arise, even from their own number, and teach perversions of the truth in order to drag away the talmidim after themselves.* Leaders must *stay alert* to internal attacks within the Messianic community *purchased by the Messiah's blood.* Sha'ul holds up his own example of diligent work among the Ephesian believers *for three years, day and night, with tears in his eyes!* Above all, he *entrusts them to the care of the Lord and to the message of his love.* He is confident all these leaders and their Messianic community will succeed because they are *set apart for God.*

These were sober warnings to the Ephesian elders, and they are strong for Messianic leaders today. We must watch out for ourselves and keep our personal life in order. This includes keeping our home in order; how can one be effective with a larger flock if the smaller flock is in disarray? (I Tim. 3:1–5)

Many times, we leaders want to focus on the positive and the many blessings within our flocks. But we would be negligent if we ignore the possible wolves outside and within. Fallen human nature can do much damage from some who would harm Yeshua's flock. We are also aware of the Adversary, Satan, who wishes to confuse or destroy any work of God's Kingdom. This only intensifies when it comes to our people Israel and spiritual ministry in the Jewish community. We are not fearful or paranoid in our spiritual life; God has given us too many promises of ultimate victory. But if you are in Messianic leadership, heed Rabbi Sha'ul's counsel to stay alert!

A final overarching point from Sha'ul is to always have a heart for serving Yeshua's flock. Again he invokes his own example and reminds the Ephesian leaders that he did *not even want for himself anyone's silver or gold or clothing.* He worked diligently not only *to provide for his own needs, but for the needs of his co-workers as well.* Even this attitude had a higher purpose in his mind as he wanted everyone *to help the weak* and needy. Here we see a beautiful balance of the ministry of the Good News and the application of *tikkun olam*, repairing the world. It is a strong Jewish value through the ages that we are divinely called to bring God's tangible blessings to our hurting society. Sometimes believers are accused of being "so heavenly minded that they are no earthly good"! This is very unfortunate and inconsistent with the balanced message of the Scriptures. Sha'ul reminds the Ephesian leaders of these values by *remembering the words of the Lord Yeshua himself, "There is more happiness in giving that in receiving."*

All this is a good reminder for Messianic Jewish leaders today. We are called to feed Yeshua's flock and protect his blood-bought sheep. This must be done in a humble spirit of serving the flock. Sometimes a spiritual leader is in the ministry for their own agenda and purposes. Sha'ul says that a good shepherd is a servant-leader, constantly looking out for the good of the sheep, not fleecing the flock. On the flip side, the sheep of the Messianic flock are exhorted, *"Obey your leaders and submit to them, for they keep watch over your lives, as people who will have to render an account. So, make it a task of joy for them, not one of groaning; for that is of no advantage to you"* (Heb. 13:17). The work of a loving shepherd has its challenges and is not always appreciated by others, but the rewards are out of this world!

In the final moments of this leadership meeting, Sha'ul and the leaders *kneeled down and prayed.* Over the centuries, true people of faith have appreciated the gift of prayer. Of course, there are many kinds of prayer in the Jewish context; everything from the *berochot* (blessings) to the intercessions of the Amidah. There are various prayer postures: bending the knee, davening, sitting. Anyway, it was a time filled with emotion as they were *all in tears as they threw their arms around Sha'ul's neck and kissed him farewell.* Such demonstrative kissing, while sometimes abstained from in Western society, is still common in the Middle East and Jewish culture. The leaders were especially *saddened by the remark that they would never see him again.* In the midst of this important closing message and emotional response, the close-knit leaders *accompanied Sha'ul to the ship.* They could only guess what would await the emissaries as they again made aliyah. But as for Sha'ul, he could have a degree of peace knowing he had imparted to them the vital focus for the growing Yeshua movement in Greece.

> *How grand is Torah! For to those who engage in it, it gives life in this world and the world to come! As it is written, "For they are life into those what find them and health to all their flesh."* (Prov. 4:22 / Pirkei Avot VI.7)

E. The Final Aliyah to Yerushalayim – 21:1–26

After we had torn ourselves away from the Ephesian elders, Luke says, the team *set sail* for Yerushalayim. It was indeed an emotional departure. Though some of the elders did not want Sha'ul to venture to the Holy City, he felt a divine calling to accomplish an important part of his ministry—to worship in Yerushalayim for the holy day of Shavuot and to bring the important love offering from the new Gentile followers in Yeshua (20:16). Luke recounts the voyage via various stops in the Mediterranean: Cos, Rhodes, Patara, Phoenicia, Cyprus *and landed at Tzor* (modern Tyre in Lebanon).

As they had a *one-week* layover, the team *searched out the talmidim* there with hopes of some ministry time. It turned out this group also was greatly concerned about Sha'ul's plan to go to Yerushalayim. We are even told that they gave this counsel *guided by the Ruach*. You'd think it would be hard to argue against such guidance, but the entire team *continued on the journey*. It is an important reminder that sometimes well-meaning believers might give counsel that is not exactly God's will. It may even be logical advice, but we are ultimately responsible to discern if we have a different path to follow (I John 4:1). In this case, the believers were likely just sharing their heartfelt concerns for Sha'ul's safety, not opposing his convictions. This seems even more evident as *the whole crowd, with their wives and children, accompanied the team outside the town*. They even have a season of personal *prayer as they are kneeling on the beach* (20:36).

The voyage continues as *they sail from Tzor* to the northern Israeli port of *Acco, known as Ptolemais* by the Romans. After an *overnight stay*, the outreach team came to Caesarea, also on the coast of Israel, staying *with Philip*, who was part of the Shamashim listed in Acts 6. This believer was well-known for actively *proclaiming the Good News and had four unmarried daughters with the gift of prophecy*. This is a reminder that many gifted women served in the early Yeshua movement. There is some debate about certain roles women may serve, but it is abundantly clear they have equal access to the spiritual gifts in the New Covenant era such as teaching and proclaiming (Acts 2:17–18; I Cor. 11:5).

While in Caesarea, a prophet named Agav came from Y'hudah to visit the team. He had a message for Sha'ul and illustrated it dramatically. He took Sha'ul's belt, tied up his own hands and feet and said, *"Here is what the Ruach HaKodesh says: the man who owns this belt—the Judeans in Yerushalayim will tie him up just like this and hand him over to the [Gentiles]."* This is reminiscent of some of the symbolic acts of the former prophets of Israel (Jer. 13:1–11; Ez. 4:1-8). Luke records the reaction from both the emissaries and local believers: All *begged him not to go up to Yerushalayim*.

As with the episode in Tzor, Sha'ul still sees the situation differently than everyone else. Even with the inherent danger, he is prepared not only to be tied up but even to die for the name of Yeshua.

The group of believers relented when they saw that Sha'ul would not be convinced otherwise and expressed their trust that the Lord's will be done. Again we find some sincere believers recommending a course of action that is not considered God's ultimate will (21:4–5). Agav does not forbid Sha'ul from going; he only speaks of what will transpire. Perhaps the group is merely expressing their personal desires, but Sha'ul believes he must follow the call to Yerushalayim. It is often beneficial for us to consider the counsel or ideas of those around us, but ultimately, we answer for our own decisions.

With this understanding, the team *went up to Yerushalayim along with some of the talmidim from Caesarea.* They connect with some of the local believers and stay at the *home of Mnason* (Manasseh) anticipating some important meetings with the top Messianic Jewish leaders. The team was *received warmly by the brothers and, on the next day, how they met with Ya'akov and all the elders.* By this time, Ya'akov is the head elder of Yerushalayim and thus the entire Yeshua movement. It's very important for Sha'ul, the Shaliach to the Gentiles, to check in with the top Jewish leaders to confirm everything is in line with Yeshua's mandate. *Sha'ul described in detail each of the things God had done among the Gentiles through his efforts.*

With some people this new outreach might be cause for concern, but Luke says those *hearing the report* were blessed and *praised God.* Some speculate that there was a philosophical division between Ya'akov and Sha'ul. Either way, clearly there is no major problem between the leaders of the Jewish community and Sha'ul's outreach work. This is key. Even with some controversy and questions, the Messianic Jewish leadership see God's hand in this. Despite the many potential barriers, it is the Jewish community who is welcoming to the new Gentile believers. Sadly, this is sometimes reversed in our day where some in the Gentile Christian majority are not very welcoming to us Jews who want to follow Yeshua within our Jewish heritage! Happily, a growing number of Christians, like these early Messianic Jews, rejoice that God is doing something wonderful outside their personal community and boundaries.

This was a great start to the meeting, but Luke honestly reflects some potential misunderstandings. The Yerushalayim elders share an important concern about the Messianic Jews in Israel. First, there are *tens of thousands* (Greek *myriads*) *of Jewish believers who are zealots for the Torah*. This is quite believable considering the early gatherings where several thousand Jews embrace the Good News of Messiah (2:41, 4:4). By all accounts, this was a major movement of newer Messianic Jews. Fascinatingly, Sha'ul is also told that this huge group remained Torah-observant. Some commentators find this puzzling, as it is often mis-taught that Yeshua came to do away with the Torah. This is still a major stumbling block that keeps many Jews today from even considering the possibility of Yeshua.

We know the Torah was given by God to Moshe. How could a Jewish messiah come to abolish this holy revelation? It should not be surprising that this Messianic Jewish community in Israel was still traditionally following (even zealous for) the Torah while fully embracing Yeshua as Messiah. Remember, he himself said came not to abolish the Torah but to fulfill (Mt. 5:17–18). Of course, this is not to imply that the new believers adhered to some kind of Jewish legalism. Sha'ul emphasized often that we follow God through the grace of Messiah (Eph. 2:8–10). Yet there is no reason why a Spirit-filled Messianic Jew cannot live their faith in the context of Torah revelation. The Spirit and the Torah are not mutually exclusive but complementary blessings for the children of God (Rom. 7:12–14).

But the Yerushalayim leaders relay their concerns that perhaps Sha'ul's outreach to the Gentiles seemed to compromise the Jewish regard for the Torah lifestyle. True, he often emphasized that Gentiles could come directly to the God of Israel through Yeshua's work. They didn't need to convert to Judaism or live within all the 613 requirements placed on Israel (Acts 15). Of course, a large portion of the Torah is simply reiterated in the New Covenant. So, it's assumed the Gentiles would observe the moral laws found in both the Torah and New Covenant.

This freedom—or rather, misunderstandings about this freedom—is what concerns traditional Jewish believers. Evidently the rumor had spread that Sha'ul *was also teaching all the Jews living among the Gentiles to apostatize from Moshe.* This confusion revolved around two specific charges: that Sha'ul was telling the Jewish believers *not to have a b'rit-milah for their sons, and secondly, not to follow the traditions.* Since b'rit-milah symbolizes a son coming into the covenant of the Torah, to forbid this would imply the Torah was unimportant now that they followed Yeshua.

The Messianic elders propose a solution. To allay the traditional Jewish believers' fears, Sha'ul is to *take four men who are under a vow,* join them in the Torah observance (Num. 6; Acts 18:18; Tractate Nazir 6.3) and *be purified with them and even pay the expenses connected with having their heads shaved.* This public act in the Temple will show *there is nothing to these rumors* about him. In fact, it will substantiate that Sha'ul himself *keeps the Torah.*

He follows the elders' directive, both to quell the false rumors and to show he loves the Torah lifestyle for himself. Some think this counsel is bad or that Sha'ul himself was confused! But there is no indication that this is wrong or against God's will, and Sha'ul's positive response affirms it's his heartfelt conviction. The theological confusion is resolved by realizing that his work among the Gentiles in no way negated the call of Jews to live a Jewish lifestyle. In fact, the elders summarize this by drawing that cultural distinctive and say the Gentile believers should follow *the decision that they should abstain from what had been sacrificed to idols, from blood, from what is strangled and from fornication* (Acts 15).

Simply put, Acts 15 and 21 give the messianic guidelines for Gentiles and Jews, respectively. This episode is informative for modern-day followers of Yeshua, both Jewish and Gentile. The simple truth is, neither side is called to convert to the other! All are free to enjoy their God-given culture and heritage in their faith walk with Messiah. Gentile believers (every tribe and tongue) are free to have myriad cultural expressions, whether days of worship, foods, or language (Rom. 14). Similarly, Jewish believers are free, even encouraged, to continue in their calling and culture as the remnant of Israel (Rom. 11:29). We should resist the temptation to judge a brother of a different culture and instead exhibit unity within diversity. This seems the heart of Yeshua's Pesach prayer for us as well (Jn. 17:21). Such unity will be a clear indicator of the power of our Messiah and even draw many people to the beauty of Yeshua!

F. The Misunderstood Rabbi – 21:27–40

Sha'ul obeyed the elders' counsel and *entered the Temple to give notice* of the requisite *purification*. His public adherence to these Torah commandments should assuage any lingering doubts (then and now) that he is anti-Torah or advocating a new religion. Still, things didn't go smoothly; toward the end of the *seven-day period, some unbelieving Jews from Asia saw him in the Temple and stirred up the crowd*. It is not the first time Sha'ul and the emissaries are harassed by other Jews who opposed their perspective. It is ironic that he is accused of *teaching things against the (Jewish) people, against this place (the Temple) and against the Torah*—all while he is diligently fulfilling a vow based in the Torah! The accusers expand their complaints, saying Sha'ul *brought some Gentiles into the Temple* (beyond the Court of the Gentiles) *and defiled this holy place*.

The Mishnah describes ten levels of increasing holiness starting at the outer walls of Yerushalayim to the Holy of Holies, with courtyards dividing each section (Tractate Kelim 1.6–9). An archaeological discovery in Yerushalayim uncovered a stone that reads in Greek, "No man of another nation shall enter within the fence and enclosure round the Temple. And whoever is caught will have himself to blame when his death ensues!" Josephus says this warning was prominently placed at the dividing wall between the Court of the Gentiles and the Court of the Women (*Of the War, Book V*). Luke explains that Sha'ul *had previously been seen with Trophimus in the city* but not in the Temple proper. Despite this, *the whole city was aroused, and people dragged him out of the Temple, some desiring even to kill him.*

At this time, *the commander of the Roman battalion* got concerned and intervened. The last thing the Romans needed was more trouble in Y'hudah; that might encourage others in their domain to do the same. As the Temple Mount had a history of being a troubled focal point, the Romans built a military installation just beyond the holy boundaries at the northwest corner. Known as Antonio Fortress, it housed at least 1000 men, as the Greek word for "commander" indicates (*Linguistic Key* 322). As the *officer and some of his soldiers* approached the crowd, *they quit beating Sha'ul*. After arresting the troublemaker, the officer tried to determine the real issue, but *the crowd was in an uproar*, so he had Sha'ul brought to the Antonio *barracks*.

Barely escaping the Temple Mount riot, Sha'ul had an interesting dialogue with his captor. The emissary addressed the officer in Greek, getting his immediate attention. The officer asked if Sha'ul was *"that same revolutionary from Egypt who led 4,000 armed terrorists into the desert"*—a situation recounted in the history of Josephus (*Antiquities* 20.8.6). *Sikarion*, the word used to describe these rebels, was a common term for the short daggers these covert assassins carried (*Linguistic Key* 323). This shows the sensitivity of the Romans regarding religious rebels. Sha'ul (who was not that terrorist) replied, *"I am a Jew from Tarsus ... and I ask your permission to let me speak to the people."*

The request was granted, and the emissary addressed the crowd in Hebrew, which no doubt got their attention. Some commentators say he spoke Aramaic, but the term *Hebraidi* here—plus confirmation from the Dead Sea Scrolls—begs to differ. What follows is a magnificent defense of the rabbi's faith in Yeshua, which he strongly believes is within the context of his Jewish faith. The responses, as usual, vary from open hostility to careful consideration. While we contemporary Messianic Jews and Gentile followers of Yeshua do not usually face such intense situation, we will face challenges to our faith. Will we stand strong or will we waiver? If Yeshua is the real Messiah for all people, we really have but one good choice!

Chapter Seven

THE MESSAGE DEFENDED BEFORE JEW AND GENTILE

*Be deliberate in judgment, raise many disciples,
and make a hedge around the Torah.*

(Pirke Avot 1.1)

XIII. A Rabbi's Testimony on the Temple Mount – 22:1–30

The Temple Mount was in an uproar over the perceived actions of the leaders of the Yeshua movement. There was enough controversy related to the claims that the true Messiah had come to Israel in the person of Yeshua. Add some grievous propaganda, like the accusations of the emissaries being anti-Torah or desecrating the Temple Mount by bringing non-Jews into the Jewish holy place (21:28–29). Some of the Jewish crowd was inflamed, and the Roman occupiers feared another Jewish problem in Y'hudah. Here Sha'ul, though under Roman arrest, asks to address the crowd. He proceeds to share his spiritual journey as a Jewish follower of Yeshua and recounts how he believes it is consistent with his Jewish heritage. He starts by *addressing the Jewish crowd in Hebrew*, which got their undivided attention.

163

His opening words are striking as he addresses the large group as *"brothers and fathers,"* emphasizing the common connection they all have as Jews, whether Messianic or any other branch of Judaism. The emissary uses a descriptive word to describe his *defense* (Greek *apologia*), a reasoned response. He further strengthens this connection to the crowd by asserting that *he is a Jew*. He does not relegate this to his past, as if he was Jew but is now something else. Sha'ul uses the present tense to emphasize that his Yeshua faith *complements* his Jewish heritage in the here-and-now. He is still living as a Jew, albeit one who has added Messiah Yeshua to his life. This is what we modern Messianic Jews wish to sincerely communicate as well, as we continue to live a practical Jewish lifestyle.

Sha'ul tells of his family life in the diaspora, *born in Tarsus of Cilicia*. This metropolis was a seat of Greek culture. We might think Sha'ul and his family were comfortable in their Hellenistic Jewish culture, but he notes he was *brought up in Yerushalayim as he was sent to train at the rabbinical school of Gamliel*. This rabbi was the leader of the Pharisees of the first century, a sect of Judaism largely related to the common people and the local synagogue. They were also known to be one of Judaism's more traditional religious groups, as their name, *Parushim*, "separated ones," implies.

It is a remarkable part of Sha'ul's testimony that he trained under Gamliel and how he got to the yeshiva rabbinical school. We often think of people signing up to follow a certain rabbi or spiritual leader, but in the first century it was often the opposite. Since the commandment was upon the rabbi to raise disciples, not vice-versa, it was often he who recruited promising students to become his talmidim (see *Pirke Avot* 1.1 above). So it makes sense that Sha'ul was of those zealous, promising students who was invited from Tarsus all the way to Gamliel's yeshiva in Yerushalayim. The Talmud semi-humorously notes heated disputes between Rabban Gamliel and an unnamed student simply called *oto ha-talmid* ("that disciple").

This zealous student takes exception with his learned rabbi on several occasions and is said to have manifested "impudence in matters of learning" (Tractate Shabbat 30b). Who could have been such a rebellious talmid? Ironically, he must have been a well-known student who became infamous if his name is deleted. Some scholars say Sha'ul's background and experience fit the description (Klausner 310).

The connection to Gamliel would have been more than enough credibility to warrant this crowd's attention. But he continues to share how this training included *every detail of the Torah of our forefathers.* In fact, he was *zealous for God just as this present crowd* is clearly serious about the values of Judaism. Sha'ul says this zeal motivated him *to persecute to death the followers of this Way, arresting both men and women*; facts *the High Priest and the Sanhedrin* could substantiate. From these religious authorities he *received letters to arrest* the new Messianic Jews *in Damascus to bring them to Yerushalayim* for their day in court. (He obviously was not concerned with any Gentiles who might be following Yeshua, as it is often portrayed that he was arresting "Christians.")

As a zealous, anti-missionary Jew, he was focused on wayward fellow Jews who embraced this so-called Messiah. Hence, these legal actions are connected to the Jewish judicial authorities and not any Roman or Greek court. All this recalls certain minority Jewish groups even today who, out of their zeal, persecute and strongly oppose the modern Messianic Jewish movement. Perhaps there are still some pre-Damascus "Sha'uls" who may yet turn out as he did.

The emissary continues by recounting *the sudden brilliant light from heaven that flashed all around* him (Acts 9). As he fell to the ground, he *heard a voice*, the famous "daughter voice" that appears in Jewish history at strategic situations. The Jewish tradition is that God himself ceased to personally speak after the last Prophet, Malachi, but this voice would echo God's message (Tractate Yoma 9b).

The message in Hebrew of this bat kol was especially troubling to the anti-Yeshua leader: *"Sha'ul! Sha'ul! Lama atah rodef oti?"* *("Why do you keep persecuting me?")* By his own admission, he asks, *"Adonee, mi atah?"* *("Sir, who are you?")* Maybe it was a sincere question, but it could also imply that he suspects it is God who is speaking. Either way, the answer is shocking to him: *"Ani Yeshua (I am Yeshua) from Natzeret, and you are persecuting me!"* Strangely, those with him saw the *bright light of the Sh'khinah but did not hear the voice.* Still, Sha'ul continues the divine dialogue with another question: *"What should I do, Lord?"* With the bat kol identified as *"the Lord,"* he is told to *continue to Damascus* but with a new agenda. This he must do humbly, led by the hand after being blinded by the light. Sha'ul often alludes to his "thorn in the flesh" and bad eyesight (II Cor. 12:7–10; Gal. 6:11). His encounter with the brilliance of the Sh'khinah could explain the source.

Sha'ul recounts meeting Hananyah, a *highly regarded Messianic Jew* with a special word for him. After miraculously regaining his sight, Sha'ul is instructed and encouraged. Hananyah prophetically shares how *the God of our fathers chose* this zealous rabbi to divinely encounter *the Righteous One and to hear his voice so he might be a witness to everyone of what he has seen and heard.* The immediate instructions are to *get up, immerse himself in a mikveh and to call on [God's] name to have his sins washed away.* He *returned to Yerushalayim,* not with arrested zealots but as a believer in Yeshua. He was told, though, to flee the Holy City before his former rabbinic associates turned against him and his new message of Messiah.

Though he was an accomplice in the recent *persecutions and even the death* of Stephen, the voice exhorts, *"Get going! For I am going to send you far away to the Gentiles!"* Note God's great sense of humor. How better to reach the pagan Roman and Greek communities than with a Torah-observant Jew? But this is in fact part of Sha'ul's amazing background that perfectly fits this unusual calling. As a zealous, educated Jew, he is ideal to share the knowledge of the God of Israel and the Messiah with anyone. With his diaspora, broad worldly experience, who better to relate as a Greek to the Greek (I Cor. 9:21). As we've seen often in Acts, Sha'ul fulfills his calling to both groups by sharing with innumerable Gentiles throughout his missionary journeys. Yet even in the Roman cities, his inevitable first stop is the local synagogue (Rom. 1:16).

Until now the Jewish crowd on the Temple Mount had been listening, but now they expressed their disapproval, shouting, *"Rid the earth of such a man! He's not fit to live!"* They showed this anger by *screaming, waving their clothes, and throwing dust into the air.* The *Roman commander*, clearly worried as the situation escalated, brought Sha'ul from the public area of the Temple Mount *to the barracks* of the Antonio Fortress adjacent to the Jewish holy place. In true Roman fashion, they proceeded to have Sha'ul *interrogated and whipped*, hoping to find out why the mob was so agitated. In Roman custom, this would be administered with leather thongs embedded with shards of metal or bone. Such an "interrogation" could easily maim or kill the accused (*Antiquities* 15.8.4).

As the soldiers were *stretching him out with thongs to be flogged*, Sha'ul spoke up with a startling question: *"Is it legal for you to whip a man who is a Roman citizen and hasn't even had a trial?"* Those in charge, obviously growing nervous upon realizing this Jew was also a citizen, further interrogated him. The commander revealed, *"I bought this citizenship for a sizeable sum of money."* Sha'ul countered with an even stronger argument: *"But I was born to it."* With this, *the soldiers became fearful and drew back from him*, knowing now the great injustice and possible consequences.

As it now had become obvious that this was a Jewish religious dispute, the Roman commander *released Sha'ul to the priests and the Sanhedrin*. Once again we see that to the outside observers like the Romans, this Yeshua group seemed just another sect of Judaism. Perhaps the Sanhedrin (or probably a smaller subcommittee) could come up with some specific charges that would merit the attention of the Roman authorities. Or at least it would become clear what the actual religious charges might be. With that in mind, they brought the messianic emissary in front of the judicial council of Israel.

If a person repudiates belief in the Resurrection of the dead, he will have no share in the Resurrection. (Tractate Sanhedrin 90a)

XIV. A Messianic Pharisee Testifies Before the Sanhedrin – 23:1–35

The Yeshua controversy took another intriguing turn. This time the issue, as represented in its top Shaliach, went from the Roman Antonio Fortress to the Sanhedrin. Both parties had a vested interest in quelling these disturbances. The Roman authorities simply wanted to keep the political peace in the tumultuous province of Y'hudah. Of course, it was a different issue for the Jewish authorities, who had a difficult time dealing with this booming Yeshua movement.

The Romans transferred Sha'ul from the Fortress and their protective custody to Israel's judicial council. Here the emissary again gives his defense for his messianic faith, albeit with some different talking points. Previously, he had addressed the volatile crowd on the Temple Mount. He was now about to address some of the top rabbis and give the reasons for his faith in Yeshua as Messiah. We are told he appears before the "Sanhedrin," but likely not the full assembly. It was rare that the formal body were all present.

The Talmud says just 23 of the 71 members were required to form an official quorum who could render judgments (Tosefta Sanhedrin VIII). This important fact is often overlooked by casual readers who think the entire Sanhedrin was represented as they responded, not only to the early disciples but to Yeshua himself. We know there were in fact several members of the Council who were sympathetic to and even supporters of Yeshua and his teachings (John 19:38–39; Acts 5:38–39).

Standing before the Sanhedrin, Sha'ul addresses the august group as *"brothers,"* again emphasizing he is still connected to Judaism even with his messianic faith. This is strongly emphasized as he says, *"I have discharged my obligations to God with a perfectly clear conscience, right up until today."* This was too much for *the High Priest Hananyah*, who was presiding over the hearing. He ordered Sha'ul be *struck in the mouth*. This kind of hot-tempered action is consistent with the description of this High Priest even in

168

secular sources (*Antiquities* 20.9.1). Never one to be timid, Sha'ul gives his own rebuke, calling the leader a *"whitewashed wall."* This image was, and still is, well-understood in the Middle East, as walls and even tombs are painted with a whitewash solution especially during the holy days. It may look good on the surface, but it would be problematic if the wall was structurally unsound (Tractate Shekelim 1.1; Mt. 23:27–28).

Here Sha'ul rebukes the action of one who, ironically, is to *judge according to the Torah yet is in clear violation of that Torah.* In a strange twist, the men nearby tell Sha'ul he is insulting the High Priest. Maybe with his dubious eyesight he didn't make that identification; or, maybe in sarcasm, Sha'ul is implying the leader is not acting like the High Priest. Either way, Sha'ul invokes the Torah verse about *not speaking disparagingly of a ruler of Israel* (Ex. 22:27).

At this tense moment, the Shaliach saw an opportunity to make his point. It was well-known that the Sanhedrin consisted of diverse religious parties. Sha'ul states his affiliation in the strongest terms: *"Brothers, I myself am a Parush (Pharisee) and the son of P'rushim."* He has made similar statements before, but here he adds, *"It is concerning the hope of the resurrection of the dead that I am being tried!"* (Dan. 12:1–2) We've seen some of the details concerning this stringent sect in first-century Judaism and Sha'ul's background within it (Acts 15). Their title "Parush" says it all, as they prided themselves on being the "separated" ones. Often, even in modern preaching, this is understood in a most negative way. No doubt this has some truth, but to be fair, even the Talmud speaks of both good and bad Pharisees. Tractate Sotah 22a&b lists seven types of P'rushim:

1. The *Shikmi* (Shoulder) Pharisee, who performs the action of Shechem (Genesis 34). Remember that Shechem pretended to convert to the God of Israel, performing good deeds visibly (worn on his shoulder), but it was only outward appearance. This seems to be part of Yeshua's reference in Matthew 23:4 as they lay burdens on men's shoulders.

2. The *Nikip* (Stumbling) Pharisee, who walks in an exaggerated manner to draw attention to his humility. How sadly ironic!

3. The *Kizai* (Bleeding) Pharisee, who is so concerned about looking upon a woman that he causes his own bleeding by bruising himself against a wall.

4. The "Pestle" Pharisee, who publicizes his own holiness as his head is bowed like a pestle in a mortar.

5. The "Ever-Reckoning" Pharisee, who constantly asks, "what is my religious duty?" as though he has fulfilled every mitzvah.

6. The *Yareh* (Fearful) Pharisee, who relationship with God is not based on reverence but an actual fear and trembling.

7. The *Ahav* (God-Loving) Pharisee, who has a balanced understanding of the Torah and his walk with God.

Like every religious group, the Pharisees have both sincere members and hypocritical ones. It's important not to make a sweeping judgment of any group. Sha'ul affirms he was sincerely seeking God through his affiliation with the P'rushim. It may surprise some that he identifies with the Pharisees in the present tense, not just as some misguided past. Though there are no Pharisees today, many of us contemporary Messianic Jews have no problem identifying as Torah-observant, traditional Jews who also embrace Yeshua as Messiah. In fact, that's the point! There is a Jewish way to follow Yeshua. This list reminds us that even today there are many Jews seeking God within the context we were brought up in. Our witness to our Jewish brothers and sisters would be more productive if we realized that many people are sincerely seeking a relationship with God but not sure how to. For many such people, there is a growing realization that Yeshua is the link for all people to get closer to the God of Israel (John 14:6). It seems we should encourage such seekers and not jump on them with judgment. We are wise to follow Sha'ul's consistent example of respectfully speaking the truth in love.

When Sha'ul mentioned the concept of resurrection, *an argument arose between the P'rushim and the Tz'dukim.* Luke, seeing a need to explain some of the Jewish theological issues, says the Tz'dukim deny the reality of *the resurrection* and doubt the *existence of angels and spirits.* As staunch Scripture believers, the P'rushim endorsed these doctrines, but the Tz'dukim doubted, mostly because of their adherence only to the Pentateuch. As Sha'ul brought up his Pharisaic beliefs, an uproar ensued. Some of the Torah-teachers supported him and saw nothing wrong with his doctrine.

As the Tz'dukim objected, *the dispute became so violent that the Roman commander* had his soldiers *take Sha'ul by force back into the barracks.* All this turmoil must have been upsetting to him, but the Lord intervened with a special word: *"Take courage! For just as you have borne a faithful witness to me in Yerushalayim, so now you must bear witness in Rome."*

The situation deteriorated. *The next day, some of the Judeans formed a radical conspiracy saying they would neither eat nor drink until they had killed Sha'ul.* All religions have radicals who fall to such animosity against those they oppose. *These forty* zealots told *the Sanhedrin leaders of their plan,* hoping to get Sha'ul released by the Romans long enough to carry it out. In a strange "coincidence," Sha'ul's own nephew *got wind of the planned ambush* and told both his uncle and the Roman authorities. This is another example of a "coincidence" that's really a "God incident"! It recalls the holiday of Purim, which celebrates the deliverance of the Jews because Mordechai "coincidentally" overheard a plot against the Persian king.

Add to this the "coincidence" of an undercover Jewish girl, Esther, being in the king's court at the right time (Est. 4:12–14). There are so many such "coincidences" in Jewish history, it's hard to stay an atheist! It's interesting that Sha'ul had a family yet seemed mostly cut off from them. The same controversy around his faith could have easily alienated him from them. He also tells of a case of a "believer" married to a "non-believer" and a resulting divorce (I Cor. 7). Most first-century rabbis were married, so he may be alluding to his own experience. All these things remind us of his unshakable faith and the incredible price he often paid as the leading Shaliach of the early Yeshua movement.

With the news from Sha'ul's nephew, the Roman commander saw he had to act swiftly before another Jewish riot and any reverberations through the territories. *At nine o'clock that very night he dispatched two of the captains along with two hundred of their infantry soldiers* to take this controversial rabbi over to the Roman stronghold of Caesarea on the coast. The commander's sentiments are clearly stated in the letter describing the situation: how Sha'ul was rescued from a developing riot on the Temple Mount; how it was learned that he's a Roman citizen who stirred up religious controversy in the city, charged *in connection with questions of their 'Torah'"*; how there was a Sanhedrin hearing but also a murderous plot by religious zealots.

It became clear the rabbi must be taken out of Yerushalayim and be sent to a higher Roman authority who could adjudicate this Jewish controversy. All this was in the letter from the commander, *Claudius Lysias,* to the *Governor of Y'hudah, Felix.* The soldiers evacuated Sha'ul to Caesarea as planned. Felix, upon learning that he was from the respected *province of Cilicia,* assured him he would *have a full hearing after the accusers have arrived.* With that, the rabbi was incarcerated *under guard in Herod's headquarters,* which would turn out to be for the next two years.

Make your study of the Torah a fixed practice; say little and do much; receive all men with a cheerful countenance. (Pirke Avot 1.15)

XV. A Messianic Jewish Testimony Before an Intermarried Governor – 24:1–27

Five days later, the High Priest Hananyah came to Caesarea *with some elders and a lawyer named Tertullus.* In normative fashion, Luke reflects the common Jewish language of *"going down"* from the spiritual apex of Yerushalayim to anywhere else. This certainly applied to Caesarea as the coastal headquarters of the local Roman government where Sha'ul was incarcerated and awaiting his civil hearing. This legal delegation finally arrived to file official charges against the leader of the Messianic movement. They previously had trouble clarifying a specific religious charge, so they'll seek a combination of charges that touch on both Jewish and Roman sensitivities. Tertullus makes his opening statement with eloquence and a bit of pandering. Addressing Felix as *"your Excellency,"* he proceeds to praise the governor for *the unbroken peace, his foresight, and his many reforms.* Then the lawyer gets to the reason for his legal team's appearance. They represent many in his district who have *found this man, Sha'ul, to be a pest.* It is he who has *incited much of the Jewish community* within the Roman *world by being a ringleader of the sect of the Natzratim.*

This is an intriguing and admittedly powerful mix of Jewish and Roman concerns. On the Jewish side, this religious sect that held to the claims of Yeshua as the promised Messiah was controversial. The group's name reflected these Jewish concepts, "Natzratim" being the Hebrew phrase from the Prophets where it is told that a *netzer* ("branch") will come from Yeshai, the family of David (Isa. 11:1). In this context, "Natzratim" applies specifically to Jewish followers of Yeshua as the Messiah. This is evident as the legal team describes the group as *a sect* of Judaism (perhaps a heretical one).

The High Priest and elders didn't care what the Gentiles were doing in their religious expressions. But these Nazarene Jews are clearly contrasted with the Gentiles who were coming to faith in Yeshua; they were specifically called *Christianos / Christians / Messianic* (11:26). Part of this binary approach can be understood by the differing cultures and languages, the difference between Antioch and Yerushalayim. The common perception was that there were two expressions of this Yeshua faith: a Jewish side where it all started, and a wild, grafted branch that welcomed non-Jews. Yet even with these cultural distinctions, the miracle of the Good News is that both groups are united in their common link to the one Messiah (Eph. 2:13–18).

Embedded within these religious allegations, the prosecuting team accuses Sha'ul of stirring up political insurrection against the Romans. Agitating the Jewish community had consequences on the Romans as the turmoil expanded. At the time of his attempt to profane the court of the Temple Mount, it got so bad that the Roman garrison had to

RABBI BARNEY KASDAN

intervene and arrest him (21:29). With tensions already high at this time of the Roman occupation of Palestine, these charges were more than enough to greatly concern the governor. Now Sha'ul was invited to present his defense. Immediately we detect a change in tone as Sha'ul states he is *glad ("good spirit")* to make his case. The Greek word implies a reasoned defense (*apologia*), yet the attitude seems key as well. This example should not be lost on believers today. It is important we know why we believe what we do.

It is also vital to share within the Jewish context to our Jewish family and friends. Yet demeanor is sometimes the most important element. Who wants the faith of an angry or contentious believer? Like Sha'ul, we have the sincere joy of sharing the Good News of what Messiah has done in our lives. He shares some of his recent background such as his *Aliyah to the Temple in Yerushalayim* and the important detail that, whether in the *Temple or in the synagogues, he was not found to be arguing or collecting a crowd.* He says the legal team can't prove any of their accusations.

With this denial of wrongdoing, Sha'ul adds in positive terms what he truly represents. He is a sincere worshiper of *the God of our fathers* through the understanding of *the Way.* He remarks that the opposition calls this messianic way *a sect.* As seen, this description could even be equated with a heretical group (not too different from how some in the Jewish community view Messianic Judaism today). Yet Sha'ul emphasizes that he *continues to have a hope in God and a resurrection of the dead*—facts the Pharisee representatives *also accept.* This is an essential affirmation by the Shaliach that, in essence, he has the same beliefs as the traditional Judaism of his day.

The main difference (admittedly a large one!) is that he believes Yeshua is the promised Messiah, while the other branches of Judaism are still waiting. This is essentially the message of modern Messianic Judaism as well. It is not so much what we take away from our Jewish background but what we add to it: Yeshua is the Tanakh's predicted One! And like Sha'ul, we say Yeshua connects us even more strongly to the God of our fathers. Both Sha'ul and we modern

174

believers can say all these things are convictions held with *a clear conscience in the sight of both God and man.* People may not agree with us, but we sincerely hold our convictions openly before society. What is even more crucial is that we hold our messianic beliefs sincerely before the God of Israel. If Yeshua is not the true Messiah, then we Jews (and Gentiles) should not follow him. But if he is...

Now Sha'ul recounts some the events of his messianic outreach in the Roman Empire. This includes his journeys of *several years* until he returned *to Yerushalayim with the charitable gift* for the Jewish believers *and to offer other sacrifices* (Acts 21). Both actions emphasize his unwavering love for his people and his Jewish heritage, both of which were being questioned. In the *latter case* of the offering, he notes he was *in the Temple to be ceremonially purified* and *not causing any disturbance.* He says it was actually *some Jews from Asia* who caused the problems, yet *they are not present to back up their charge*—perhaps because of the weakness of their accusations.

The alternative is to let this present legal team *say what crime they found him guilty of in front of the Sanhedrin.* The only thing Sha'ul claims is that he *shouted out, "I am on trial before you today because I believe in the resurrection of the dead!"* At this climatic moment, the governor *shut down the hearing,* seeking to deflect his responsibility, stating that *Lysias the Commander will decide the case.* Luke inserts an intriguing note that perhaps this was because *Felix had detailed knowledge of things connected with the Way.* Maybe he'd seen enough controversy to opt out of this legal proceeding. Still, he ordered the *captain to keep Sha'ul in custody yet with considerable liberty and visitation from friends.*

Felix coincidentally had *a Jewish wife named Drusilla,* which is likely why he had some knowledge of this Jewish sect. *He sent for Sha'ul, and they listened as he spoke about trusting in the Messiah Yeshua.* When the rabbi touched on some topics that would not be popular with a pagan (thrice-married) Roman (e.g., *self-control and coming judgment!), Felix became frightened.* This is not surprising; he had encouraged his current wife to leave her husband to marry him and was notoriously unjust (*Antiquities* 20:7.1; 8.9). It's still true today that many like the Good News of a Messiah, but attitudes change when they realize some of the implications of the rest of the Tanakh! In Felix's case, he insists this controversial rabbi *get out* of his presence. Felix actually hoped Sha'ul *would offer a bribe*, resulting in multiple visits with Sha'ul as he *kept talking with him* about the spiritual life found in Yeshua. This went on for about *two years until Felix was succeeded by Porcius Festus*, who inherited the Jewish prisoner Sha'ul. No doubt there were some interesting discussions between the pagan governor and his Jewish wife regarding the possibility of the true Messiah coming in their day.

> *The Holy One, Blessed be He, will sit and expound the New Torah which he will give through the Messiah. "New Torah" means the secrets and the mysteries of the Torah which have remained hidden until now.* (Midrash Talpiyot 58a)

XVI. A Messianic Jew Appeals to Caesar – 25:1–27

Three days after Festus had entered the province, he went up from Caesarea to Yerushalayim. The case against Sha'ul was both civil and religious, though there was no consensus on either issue. The legal team had pressed the civil case, accusing him of instigating community unrest and potential insurrection against Rome. Festus, as the new governor who inherited this case, was certainly concerned about any political turmoil emanating from Y'hudah. But here it is some of the Jewish leaders who wish to pursue their priorities of stopping this leader of the Yeshua movement. Luke says it was the *leading cohanim and the Judean leaders who made their case* to the governor and asked *Sha'ul be sent to Yerushalayim* to face the religious authorities.

Perhaps Festus saw it as problematic to hear the case in the intense religious climate of the Holy City. So he told the legal team to *come down with him* to the Roman secular court in Caesarea where *they could press their charges. Eight or ten days later, Festus finally journeyed down* to the coastal capital and commenced to oversee the legal proceedings surrounding Sha'ul. The Yerushalayim legal team brought *many serious charges* against him, but Luke says *they could not prove* any of them. Add to this the rabbi's firm statement: *"I have committed no offense; not against the Torah nor against the Temple* [both religious charges] *or against the emperor* [the civil charge]. Accusations are one thing, but proving them is quite another. No doubt there was controversy regarding this nascent Yeshua movement and its claims of a risen Messiah. As seen before, there were also fears that this new sect of Judaism was anti-Torah or deliberately infringing upon Jewish sensitivities at the Temple Mount (21:28–29). Though there was political turmoil in the city, it was unclear whether this Shaliach was the source. All the charges were categorically denied by Sha'ul and could not be proven by his accusers.

With this standoff, Festus had a proposal that might defuse the situation. Was Sha'ul *willing to be tried in Yerushalayim?* It sounded good on the surface, but the emissary could already see the problem. He had clearly done nothing wrong and demanded to be *tried in the court of the Emperor. "If I am a wrongdoer ... if I have done something for which I deserve to die, then I am ready to die."* But if the charges amount to nothing, *"no one can give me over to [the Jewish authorities.]"* With that in mind, along with the fact of his Roman citizenship, Sha'ul officially *appeals to the Emperor.*

With Festus' hands seemingly tied, the governor pronounces, *"You have appealed to the Emperor; you will go the Emperor!"* It is quite revealing that Sha'ul would rather take his chances in the Roman court (and the notorious Emperor Nero!) than face the obvious bias of the Yerushalayim zealots. One also senses that he feels a strong calling to take this message of Yeshua to the capital of the Roman Empire and to the highest leadership of the land.

At about this time, some Roman friends, *King Agrippa II and his sister Bernice*, paid a visit to their political colleague. Naturally, the governor sought the counsel of these representatives from the House of Herod. Festus told the king of Sha'ul's situation, including the accusations of the *religious leaders in Yerushalayim* and his rejection

of their request *to judge* the messianic leader. The governor instead
relates his discomfort in hosting a trial of a any person *before he has
met his accusers face to face.* So he continued with his court in
Caesarea and ordered Sha'ul brought in. Festus continues by noting
that *the accusers did not have any serious crime* to throw against the
emissary, just some objections *from their own Jewish religion.*

Especially strange, Festus said, is this faith in *somebody called
Yeshua, who had died, but who Sha'ul claimed is alive.* As this was
considered beyond the expertise of a secular ruler, Festus says he
made offered a trial in Yerushalayim, but Sha'ul *appealed to be kept
in custody and have his case decided by the Emperor Nero.* At this
point *Agrippa interjected that he had also wanted to hear* from this
rather famous man, so the governor arranged for a personal interview.

The next day, the Herods made their entrance in a most Herodian
manner, with *much pageantry, including military commanders and
other prominent men of the city.* It must have been quite a scene as
this royal audience looked on as a lone rabbi was brought in. With
all in place, Festus addressed the aristocratic crowd with the main
point of contention: *The whole Judean community has complained*
about this man, even calling for his death. But the problem was, he
had done nothing that deserves a death sentence. Since he *appealed
to the Emperor,* Festus says he conceded *even though he had nothing
specific to write* in his charges. Evidently the governor hoped this
hearing in Caesarea might shed more light and reveal a charge that
would impress the Roman legal authorities.

In a humorous addendum, Festus adds, *"It seems irrational to me to
send a prisoner to Rome without also indicating what the charges
against him are."* Irrational indeed! But some solution must be found
for dealing with this zealot. Even if the pagan officials had a hard time
understanding the theological objections to Sha'ul and the Yeshua
movement, the last thing the Romans wanted was another troublemaker
stirring up turmoil in Y'hudah. The stage was set for another dynamic
encounter between the Spirit of God and the spirit of a skeptical world.

I believe with complete faith in the coming of the Messiah, and even though he may delay, nevertheless I anticipate every day that he will come. (Principle #12 of "Maimonides' "13 Principles of Faith")

XVII. The Rabbi Before the Jewish-Roman King – 26:1–32

Sha'ul received Agrippa's *permission to speak* at the legal hearing and *began his defense*. Once again, the word used, *apologia*, describes a reasoned explanation and not just an emotional response. Sha'ul opens with his appreciation for the opportunity, especially before such a leader *so well informed about all the Jewish customs and controversies*. This important court hearing is now presided over by someone from the Herod family, whose forefathers in past generations had converted to Judaism around 200 B.C.E. in their home province of Idumea. Because of this, the Herods were a rather eclectic mixture of Roman heritage and Jewish religion.

This also explains why, at several junctures, the Herods were called on to rule over Roman-occupied Y'hudah. Sadly, it also led to powerful conflicts of interest, as in the slaughter of the Jewish babies who were a perceived threat to the Roman king (Mt. 2). Add to this the public perception that Herod "the Great" was more like Herod "the Paranoid," at one point murdering two of his own sons so they could not usurp his throne. A saying arose: "It is better to be Herod's pig than son!" Though Herod the Great died in 4 B.C.E., this grandson carried on the Jewish-Roman connection as noted by Sha'ul.

Sha'ul summarizes his religious background and some of the current events that brought him to this hearing. Central to his testimony is that *it is well-known* about his affiliation with *the strictest party of Judaism, the Pharisees*. He says his Jewish brothers who are present can affirm he lived this Torah-observant lifestyle *from his youth, both in Tarsus and in Yerushalayim*. The emissary also makes the strong connection between historic Judaism and this newer messianic branch by affirming they are both part of "our religion."

Because of these things, Sha'ul points out *how ironic it is that he is standing trial because of his hope in the promise made to the fathers! This promise* (the hope of the resurrection) *was made to "our" twelve tribes, and they resolutely carry on their acts of worship in connection with this hope.* Yet it is this Jewish legal team (comprised of Pharisees) that is pushing the accusations that this leader somehow opposed Judaism. The real issue, Sha'ul says, is that some of these *same people now think it is incredible that God could raise someone from the dead.* No doubt this was a radical new thought about Yeshua, but the belief in the resurrection of the dead has always been one of the foundations of historic Judaism (Isa. 26:19; Dan. 12:1–2). With this key point driven home, Sha'ul recounts his spiritual journey leading to Yeshua.

He starts by sharing his past attitude regarding the new messianic movement. As a zealous Torah-observant Jew, he sincerely *thought it was his duty to do all he could to combat the name of Yeshua from Natzeret.* During his rabbinical studies *in Yerushalayim* under Gamliel he *received authority from the head priests* to harass the Jewish followers of this self-proclaimed Messiah. This included *putting many of God's people in prison and even casting his vote for their death.* The phrase "casting his vote" literally means "set down a stone or pebble," which alludes to the classic way of casting lots in biblical times (Prov. 16:33; Lk. 1:9; Tractate Sanhedrin 5.5).

This certainly recalls the stoning of Stephen (Acts 7), but he speaks in the plural, so evidently many others were impacted as well. *From one synagogue to another* Sha'ul pursued them, *trying to make them blaspheme*; that is, claiming Yeshua to be the divine revelation of God. Today it's often said that Sha'ul was persecuting "Christians," which many would assume to be non-Jews as well. But his testimony makes clear that he was solely concerned about his fellow Jews following a false messiah. Within traditional Judaism even today, there is little concern for Gentiles who become Christians. They'll probably even become better people if they do!

But the long-standing Jewish belief is that if a non-Jew simply follows the Seven Laws, they are righteous enough for the coming

Kingdom of God (Gen. 9; Acts 15). Clearly Sha'ul also had this philosophy at that point, searching local *synagogues* with a *wild fury* against these apostate Jews. This also explains why modern Judaism is not evangelistic toward the non-Jewish world. It was not always this way, and Israel still has a mandate to bring spiritual light to the Gentiles (Gen. 12:3; Isa. 49:6). It is also true that the Roman government and even the Church of the Middle Ages later forbade Jews to seek converts. Still, in the early decades of the Yeshua movement, it was solely the Jewish adherents who received the scrutiny of the Jewish religious authorities.

The emissary now segues into his encounter with the divine Messiah. On one of his anti-missionary trips he was stopped in his tracks. He was *on the road* to Dammesek when *he and his traveling companions saw a light even brighter than the noontime sun.* For a traditional Jew, this could only have one explanation: It was the brilliance of the Sh'khinah of God. So bright was this manifestation that *Sha'ul and his companions all fell to the ground.* Yet only the Shaliach heard a voice saying, *"Sha'ul, Sha'ul! Why are you persecuting me?"* The voice from heaven spoke in Hebrew, getting the young rabbi's attention. It is noteworthy that he is addressed by his Hebrew Jewish name and not his diaspora name (13:9).

Add to this the belief that a special bat kol was manifested after the last of the Jewish prophets when it was believed that God stopped speaking directly to the people (Tractate Yoma 9b). The bat kol further rebuked the rabbi, saying his actions were like *one kicking against the ox-goads.* This analogy refers to an ox being directed by its master with pokes of a sharp stick. In this case, Sha'ul was fighting even the correction of God himself! The rabbi recounts responding with his own question: *"Who are you, Lord?"* The usage of "Lord" can have two inferences here. It can be a simple address ("sir"), but Sha'ul is using it in the other way as "my Lord," meaning he assumed the bat kol voice was a divine revelation of God. This was confirmed as it is written that *the Lord answered, "I am Yeshua, and you are persecuting me."*

Sha'ul shares further details of the divine message. He is to *get up as the Messiah has appointed him to serve and bear witness to what he has seen and what he will see in the future.* As Israel itself was called to be a light to the nations (Isa. 49:6), this rabbi would become a special witness to all. He will be sent as a Shaliach *to both the People (Jewish world) and the Gentiles.* The Hebrew word for "one sent" is far stronger that the Greek word. The latter means "one sent" for a task, while the former means "a direct representative," as reflected in the Talmud: "A shaliach is equal to the sender himself." This is why all followers of Yeshua should accept Sha'ul's writings as inspired and directly from our Messiah himself (II Kefa 3:15–16). Sha'ul will be *sent out to open the eyes* of various communities *so that they might turn from darkness to light and receive the forgiveness of sins.* This spiritual light and forgiveness comes through personal trust and faith in Yeshua as the promised Messiah.

Sha'ul addresses Agrippa with a bit of personal application. He affirms he has been attempting to fulfill this calling from that point on. It started for him *in Dammesek, then in Yerushalayim and throughout Y'hudah,* thus covering the center of first-century Israel as the home of the Jewish people. This Good News of Messiah has gone even well beyond the Jewish world to *the Gentiles so that they too could turn from their sins and do deeds consistent with that repentance.* The emissary tells the king that this is the real reason why *some of the Jews seized him in the Temple and even tried to kill him* (22:22–24).

But *with God's help, he can testify before all that he is saying nothing but what both the prophets and Moshe said would happen—* first, that *the Messiah would die.* Though this teaching is often forgotten, the Messiah's suffering and death is well substantiated in the Tanakh (Isa. 53; Zech. 12; Dan. 9). It may surprise some folks to learn that it is also a significant teaching among the sages of the Talmud. The rabbis, seeing some of these same truths, even gave a special name to the suffering Messiah: Mashiach ben Yosef. This title was chosen as it was believed that in some mysterious way, the patriarch of Genesis is a type of the future Redeemer. Both will suffer; both will be rejected; yet both will ultimately be reconciled to their Jewish brothers (Tractate Sukkah 52a commentary on Zech. 12:10). It is this teaching Sha'ul affirms as part of his own understanding as a faithful Jew.

Yet there's more to the story. Sha'ul affirms that the experience of Yeshua also fulfills a second ministry of the Messiah—namely, that he would be *the first to rise from the dead*. While the doctrine of the general resurrection is clearly entrenched in traditional Judaism, there is significant debate as to how and when this will all take place (Dan. 12:1–2; Isa. 26:19; Rambam Principle #13). This last-day resurrection from the dead was to be led by the Messiah himself, who was to be risen from the dead in his own day.

This speculation appears as the Talmud considers the Isaiah 53 passage that says the suffering one "will see his offspring," applying this to the Messiah (Tractate Sanhedrin 98a). However, the sages also see all the promises of the King Messiah and give him the special name Mashiach ben David, the future king from the line of David (II Sam. 7:13). This led to some interpretations that held to the possibility of two Messiahs coming for the two different missions— suffering and kingship. One especially intriguing view states:

> *When Messiah ben Yosef is killed, his body will remain cast out in the streets for forty days, but no unclean thing will touch him until Messiah ben David comes and brings him back to life, as commanded by the Lord. And this is the beginning of the signs which he will perform and this is the resurrection of the dead which will come to pass.* (Hai Gaon, *Responsum*, in Patai, 169)

As this later midrash reflects, there is some mystery as to how a messiah might suffer and yet how a king messiah would also appear. Will two different messiahs will come for two different purposes? Or could it be one Messiah who could somehow accomplish both goals? At this point in Sha'ul's testimony, he says that in the person of Yeshua, both of these have now been fulfilled! That *Messiah would die* (Mashiach ben Yosef) was fulfilled by Yeshua's death on the Roman cross on Pesach. Yet because he is also *the first to rise from the dead*, Yeshua can fulfill the second work of Messiah as he returns as our King. Is it two messiahs at two different appearances or one Messiah who is risen to fulfill both missions?

Implied in Sha'ul's response is not only the reality of Yeshua being raised but also the precise timing of this momentous event. By alluding to Yeshua as the "first to rise" we can see a reference to Bikkurim, the Jewish holy day that falls on the third day of Pesach (Lev. 23:15–17). So, Yeshua died precisely on the first afternoon of Pesach when the Minchah lamb offering was given for the entire nation. Likewise, he rose from the dead on Bikkurim when the sheave offering, previously in the ground, was to be lifted up for all to see. Sha'ul confidently shares with the king this great fulfillment. Students of Judaism and the Torah should contemplate these prophetic pictures as well!

The two Roman leaders who listened to Sha'ul's defense were not so sure and even mystified by this messianic message. *At this point* of declaring the risen Yeshua, Governor Festus objects and shouts, *"You're out of your mind! So much learning is driving you crazy!"* In Festus' secular way of thinking, this educated Pharisee was mad. One has to be somewhat amused by this accusation. In an earlier context, the Yeshua disciples are mocked as being ignorant Jews, untrained in formal rabbinic yeshiva (Acts 4:13). Here the rabbinically trained Sha'ul is mocked for being *too* educated!

Even today there are those who seek to find a loophole to explain how some of us contemporary Jews have become sincere followers of the risen Yeshua! Sha'ul's response to the charge is both logical and respectful. While denying he is *crazy*, the emissary affirms he is *speaking words of truth and sanity*. But the pagan governor seems unswayed from his superficial convictions. Perhaps the Shaliach had this response in mind when he later wrote that the Good News of a Messiah is "foolishness to the Gentiles" (I Cor. 1:23). But it's a different story with the Jewish-Roman King Agrippa.

Sha'ul turns his attention to him as *one who understands these matters*—the promise of a coming Messiah and the resurrection of the dead. None of these things would be *hidden from him*, as they are all spoken in Tanakh and have taken place recently in public. That being so, the emissary asks Agrippa a compelling question: *"Do you believe the prophets?"* Sha'ul answers his own rhetorical question with the strong affirmation, of course *you believe!* The pagan may mock in bewilderment, but to any educated Jew, these things ring familiar.

King Agrippa's response is succinct but powerful. He answers with his own question (sounds like two Jews dialoging!): *"In this short time, you're trying to convince me to become Messianic?"* We weren't there to hear the tone of this response, so we can't be sure if he was skeptical or sincere. Part of the answer may lie in the specific usage of "Messianic," which is from the Greek *Christianos*. The only other usage of the term in Acts is a derisive description of the non-Jewish followers of Yeshua in Antioch (11:26). "Christian" is rarely used, and never of Jewish followers of Yeshua.

Part of this may be because it is the actual Greek language for what the Jews called "followers of Messiah." But there is a definite nuance to the term "Christian" applying to Gentile believers of the first century while Jewish believers are called followers of "The Way" or the Jewish sect of the Nazarenes (24:6). True, both terms essentially mean the same thing, albeit in different language and culture. But this interaction between Sha'ul and Agrippa illustrates some of the confusion that remains to this day.

Frankly, the great majority of Jews are not interested in converting cultures and becoming Gentile Christians. But many of the same people might be a little more open if the discussion was similar to what we find in Acts. Jews need not convert to a new culture. We can simply be Jews who believe Yeshua is the promised Messiah. This is an oft-neglected emphasis the modern Messianic Jewish movement is trying to correct. This is why we have "synagogues" (not churches) for Yeshua and prefer to call ourselves "Messianic Jews" instead of the culturally confusing term "Christian." Perhaps it was this early confusion of terms that elicited the interesting question from the Jewish King Agrippa as to becoming a "Messianic" or not.

Sha'ul's reply is honest and forthright. *A short time or long time* is not really the issue. His primary hope is that *all the listeners* (the Roman officials as well as the assistants) might *become like the messianic believer except for his chains.* This transparent desire of the rabbi went unheeded, though the king and the governor seemed to agree that *this man is doing nothing wrong.* Certainly *nothing that deserves either death or prison.* In fact, their debriefing leads them to conclude that if Sha'ul *hadn't appealed to the Emperor, he could have been released.* The various responses of the diverse individuals in this section of Acts still inform us today.

As Sha'ul works his way through the Roman judicial system, his message remains consistent. The Good News of Yeshua is totally consistent with the promises of the Torah and entire Tanakh. This remains the foundational message of modern Messianic Judaism as well. It is tragic that many believe the New Testament message is only for Gentile Christians. There is in fact a Jewish way to follow Yeshua and live a beautiful spiritual life within the boundaries of historical Judaism. It is not surprising, however, that as with the experience of the first-century rabbi, it is often the case today.

The message does not change, but the responses are varied. Some today are like Governor Felix, who seems to react to the message out of fear of his friends, community and even his Jewish wife (Acts 24). Others, like Governor Festus, seem to respond to the negative peer pressure around them. The whole thing seems a bit crazy to him, so he passes the issue on to others (Acts 25). There are also many today like Agrippa who, when faced with the logical evidence of Yeshua as Messiah, come close to also believing. We are not told, but evidently the king never did make a concrete decision to receive the gift of Messiah (Acts 26). There are many "fans" of the Jewish Jesus today (even in the Jewish community), but he is looking for a deeper commitment. Yeshua is still looking today for disciples who will unashamedly follow and serve him. Sha'ul will continue his strong testimony all the way to the Emperor in Rome. Who do you relate to in this series of encounters?

It is appropriate for a High Priest to bow at the end of each and every blessing; and for a king to bow at the beginning of each and every blessing and at the end of each and every blessing. This is because the more lofty one's status, the more important it is to demonstrate his subservience to God. (Tractate Berakhot 34b)

Sha'ul's Journey to Rome – Acts 27:1–28:31

XVIII. Facing a Crisis God's Way – 27:1–44

After the powerful defenses before the various Jewish and Roman authorities, Sha'ul again embarked on his ultimate journey to Rome. This would involve an extensive voyage from the eastern Mediterranean over the course of about 1350 miles, with the last leg traversing land to reach the capital. It would usually be a journey of about five weeks, and it is probably the fall of 60 C.E. (Bock 731). The emissary had given testimony at several judicial hearings and endured a two-year incarceration in the Caesarean brig. With no local decision on the charges against him, *Sha'ul and some other prisoners are now handed over* to Julius, the next Roman officer.

Luke again uses the word *"we"* to note he is part of the team. As was common practice in the Mediterranean, many ships would be navigating the sea for commerce and travel purposes. The messianic team embarked in *a ship from Adramyttium*, a busy seaport in northwest Asia Minor. Catching this ship in Caesarea, it evidently was on a journey that would take the group in the direction of the Italian mainland. A Messianic Jew named *Aristarchus* was also part of the team, but beyond that, it is not clear who else may have accompanied Sha'ul (Col. 4:10; Phlm. 24). Many of the ports of call for this voyage are about one day's sailing. Hence the next major stop is Tzidon. That Sha'ul is allowed to *visit his friends and receive what he needed* suggests he was considered a low-security prisoner with some freedom. He certainly was not perceived as a regular prisoner, as he had confirmed his Roman citizenship. *Chaverim*, the root word for "friends," may even indicate he was allowed to visit an organized *chavurah* of fellow messianic believers (Col. 4:15).

From Tzidon, the group continues sailing *close to the sheltered side of Cyprus*. As the *winds were against them*, the island's northern side offered some protection. The ship set out *across the open sea along the coasts of Cilicia and Pamphylia* (the coast of southern Turkey) until they *reached Myra in the coastal province of Lycia*. This seems to be the end of the line for this ship, but *the Roman officer found an Alexandrian vessel sailing to Italy*. Sha'ul, Luke and Aristarchus (and perhaps others) are transferred to this new ship with the hopes of reaching their destination for their appeal to Caesar. But the coastal winds remain strong, and they *made little headway* and finally *arrived off Cnidus only with difficulty* (far southwestern coast of Asia Minor).

The prevailing winds *did not allow the ship to take a direct route* toward Italy, so they adjusted the course south *along the sheltered side of Crete*. It is described as a *continuing struggle to hug the coast* of the island until they finally reached *a place called Pleasant Harbor*. Some have questioned the rather tedious details given to this voyage and even wondered why Luke would note such things. It goes to show his historian's mind for detail was part of Luke's perspective and likewise gives us great confidence in his entire account of Acts.

The nautical details are so precise that it even led a yachtsman and scholar to try to replicate the voyage in 1848. His confirmation of Luke's account and his successful Mediterranean voyage is recorded in his book *The Voyage and Shipwreck of St. Paul*.

The group had lost precious time due to the adverse conditions. Luke now turns his focus to the interpersonal details of those on the voyage. With this loss of time, the voyage was *now risky because it was already past Yom Kippur*. The exact phrase is "the Fast," which might lead some people to speculate. But to any educated Jew, it is clearly the great annual Fast of the Day of Atonement. This reference is significant for a couple of reasons. First, it tells us the voyage was taking place in the late fall, as the Jewish holy day falls on the 10th of Tishrei (late September or October). This timeframe was commonly considered the very edge of the safe sailing season in the Mediterranean as the winter weather and rough seas would soon encroach (Genesis Rabah 6.5).

Second, we again see Luke's awareness of Jewish details. He does not use the Roman or Greek calendars in his writings but the distinctive Jewish lunar calendar; this and other evidence leads us to assert that Luke is a Hellenistic Jew or proselyte to the faith with an in-depth Jewish education (Acts 1:1). A careful reading of the New Testament reveals that the early Yeshua believers (both Jews and non-Jews) followed the Jewish biblical calendar along with its directed holy days (Acts 2:1; I Cor. 5:6–8). For Jews, this is the natural expression now that we believe Messiah has come. For Gentile Christians, there is more of a learning curve, but it also makes sense as these days are God's appointed times to teach everyone about great spiritual truths.

In this context of Yom Kippur, Sha'ul feels the need to address his shipmates. With all the struggles to this point, he wonders if *the voyage might be a catastrophe*. It is clear this is not a divine, prophetic prediction but a premonition from his own spirit. He fears there might be not only *huge losses to the cargo and the ship but with loss of life as well*. Even with these dire warnings, *the ship's crew paid more attention to the pilot*. What could a rabbi know?

It was true that the *harbor was not well suited for sitting out the winter*, so they decided *to sail on from there in the hope of reaching Phoenix, a better harbor* for protection from the winter winds. When a *gentle southerly breeze* began to blow, the crew thought they *could sail and reach this goal*. But before long, they were hit with a *full gale from the northeast*. Luke describes this storm as "typhonic." So strong were the gale-force winds that *the crew gave way to it and let the storm carry* the ship off-course and into the middle of Mediterranean Sea. This new course would take the ship southward toward the treacherous reefs and sandbars of the coast of Libya in North Africa. This area, *Syrtis*, could be called the Bermuda Triangle of the Mediterranean, with innumerable shipwrecks and disasters recorded.

As the crew *feared that they might run aground, they lowered the topsails hoping to drift* by the shallows. Even this did not work, so *the next day they began to jettison non-essentials* in hopes of lightening the load and raising the level of the ship. *By the third day*, they were so desperate that the crew *threw the ship's sailing equipment overboard with their own hands*. A fitting targum on *Kohelet* (Ecclesiastes) 3:6 says, "There is a time for throwing a thing into the sea—namely the time of a tempest." To add to the fear and trauma, *the storm intensified so that the sun and the stars did not appear for many days*. With the loss of equipment and nature's guidance, it is not surprising that virtually all crew and passengers *lost any hope of survival*.

At this lowest point of desperation, *Sha'ul stood up in front of them* to give his perspective as a man of faith. The emotions could not go any lower, and *they went a long time without eating*. Body, soul and spirit were exhausted, but the rabbi had a word of encouragement to minister to every part. He starts his address by reminding the crew that *if they had listened to him about not setting out from Crete, they would have escaped this disastrous loss*. This is not an "I told you so" shaming but the emissary reminding them of the truth of God's word. Until now, the pagan crew likely had little interest in this Jewish prisoner and his message of one God with a risen Messiah. But now these warnings were being fulfilled before their eyes.

Often, when a person's life hits rock bottom, they can be more open to those things previously ignored. God has a way of getting our attention, especially in times of crisis. Instead of beating them down with guilt, the rabbi shares another word from his God, the God of Israel. His advice to them is to *take heart* because, even in this life-threatening typhoon, *there will be no loss of life*. They will not come through this voyage unscathed, but it is *only the ship that will be lost*, according to this prophetic word. Sha'ul emphasizes that this is not his personal opinion but a direct message *from an angel of the God to whom he belongs*. The message was this: *"Don't be afraid, Sha'ul! You have to stand before the emperor. God has granted all those who are sailing with you as well."* The rabbi adds his conviction that he *believes what he was told will come true*. The crew is exhorted again to *take heart* even though *their ship will run aground on some island*.

While this spiritual perspective and encouragement was helpful, the crew, passengers and prisoners still had to face the immediate challenge. Luke says, *"It was the fourteenth night, and **we** were still being driven about in the Adriatic Sea, when around midnight the sailors sensed that **we** were nearing land"* (literally "hearing the breakers"). The sailors started checking the depths of the water, *first finding it to be 120 feet deep and then later 90 feet*. It was evident they were approaching the shallows and *might run on the rocks*.

In another desperate act, they *let out four anchors from the stern and prayed for daylight to come*. The crew decided to *abandon ship*, so they *lowered the lifeboat into the sea, pretending that they were letting out some anchors from the bow*. The rabbi had an urgent new word for the officers. The Lord revealed to him that *unless everyone remains on board the ship, they will not be saved*. Though there are various levels of "salvation" (physical or spiritual) in the Jewish tradition, Sha'ul seems to have physical deliverance in mind here.

Sometimes these concepts intermingle, as in the case of the first Pesach or the last Tribulation before the return of Messiah (Ex. 14:13; Mt. 24:22). This time, the crew takes the words of the Jewish prisoner seriously. It must have seemed counter-intuitive, but *they cut the ropes holding the lifeboat and let it go.* How many times today do we believers also discover that it is wise not to follow our own wisdom but finally listen to God (Prov. 3:5–6)? The hardest challenges are often ones of letting go of our perceived lifeboats!

This climactic struggle took place from *midnight* to *just before daybreak.* The group of sailors had already been "praying" in the night, perhaps in their accustomed manner to the plethora of Roman gods. But perhaps after this extreme time of testing, they joined the rabbi for an earnest Shachrit morning prayer! *Sha'ul urged them all to eat,* as they no doubt expended so much energy battling the storm. They'd need renewed strength with a shipwreck imminent. But Sha'ul said, *"Not one of you will lose so much as a hair from his head."* Then *he took bread* [and] *said the b'rakhah (blessing) to God in front of everyone.* Jewish tradition calls Jews to say at least 100 berakhot per day, which is actually easy to fulfill. There is an entire Tractate of the Talmud that teaches the details, and it is said to have been a practice started by King David (Tractate Berakhot; Menachot 43b).

There are blessings of waking up, going to sleep, for personal safety, even for enjoying the ocean (said as a Californian surfing rabbi)! There is something encouraging about giving thanks to God in all situations (I Thes. 5:16–18). This particular blessing was the traditional *hamotzi* over bread: *"Barukh atah Adonai Eloheinu, melekh ha'olam, hamotzi lechem min ha'aretz"* ("Blessed art Thou, Lord our God, King of the universe, who brings forth bread from the earth"). Sha'ul says this blessing publicly as a testimony of his faith and an encouragement to the others, probably with some new believers in the crowd. He *broke the bread and began to eat.* Some Christian interpreters see this as a reference to Christian Communion or the Eucharist. But it's clearly the more-common "breaking of bread" that is literally done to start a meal (Tractate Berakhot 46.1; Acts 2:46).

With this important prayer, *courage was restored and they ate some food.* For the first time we are told that *there were 276 people on board,* which is consistent with historical records describing some of the large commercial ships of the Roman Empire. Josephus documents a ship holding 600 people (*Life* 3.15). Preparing for the inevitable, the crew *dumped into the sea* the last important element, their *grain* cargo. *When day broke*, they didn't recognize the island, but they judged that *the bay with a sand beach* was their best hope of survival. Luke gives some amazing nautical details here: *they cut away the remaining anchors and loosened the ropes that held the rudders*. The crew *hoisted the foresail to the wind and headed for the beach.*

The landing was not going to be as easy as hoped, as they encountered *two currents which forced the vessel to run aground on the sandbar*. With *the bow stuck in the sand, the stern started breaking up* as it was exposed to *the pounding surf*. Luke observes that at this hopeless juncture, *the soldiers considered killing the prisoners so none of them could escape*. But since the rabbi had proven so helpful, *the head officer kept them from carrying out their plan*, thus preserving Sha'ul's life. With that, the order was given for *those who could swim to throw themselves overboard first and head for shore*. All others would have to fend for themselves by *using planks or whatever they could find from the ship* as floatation devices. Miraculously, *everyone reached land safely*, just as the rabbi had predicted. Today the place is appropriately called St. Paul's Bay.

Through this harrowing ordeal there are spiritual lessons to be learned. Though it was clearly God's will for Sha'ul to travel to Rome, the process was far from easy. This is often the case in our own spiritual journey with Yeshua. His plan can be clear and the intentions good, but there usually are tests along the way. God was not mad at Sha'ul (or us today). In fact, it is his love that seeks to mold us into the image of our Messiah by taking off some rough edges. Sha'ul was well aware of these dynamics and even had a positive perspective it all. In his letter to the Romans, he sums it up:

> *We know that God causes everything to work together for the good of those who love God and are called in accordance with his purpose; because those whom He knew in advance, He also determined in advance would be conformed to the pattern of his Son.* (Rom. 8:28–29)

If Sha'ul could have such a perspective amidst a life-threatening shipwreck, maybe we too can see God's work in our own lives. We will all face crises (tzuris) in our lives, often a result of things beyond our control. We do not know the future, but we do know the One who holds the future! We can take things into our own hands, or we can face a crisis God's way. Many times we don't have a say on what happens around us, but we do have a say in how we respond. Perhaps a well-placed b'rakhah is one key to getting us through!

> *Abaye said to Rabba: What is the reason that you are so concerned? If we say it is due to the pains preceding and accompanying the coming of the Messiah, but isn't it taught in a baraita that Rabbi Elazar's students asked Rabbi Elazar: What shall a person do to be spared from the pains preceding the coming of the Messiah? Rabbi Elazar said to them: They shall engage in Torah study and acts of kindness.* (Tractate Sanhedrin 98b.4)

XIX. Arrival in Rome – 28:1–31

It had now been over two years since Sha'ul's arrest in Israel and the legal proceedings against him. The various hearings (both Jewish and Roman) led to this rabbi being shipped to Rome for his highest legal appeal. After the treacherous storm and resultant shipwreck, everyone miraculously survived and swam to shore. They discovered it was *the island of Malta* where the voyage ended, just south of mainland Italy. The older first-century name is Melite, meaning "refuge." The weather was still bad with *rain and cold*, but some locals *showed extraordinary kindness by welcoming the group with a bonfire*. The word describing the people, "barbarians," simply means "non-Greek."

The common implication was that such people were uneducated and below the cultured Greeks or Romans of that day. Evidently, God was not done working on Sha'ul yet, nor was he done teaching spiritual lessons to the Roman and pagan crowd. As the rabbi was *adding sticks to the fire, a poisonous snake fastened itself to his hand!* Luke says that *to the islanders*, this was a sure sign that the man was *a murderer*. They said, *"Even though he escaped the sea, justice has not allowed him to live."* Still today it is easy to find people who believe their misfortune must be God's judgment. While that is always possible, it is also true that many times people are simply reaping the bad fruit of what they have sown (Gal. 6:7–8).

We could translate the word "justice" here with a capital J as it likely refers to Dike, a pagan goddess depicted as holding a scale and sword. The later European version also depicted her as blindfolded, inferring that Lady Justice is equal before all people. In this case, the islanders waited, *expecting [Sha'ul] to fall down dead; but after waiting a long time and seeing that nothing amiss was happening to him, they reversed their opinion and said he was a god!*

Of course, for Sha'ul and his team, it was not that surprising that the God of Israel was again confirming the message of Yeshua with signs and wonders. This was expanded as *the governor of the island*, Publius, *received us in a friendly manner and put us up for three days*. In another "coincidence," *Publius' father was lying in bed* with *dysentery*. Luke says the rabbi *went to him, prayed, placed his hands on him and healed him*. After his miraculous recovery, *the rest of the islanders who had ailments came and also were healed*.

Luke says, *"They heaped honors on us; and when the time came for us to sail, they provided the supplies we needed."* The miraculous interventions and supernatural signs were following the messianic team, yet with it was not unconditional. As we see many times in Scripture, there are those who do not receive a healing. Sometimes the reason is a mystery; sometimes it is obvious. Recall Sha'ul's own "thorn in the flesh." While he often prayed successfully for God's healing, it did not come in his own personal life.

God answered his prayer with the promise, *"My grace is sufficient for you"* (II Cor. 12:7–10). But ultimately, it is best to trust God even when the answer is not to our liking. I am sure all of us would love to see 100% healing guaranteed, but sometimes God's plan has an even higher purpose. Physical healing or not, it is comforting for us Yeshua believers to know that God promises to give us the resources to walk through any valley or test until we are in his future Kingdom!

Luke's account continues some *three months* later as the Jewish team *sets sail on a ship from Alexandria* called *"Twin Gods."* It was named for Castor and Pollux, the Romans' patron gods of sailors. On this new vessel, the group *landed at Syracuse and stayed three days.* From there they progressed *to Rhegium* (on the toe on Italy), then caught a favorable *south wind* that took them quickly *to Puteoli* (the modern Bay of Naples). Luke says, *"We found brothers who invited us to spend a week with them."* It was a blessing that the team connected with other Messianic believers already established in Italy. Perhaps they were part of the early Yeshua community who became believers in Yerushalayim at one of the required Shalosh Regalim and returned to their native country to establish the faith (Acts 2:10).

The group presses on to their ultimate destination of *the city of Rome*, traveling on the famous highway known as the Appian Way. Along this route (some 43 miles from the capital), the group met some more messianic *brothers*, who planned to meet them *at the Appian Market and Three Inns. When Sha'ul saw them, he thanked God and took courage.* When the team finally *arrived in Rome*, the *officer allowed Sha'ul to stay by himself, though guarded by a soldier.* Most likely this was following the Roman military custom of a guard chained to an important prisoner. One wonders how many Roman soldiers essentially became the captive audience of this zealous rabbi!

Through it all, we see how important the fellowship of believers was to Sha'ul. Despite being the top leader of his day, he appreciated and needed the personal connection to other Messianic brothers and sisters. In his rabbinic background, he would have been familiar with the saying *"Al tifrosh min ha-tzibur"* ("don't forsake the community"; Pirkei Avot 2.5). We may have personal faith in Yeshua, which is vitally important. But it is also crucial that all Messianic Jews and like-minded Gentiles be involved in the Messianic Jewish community and local synagogue. You need it like Sha'ul, but don't overlook the fact that you are needed to bless the community as well (Heb. 10:25)!

After three days Sha'ul called a meeting of the local Jewish leaders. We have seen the consistent theme through Acts that the early Messianic Jews considered themselves still connected to the larger Jewish community. This is again affirmed even at this late point as Sha'ul addresses the Jewish group as "brothers." Add to this personal connection his statement that he has *done nothing against either our people or the traditions of our fathers.*

This declaration gives great insight into the perspective of the early Yeshua followers. First, though they held fast to their conviction of Yeshua as the promised Messiah, they held that this should not be considered a crime against the people. Note again the use of *"our"* people, not *"your"* people. There is certainly debate and much disagreement from the larger Jewish community about this possible Messiah, but his followers naturally remain faithful Jews. Sha'ul takes it a step further and affirms that there has not even been an infringement upon the "traditions" of "our" people. This seems to apply to doctrines and practices even beyond the written Torah.

For example, where the Written Torah (*Torah Shebiktav*) clearly commands the observance of Shabbat, the Oral Torah (*Torah Shebaal Peh*) explains many traditions on how to observe Shabbat. Technically, the Torah does not command the lighting of candles or wearing of a kippah. These are traditions that some may not observe and that certainly inspire sincere debate among various denominations within Judaism. Messianic Jews even today tend to have a high regard to the Torah and appreciation for many of the traditions of our heritage. That's why we live a Jewish lifestyle, follow the Jewish calendar and have synagogues instead of churches. This does not mean the messianic community worldwide agrees on some of these details, and like the broader Jewish world, we also see considerable debate about these things. But Sha'ul's declaration should get our attention. It is quite an insight that one of the top messianic leaders claims to be a faithful Jew to both the people and traditions.

Despite his faithful Jewish observance, Sha'ul was nonetheless *made a prisoner in Yerushalayim and handed over to the Romans.*

The *authorities examined the accusations and were ready to release* him, but some of the Jewish leaders objected and continued to press the case forward. Because he is a Roman citizen, the emissary says he was *forced to appeal to the Emperor* for an impartial judicial hearing. Sha'ul openly shares this background with the current group of Jewish leaders in Rome in hopes they will understand his situation more accurately. In short, it is not for any crime against the people or the government that he is *bound by this chain*. It is because of *the hope of Isra'el* (his understanding of Yeshua being the Messiah) that he is in this legal controversy.

Surprisingly, the Jewish leaders say they have *not received any letters from Y'hudah* about this case, not even a complaint of *anything bad* about Sha'ul. Commentators speculate how this could be. Perhaps over the long journey to Rome the accusers dropped out of sight or simply had not caught up with the messianic group quite yet. They do concede that they *all know about this sect and that many people speak against it*. Even in this admission, the leaders seem to perceive the Yeshua movement as a sect of Judaism. Why else would they care or bother to investigate? Though they have not received any direct information about Sha'ul and his work, the Jewish leaders agree it would be appropriate to hear his views directly from the source.

With this sense of openness and sincerity, the leaders *arranged a day* with Sha'ul *and came to his quarters in large numbers*. Luke, the resident historian, says *from morning until evening he explained the matter to them*, including a traditional focus on issues of Jewish interest such as *the Kingdom of God and how Yeshua* of Nazareth might be King Messiah. This was not just numerous rabbis and leaders sharing their personal opinions. Sha'ul used as his sources *both the Torah of Moshe and the Neviim to try to persuade them about Yeshua*. As was often the case in Sha'ul's ministry to his Jewish brothers, *some were convinced*. The evidence becomes overwhelming as one considers the statements of Tanakh about the promise of Messiah. A small sample of what the emissary may have discussed his Jewish brothers could have included the following:

- Messiah must come from the tribe of Y'hudah – Gen. 49:10

- Messiah must come from the smaller family of King David from within Y'hudah – II Sam. 7:12–13

- Messiah must be born in the city of King David, Beit-Lechem – Mic. 5:1 (Hebrew)

- Messiah will suffer and be rejected by many – Isaiah 53; Talmudic name "Mashiach ben Yosef"

- Messiah will ultimately rule over a kingdom of peace and blessing – Isa. 11; Talmudic name "Mashiach ben David"

Taken together, the odds become ludicrous that any one person could fulfill all these Tanakh conditions. And these are just five descriptions out of dozens. The Messiah must be a Jew, whose people represent 0.1% of the world's population. In other words, 99.9% of people can step aside. Subtract from this that the Messiah must come from one of the twelve tribes. Now 11 out of every 12 Jews can step aside. That he must descend from the Jewish family of David—you get the point!

The conviction that Yeshua of Nazareth is the promised Messiah is not just a "blind faith" spiritual experience. The God of Israel has not only foretold the coming of Messiah but given us specific ways to confirm his true identity. No wonder the last chapter of Acts speaks of some of the Jewish brothers and sisters becoming convinced that Yeshua is the One. Many contemporary Messianic Jews have also become convinced based on the predictions from Moshe and the Prophets.

While there were new believers in this crowd, *others refused to believe*. To an open-minded seeker, the evidence is more than adequate. But there are other factors involved in having faith in Yeshua. No doubt the Jewish experience with "Christianity" over history has made it difficult for many Jews to even entertain the thought. Add to this the Westernized representation of "Jesus Christ" that basically removes him from his original Jewish root. If these weren't difficult enough, there are also the issues every person, Jew or Gentile, faces regarding the person of Yeshua.

Are we willing to repent of sin? Are we willing to make him Lord of our life instead of a mere appendage? Are we willing to die to self? There is a plethora of reasons for Jews not to follow Yeshua, so it has always been a split decision. We should not be surprised that there are various responses today as we present Yeshua. Ultimately, believers are called to be ambassadors of the message and leave the rest between God and the other person. This is not only the ultimate reality, but it also takes the undue pressure off us to bring someone to faith.

In this Acts 28 situation, we are told that the Jewish *group left* the messianic Torah study even *disagreeing among themselves*. We Messianic Jews often walk a tightrope of our faith in Yeshua along with the rejection of some of our family and friends. Some even cave into the intense social pressure to deny being a follower of Yeshua. But where else can we go? If he is the true Jewish Messiah, we must stand strong even amidst opposition and strong disagreement. Luke says Sha'ul now makes *a final statement* to the Roman Jewish community leaders. For this he simply invokes *Yesha'yahu the prophet* as he addressed *the fathers* of his generation. The rabbi points out that it was not just Isaiah's opinion but also the perspective of *the Ruach HaKodesh when he said*:

> *"Go to this people and say, 'You will keep on hearing but never understand, and you will keep on seeing but never perceive, because the heart of this people has grown thick—with their ears they barely hear, and their eyes they have closed, for fear that they should see with their eyes, hear with their ears, understand with their heart, and do t'shuvah, so that I could heal them.'"* (Isa. 6:9–10)

These can seem harsh words, and some have even tried to use such phraseology as fodder for their anti-Semitic darkness. But these words are from the Tanakh and from one of our revered prophets. It does not represent xenophobia but an in-house family debate among Jews. That Sha'ul quotes Isaiah merely emphasizes that what has happened so often before in Jewish history is in danger of happening again in the first century. In the Prophets' generation, most of the

Jewish community rejected Isaiah's message, thus bringing the Assyrian invasion and captivity. In Sha'ul's generation, there was a risk of similar consequences if most of the Jewish community rejects the true Messiah sent from God. In both cases there is plenty of evidence, yet so many were unwilling to believe.

As a final application of Sha'ul's message, the emissary declares that *this salvation of God has now been sent to the Gentiles*. It is ironic that this thoroughly Jewish message would be largely rejected by the Jewish community, yet the non-Jews *will listen*. As with the generalized statements about the Jewish rejection of Yeshua, one must be careful to contextualize the statements of the Gentile acceptance. Even with the majority rejection of Yeshua, there was always a strong remnant of Jews who embraced him as the promised Messiah (Rom. 11:1–5). How else can we understand the tens of thousands in first-century Israel as well as the growing tens of thousands even in today's modern Messianic Jewish movement?

And it's not as if all Gentiles welcomed this news of the Messiah. There were riots in the streets of Ephesus and strong opposition from the Roman community (19:28–29). The fact is, the great majority of Gentiles did not follow Yeshua and continued in their various pagan expressions. A balanced understanding of the history should note that the early Messianic Jews continued to go to their Jewish cousins despite much opposition (Rom. 1:16). It is a blessing to all Gentile believers (even today!) that the Good News has now come to them. To bring the message to the Gentiles is not to the exclusion of continuing to share these blessings with the Jewish world.

The last statement of Acts 28 clearly affirms that the Messianic message is not withheld from the Jewish community both then and to this day. Luke says *Sha'ul remained two whole years in a place he rented for himself; and he continued receiving all who came to see him*. This seems to be a somewhat flexible house arrest as the Shaliach awaits his trial in Rome. The content of his message remained consistent from beginning to end. He proclaimed the focal point of all the Scriptures, the promised *Kingdom of God*. Connected to this is the all-important question of who the King might be, so he continued his *teaching about the Lord Yeshua the Messiah.*

It is with this rather abrupt ending that the Book of Acts draws to a close. One might think Luke would record other details concerning Sha'ul's trial or even the 70 C.E. destruction of Yerushalayim. This evidence seems to indicate that Luke concludes his history at this point, because it is before those events around 65 C.E. There is speculation that the emissary was ultimately executed by treacherous Emperor Nero in 66 C.E. There are also conjectures that Sha'ul was released from Roman arrest and made it to one of his stated goals of reaching the Iberian Peninsula (Rom. 15:28). The second-century historian Eusebius says Sha'ul was imprisoned twice in Rome before being martyred there (*Ecclesiastical History* 2:22.1–7). Perhaps it is most fitting that Luke leaves the Book of Acts with an open ending?

Maybe his intention is to imply that there will be more amazing history yet to be written in both the Gentile world and the Jewish community. We are currently witnessing in our day the rebirth of the modern Messianic Jewish movement along with many segments of the Gentile Church who appreciate Israel and their inherited Jewish roots!

Either way, the return of Messiah is 2000 years closer. The birth pains of Messiah (*chevlei shel Mashiach*) are getting stronger and more obvious in our day (Mt. 24; Tractate Sanhedrin 98b). There are some troubling and striking signs in our generation that should get our attention. There are also many exciting doors opening with renewed dialogue and understanding within the Jewish and Christian communities. It seems we are in one of the last generations before the return of Messiah.

This Good News of Yeshua must accordingly go to the ends of the earth, yet we are told there will be a special, last-day focus on God's beloved chosen people of Israel. With a miraculous revelation of God himself, all Israel will call out for Messiah with the famous words, *"Baruch haba b'shem Adonai"* ("Blessed is he who comes in the name of the Lord!") (Mt. 23:39; Ps. 118:26). Are you fulfilling your calling to be part of the Yeshua movement in our day?

TANAKH REFERENCES IN ACTS

Genesis 9:1–7 — 15:19–21
Genesis 12:1, 7; 15:13 — 7:3
Genesis 22:18 — 3:25
Genesis 37–45 — 7:9
Exodus 1:7–8 — 7:18
Exodus 3:6, 15 — 3:13
Exodus 6:6 — 13:17
Exodus 22:27 — 23:5
Numbers 6:1–8 — 18:18; 21:22–26
Deuteronomy 18:15–16 — 3:22–23; 7:37
Deuteronomy 21:22–23 — 5:30; 10:39
Psalm 110:1 — 2:35; 5:31; 7:56
Psalm 2:1–7 — 4:25; 13:33
Psalm 16:8–11 — 2:25; 13:35
Psalm 69:26 — 1:20
Psalm 89:21 — 13:22
Psalm 109:8 — 1:20
Psalm 118:22–25 — 4:11; 16:25
Psalm 146:6 — 14:15
Isaiah 11:1 — 11:26
Isaiah 49:6 — 13:47
Isaiah 53:7–8 — 8:32–33
Isaiah 66:1–2 — 7:51
Daniel 7:13 — 7:56
Joel 3:1–5 — 2:16
Amos 5:25–27 — 7:42–43
Amos 9:11–12 — 15:15–18
Habakkuk 1:5 — 13:41

GLOSSARY

Adonai Echad	The Lord is One (Deut. 6:4)
afikoman	the broken middle matzah of the Passover Seder
aliyah	going up, especially to Jerusalem
Amidah	18 benedictions (plus one added after 70 C.E.)
ashrey	happy are those; opening phrase of many Psalms and prayers
asur	rabbinic term for forbidden actions
avot/toledot	Fathers. 39 Father commandments; many descendants
b'rakhah	blessing
b'ris	covenant (Ashkenazi pronunciation)
b'rit	covenant (Sephardic pronunciation)
b'rit milah	covenant of circumcision, often referred to as just *b'ris* or *b'rit*
bar	son (Aramaic)
Bar/Bat Mitzvah	Son/Daughter of the Commandment
barukh haba	blessed is he who comes in the name of
b'shem	Adonai the Lord
bat-kol	lit. "daughter voice" but used to describe a voice coming from the heavens
ben	son (Hebrew)
beit	house
Beit-Din	house of judgment; local rabbinic court
Beit Ha-Mikdash	The Holy Temple
Beit-Hillel/Shammai	House of Hillel/Shammai; opposing first-century rabbis
bimah	pulpit, platform
birkat ha'mazon	blessing after a meal
b'nai Yisra'el	sons of Israel
challah	Sabbath bread

chametz	leaven
chevra kaddisha	burial society
Cohanim	Priests, the sons of Aaron
Cohen hagadol	The High Priest
davvening	Yiddish for praying
Eretz Yisrael	The Land of Israel
erusin	betrothal; engagement
Gemara	commentary on the *Mishnah*
get	divorce decree
Gei-Hinnom	Hell
goyim	non-Jews, Gentiles
Haftarah	section read from the Prophets
haggadah	Passover booklet of liturgy and readings used during seder
halakhah	rabbinic interpretive law
hallel	praise Psalms 113–118
HaShem	The Name; substitute for the name of God (*YHVH*)
huppah	wedding canopy
Josephus	first-century Jewish historian
kal v'chomer	light to heavy; how much more
kashrut	dietary laws
Kefa	Peter
kehilah	congregation
ketubah	marriage contract
kiddush	sanctification, often a cup of wine to "set apart" an event
kippah (kippot)	Hebrew for skullcap(s)
klal	rabbinic general principle
kosher	fit for consumption, clean (primarily used to describe food, but can be applied to situations that are "fit," or "clean," like "kosher behavior")
kosher l'Pesach	kosher for Passover
Levi'im	sons of the tribe of Levi

lulav	palm branch of *Sukkot*/Feast of Tabernacles
maror	the bitter herb eaten at Passover; usually ground horseradish
mashal	parable
Mashiach	Hebrew for Messiah
Mashiach ben David	Son of David, refers to King Messiah
Mashiach ben Yosef	Son of Joseph, refers to the Suffering Messiah
matzah	the unleavened bread used for Passover (and other times)
m'zuzah	doorpost, but used to describe a small box containing two handwritten biblical passages (Deut. 6:4–9, 11:13–21) on parchment; the box attached to the doors of homes
midrash	rabbinical commentary on the *Torah*
mikveh	special pool constructed for ritual water immersion
minchah	afternoon Temple sacrifice
Mishnah	the Oral Law written down about 200 C.E. based on the *Torah* (the Written Law)
mitzvah (mitzvot)	commandment(s), good deed(s)
mutar	rabbinic term for permitted actions
natilat yadaim	washing the hands
niddah	removed, separated (the period when a woman is forbidden to have sexual contact with her husband)
nisuin	marriage
olam haba	the age to come
olam hazeh	this age
ol ha-Torah	the yoke (responsibility and blessing) of the *Torah*
oneg	joyful celebration, often refers to a meal after Shabbat morning services.
oy!	woe (but untranslatable!)
P'rushim	Pharisees
Pesach	Passover
Rashi	acronym for Rabbi Shlomo Yitzaki (1040–1105 C.E.), a famous and influential rabbi

Rambam	acronym for Rabbi Moshe ben Maimon, also known as Maimonides (1135–1204 C.E.), a famous and influential rabbi
Rosh Hashanah	Jewish New Year, head of the year
Ruach HaKodesh	Holy Spirit
Sanhedrin	Israel's religious supreme court until 70 C.E.
seder	order (Passover meal)
Sh'khinah	Glory of God
sh'khitah	ritual slaughtering procedure
Sh'ma	refers to Deut. 6:4-6; Hear (O Israel)
Sh'ol	the place of the dead
Shabbat	Sabbath
shadkhan	marriage broker, matchmaker
shakharit	daily morning prayer services
shaliach (Sh'likhim)	representative(s), apostle(s)
shalom	peace, health, contentment
Shavuot	Pentecost, Feast of Weeks
shel rosh	head *t'fillin*, designated for the head
shel yad	hand *t'fillin*, designated for the hand
sheva b'rakhot	seven blessings at a Jewish wedding
shiddukhin	arrangements preliminary to betrothal
Shim'on	Simon
shofar	ram's horn (other animals' horns are sometimes used)
shokhet	kosher butcher
siddur (siddurim)	prayer book(s)
simcha	joyous occasion
s'mikhah	laying on of hands or ordination
sukkah	booth for Feast of Tabernacles
Sukkot	Feast of Tabernacles
t'fillah	prayer
t'fillin	phylacteries, leather boxes strapped to the forehead and hand used for prayer

t'shuvah	repentance
t'vilah	to totally immerse
tallit	prayer shawl
tallit katan	small prayer shawl worn under shirt
talmid (talmidim)	disciple(s) or student(s)
Talmud	codified body of rabbinic thought; *Mishnah* plus *Gemara*. Completed in 6th century.
Tanakh	acronym for The Hebrew Scriptures: *Torah* (Law), Neviim (Prophets), Ketuvim (Writings)
Targum	translation into another language
tashlikh	ceremony of repentance that takes place at a body of water on Rosh Hashanah
Torah	Law or Instruction; five books of Moses
Tractate	a book of the Talmud
treif	non-kosher
Tz'dukim	Sadducees
tzedakah	righteousness, charity
tzitzit, tzitziyot	fringe(s) worn on a garment
yarmulke	Yiddish for head covering
Yerushalayim	Jerusalem
Yeshua	Jesus, salvation
Yeshua HaMashiach	Jesus the Messiah
yetzer ha-tov (ha-ra)	the good (or evil) inclination of mankind
YHVH	(Yud-Heh-Vav-Heh) the Hebrew letters for the ineffable Name of God
Yom Kippur	Day of Atonement

Bibliography

Abbott-Smith, G. *A Manual Greek Lexicon of the New Testament.* Edinburgh, Scotland: T&T Clark, 1973.

Birnbaum, Philip. *A Book of Jewish Concepts.* New York: Hebrew Publishing Company, 1975.

Birnbaum, Philip (ed). *Maimonides Code of Law and Ethics: Mishneh Torah.* New York: Hebrew Publishing Company, 1974.

Bock, Darrell L. *Acts.* Grand Rapids: Baker Academic, 2007.

Boteach, Shmuley. *Kosher Jesus.* Springfield, NJ: Gefen Books, 2012.

Boyarin, Daniel. *Border Lines: The Partition of Judaeo-Christianity.* Philadelphia: University of Pennsylvania Press, 2004.

Boyarin, Daniel. *The Jewish Gospels.* New York: The New Press, 2012.

Brown, Michael. *Answering Jewish Objections to Jesus (5 Volumes).* Grand Rapids: Baker Books, 2003.

Bruce, F. F. *The Book of Acts.* Grand Rapids: Eerdmans Publishing, 1986.

Budoff, Barry & Gliebe, Kirk. *Messianic Jewish Siddur for Shabbat and Festivals.* Skokie, IL: Devar Emet Messianic Publications, 2017.

Buxbaum, Yitzhak. *Jewish Spiritual Practices.* Northvale, NJ: Jason Aronson, Inc., 1994.

Carroll, James. *Constantine's Sword: The Church and the Jews.* New York: Houghton Mifflin Company, 2001.

Cohen, Abraham. *Everyman's Talmud.* New York: Schocken Books, 1975.

Cohen, Abraham. *The Twelve Prophets.* New York: Soncino Press, 1985.

Cohen, Shaye. The Beginnings of Jewishness. Berkeley: University of California Press, 2000.

Cohn-Sherbok, Dan (ed). *Voices of Messianic Judaism.* Baltimore: Messianic Jewish Publications, 2001.

Danby, Herbert. *The Mishnah.* New York: Oxford University Press, 1991.

Daube, David. *The New Testament and Rabbinic Judaism.* Peabody, MA: Hendrickson Publishers, 1956.

Dauermann, Stuart. *Converging Destinies: Jews, Christians, and the Mission of God.* Eugene, OR: Cascade Books, 2017.

Davies, W. D. *Paul and Rabbinic Judaism.* Philadelphia: Fortress Press, 1980.

Edersheim, Alfred. *The Life and Times of Jesus the Messiah*. Grand Rapids: Eerdmans Publishing, 1984.

Epstein, Isidore (ed). *The Soncino Talmud*. Brooklyn: Soncino Press, 1995. CD-ROM.

Eisenbaum, Pamela. *Paul Was Not a Christian*. New York: HarperCollins Publishers, 2009.

Eisenman, Robert, and Michael Wise. *The Dead Sea Scrolls Uncovered*. New York: Barnes & Noble, 1992.

Feinberg, Jeffrey. *Walk! Genesis Through Deuteronomy*. Baltimore: Lederer Messianic Publications, 1999.

Fischer, John. *Siddur For Messianic Jews*. Palm Harbor, FL: Menorah Ministries, 1988.

Fischer, John. *The Epistles from a Jewish Perspective*. Clarksville: Messianic Jewish Publishers, 2011. MP3 / DVD-ROM series.

Flusser, David. *The Sage from Galilee*. Grand Rapids: Eerdmans Publishing, 2007.

Fredriksen, Paula. *When Christians Were Jews*. New Haven: Yale University Press, 2018.

Friedman, David. *At The Feet of Rabbi Gamaliel*. Clarksville: Messianic Jewish Publishers, 2013.

Glaser, Mitch. *Isaiah 53 Explained*. New York: Chosen People Productions, 2010.

Harink, Douglas. *Paul Among the Postliberals*. Grand Rapids: Brazos Press, 2003.

Heschel, Abraham Joshua. *God in Search of Man: A Philosophy of Judaism*. New York: Noonday Press, 1993.

Hilton, Rabbi Michael, and Father Gorian Marshall. *The Gospels and Rabbinic Judaism*. Hoboken: Ktav Publishing House, 1988.

Jeremias, Joachim. *Jerusalem in the Time of Jesus*. Philadelphia: Fortress Press, 1988.

Juster, Daniel. *Jewish Roots*. Pacific Palisades, CA: Davar, 1986.

Kaiser, Walter, et al. *Three Views on the New Testament Use of the Old Testament*. Grand Rapids: Zondervan, 2008.

Kasdan, Barney. *God's Appointed Times*. Baltimore: Messianic Jewish Publishers, 1993.

Kasdan, Barney. *God's Appointed Customs*. Baltimore: Messianic Jewish Publishers, 1996.

Kasdan, Barney. *Matthew Presents Yeshua, King Messiah*. Baltimore: Messianic Jewish Publishers, 2011.

Kasdan, Barney. *Rabbi Paul Enlightens the Ephesians on Walking with Messiah Yeshua*. Baltimore: Messianic Jewish Publishers, 2015.

Kinzer, Mark, & Russell Resnik. *Besorah: The Resurrection of Jerusalem and the Healing of a Fractured Gospel*. Eugene, OR: Cascade Books, 2021.

Klausner, Joseph. *From Jesus to Paul*. New York: Menorah Publishing Company, 1979.

Klein, Isaac. *A Guide to Jewish Religious Practice*. New York: The Jewish Theological Seminary of America, 1979.

Lachs, Samuel Tobias. *A Rabbinic Commentary on the New Testament*. Hoboken: Ktav Publishing House, 1987.

Levine, Amy-Jill, and Marc Zvi Brettler. *The Jewish Annotated New Testament*. New York: Oxford University Press, 2011.

Lightfoot, John. *A Commentary of the New Testament from the Talmud and Hebraica, Vol. 4*. Grand Rapids: Baker Book House, 1979.

Messianic Jewish Family Bible (Tree of Life Version). Syracuse, NY: Messianic Jewish Family Bible Society, 2014.

Nanos, Mark. *Reading Paul Within Judaism*. Eugene, OR: Cascade Books, 2017.

Neusner, Jacob. *A Rabbi Talks with Jesus*. New York: Doubleday, 1994.

Oliver, Isaac. *Luke's Jewish Eschatology: The National Restoration of Israel in Luke-Acts*. New York: Oxford University Press, 2021.

Cross, F. L., and E. A. Livingstone (eds). "Didache." In *Oxford Dictionary of the Christian Church*. New York: Oxford University Press, 2005.

Patai, Raphael. *The Messiah Texts*. New York: Avon Books, 1979.

Prager, Dennis, and Joseph Telushkin. *Why The Jews?* New York: Simon & Schuster, 2003.

Rienecker, Fritz, and Cleon Rogers. *Linguistic Key to the Greek New Testament*. Grand Rapids: Zondervan, 1982.

Roth, Cecil, and Geoffrey Wigoder. *Encyclopedia Judaica*. Jerusalem: Keter Publishing House, 1972.

Rudolph, David, and Joel Willetts (eds). *Introduction to Messianic Judaism*. Grand Rapids: Zondervan, 2013.

Sadan, Tsvi. *The Concealed Light*. Marshfield, MO: Vine of David, 2012.

Safrai, Shmuel. "The Value of Rabbinical Literature as an Historical Source." *Jerusalem Perspective*. 29 September 2009. https://www.jerusalemperspective.com/4669.

Sanders, E. P. *Judaism: Practice and Belief, 63 B.C.E. – 66 C.E.* London: SCM Press, 1992.

Sanders, E. P. *Paul, the Law, and the Jewish People*. Philadelphia: Fortress Press, 1983.

Scherman, Nosson. *The Rabbinical Council of America Edition of the Artscroll Siddur*. Brooklyn: Mesorah Publications, 1990.

Scherman, Nosson. *Tanach: The Torah, Prophets and Writings*. Brooklyn: Mesorah Publications, 1996.

Spangler, Ann, and Lois Tverberg. *Sitting at the Feet of Rabbi Jesus: How the Jewishness of Jesus Can Transform Your Faith*. Grand Rapids: Zondervan, 2009.

Spitz, Elie Kaplan. *Does the Soul Survive?* Woodstock, VT: Jewish Lights Publishing, 2001.

Stendahl, Krister. *Paul Among Jews and Gentiles*. Philadelphia: Fortress Press, 1976.

Stern, David. *Complete Jewish Bible*. Clarksville: Jewish New Testament Publications, 1998, 2016.

Stern, David. *Jewish New Testament Commentary*. Clarksville, MD: Jewish New Testament Publications, 1992.

Stern, David. *Messianic Judaism: A Modern Movement with an Ancient Past*. Baltimore: Messianic Jewish Publications, 2009.

Thiede, Carsten Peter. *The Dead Sea Scrolls and the Jewish Origins of Christianity*. New York: Palgrave, 2001.

Vermes, Geza. *Jesus in His Jewish Context*. Minneapolis: Fortress Press, 2003.

Wagner, Jordan. *The Synagogue Survival Kit*. Northvale, NJ: Jason Aronson Inc, 1997.

Whiston, William. *Josephus' Complete Works*. Grand Rapids: Kregel Publications, 1960.

Wright, N.T. *Paul in Fresh Perspective*. Minneapolis: Fortress Press, 2009.

Young, Brad H. *Meet the Rabbis: Rabbinic Thought and the Teachings of Jesus*. Peabody, MA: Hendrickson Publishers, 2007.

INDEX

Printed in the United States
by Baker & Taylor Publisher Services